STRUCTURING
YOUR
BUSINESS

From Corporations to LLCs—Everything You
Need to Set Up Your Business Efficiently

MICHELE CAGAN, C.P.A.

Adams Media
Avon, Massachusetts

D0945611

A Streetwise® Publication.
Streetwise® is a registered trademark of Adams Media.

Published by Adams Media
57 Littlefield Street, Avon, MA 02322 U.S.A.
www.adamsmedia.com

ISBN: 1-59337-177-2

Printed in the United States of America.
J I H G F E D C B A

Library of Congress Cataloging-in-Publication Data
Cagan, Michele.
Streetwise structuring your business / Michele Cagan.
p.   cm.
ISBN 1-59337-177-2
1. Business planning—United States. 2. Industrial management—United States.
3. Business enterprises—Law and legislation—United States. I. Title.

HD30.28.C33 2004
658—dc22
2004013575

This publication is designed to provide accurate and authoritative information with regard to the subject matter covered. It is sold with the understanding that the publisher is not engaged in rendering legal, accounting, or other professional advice. If legal advice or other expert assistance is required, the services of a competent professional person should be sought.
— From a *Declaration of Principles* jointly adopted by a Committee of the American Bar Association and a Committee of Publishers and Associations

This publication is intended to provide current and prospective business owners with useful information that may assist them in preparing for and obtaining business capital loans and investment funding. This information is general in nature and is not intended to provide specific advice for any individual or business entity. While the information contained herein should be helpful to the reader, appropriate financial, accounting, tax, or legal advice should always be sought from a competent professional engaged for any specific situation regarding your enterprise.

Many of the designations used by manufacturers and sellers to distinguish their products are claimed as trademarks. Where those designations appear in this book and Adams Media was aware of a trademark claim, the designations have been printed in initial capital letters.

Illustration by Eric Mueller.

This book is available at quantity discounts for bulk purchases. For information, call 1-800-872-5627.

Contents

Contents

Introduction

I've been working with small business clients, and preparing their tax returns, for many years now. Their businesses are quite diverse—from hairdressers to landscapers to concert violinists. But most of them have one thing in common: They came to me for advice after they had already started their companies. And though it's not terribly difficult to restructure an existing business, it's much easier (and cheaper) to do it right the first time.

That's why this book is so important. Setting up your company in the form that's best for your unique personal situation can save you a lot of headaches, time, and money. This book will explain how each type of business entity works, from starting it up to shutting it down. It will help you decide which structure will work the best for your business today, and it will teach you how to tell when it is time to make a change.

Once you have chosen the structure you'll initially use for your business, the book will help you through the process. You'll learn how to form a team of business professionals (like accountants and attorneys) so you can concentrate on running your company. You'll learn some tax basics, a little bit of business law, and some very practical ways to protect both your personal and business assets.

Most important, though, this book will empower you. It's hard to start a business, and even harder to make it successful. Building your company on a strong foundation will provide it with the stability it needs to grow. When you've read through this book, you will know how to build the right foundation by choosing the best structure for your business.

> **Chapter 1**

Choosing the Best Business Structure

Part One

Part Two

Part Three

Part Four

Part Five

Part Six

PART ONE   HOW TO GET STARTED IN BUSINESS

■ **CHAPTER 1   Choosing the Best Business Structure**   ■   CHAPTER 2   Things You Need to Do for Any Structure

■ CHAPTER 3   Get Professional Help Before You Start

Why Does the Structure Matter?

You want to start your own business. Maybe you've been in the industry, working for someone else for a while and you just want to be your own boss. Or perhaps you have a natural talent or calling that is leading you to create your own company. You're passionate about what you want to do—and you just can't wait to get started. Passion and self-motivation are crucial to the success of any new business. But they can only take off within a sound framework; without it, your company will likely crash and burn.

The decisions you make now, at the outset, will have long-reaching implications for both you and your business. The location you pick, where you get your start-up funding, who you plan to sell to—all of these choices are long-term, and they have long-term side effects. But perhaps the most crucial choice you'll make for your company is its business structure, so it's not a decision to be made lightly.

The business structure you choose will have a major impact on the future financial health of both you and your business. While making the right choice can significantly enhance your success, the wrong choice can cause a lot of problems. The potential problems aren't pint-sized, either; they include serious tax consequences and legal liability issues.

Many would-be entrepreneurs get a great business idea and just run with it. But neglecting to lay a strong foundation for a great business idea can lead to failure. By considering, choosing, and implementing the best possible structure for your business, you're setting the stage for success. This key decision should be made before you actually open your doors, and not be a default choice after the fact.

This decision will take a lot of time and thought. There is no "one size fits all" perfect entity that will suit every business. But you will find, as you begin to compare the different structures, that one will stand out as the best choice for you.

An Overview of Business Structures

For decades, the business world managed with three basic structures: the proprietorship, the partnership, and the corporation. Then "substructures" were created, adding small variations on the original themes. Finally, in the late 1980s, a fourth major structure (the limited liability company) was added to the roster.

Today, there are myriad entities to choose from. Some of the distinctions are huge and obvious, others small and subtle. But even the smallest difference in structural characteristics can make a large difference to the future health of your company.

Each business structure has a unique combination of features, and each has inherent advantages and disadvantages. Below is a brief description of each of the four main business structures.

Sole Proprietorship

A *sole proprietorship* is defined as a one-person unincorporated business. This very basic structure is by far the most common form of business organization. What it lacks in bells and whistles, it makes up for with ease and informality. If you're looking for simplicity and autonomy, this entity fills the bill: A sole proprietorship is easy to form, easy to maintain, and easy to

A Look at the Numbers

Each year the IRS publishes information about all tax returns filed, including the numbers of each type of return. This data shows how many of each type of business entity exist. In 2002 (the last year with full figures available), 18,336,500 Schedule Cs were filed, meaning there were that many sole proprietors (not including farmers, who file Schedule F); 2,361,600 regular (or "C") corporations filed returns on Form 1120; and 3,191,100 "S" corporations filed returns on Form 1120S. The count for Form 1065, which covers all types of partnerships and most LLCs, was 2,271,800.

The projected numbers for 2003 show a lot of business start-ups. When the overall U.S. economy is in a bit of a slump, more people create their own jobs by turning to entrepreneurship. Projected numbers for sole proprietors are about 350,000 higher, and increases are also projected for partnerships and for S corporations. The only expected decrease comes with C corporations, projected to drop down about 2 percent from 2002.

dissolve. This ease of set-up and get-out offers a corollary advantage—minimal paperwork and negligible start-up costs. Since there is only one owner, there is only one person in charge of the major decisions. There are also some serious potential drawbacks to this entity, the biggest of which is unlimited personal liability for all of the business's financial obligations. Taxation scores on both sides of the equation. Profits are only taxed once, on the owner's personal return; but self-employment taxes eat up a lot of those profits.

Partnership

A *partnership* is an unincorporated business co-owned by at least two individuals. There are three basic variations of partnership: general, limited, and limited liability. The main distinction among the three is each partner's liability. In a *general partnership,* each partner is 100 percent personally liable for all debts of the business and all business-related actions of the other partners. In a *limited partnership,* at least one partner acts as a general partner while the others enjoy limited liability protection similar to that of corporate shareholders. *Limited liability partnerships* theoretically protect all partners from personal liability for business debts, but the protection varies widely from state to state. Favorable tax treatment, extremely low audit risk, and simple formation and maintenance make partnerships appear attractive to multiowner companies. The biggest drawback of both general and limited partnerships is that at least one partner must be fully personally liable for all business-related debts. The biggest drawback of limited liability partnerships is the newness of the structure, meaning the liability protection promised has not been tested widely in the courts and is, therefore, a bit uncertain.

Corporation

A *corporation* is a business that is a legal entity on its own, separate from any and all owners, and literally counts as a legal "person." There are two main types of corporations: *C corporations* and *S corporations;* and there are some additional minor subcategories, like the *personal service corporation (PSC).* The basic distinction between the two major types is federal tax treatment. C corporations pay their own taxes on income (although the owners also pay tax on any dividends they receive, the dreaded "double taxation") while S corporations pass all tax benefits and tax liabilities through to their owners. The best thing about corporations is personal protection—the owners of corporations have no personal liability for any business obligations, and they can never lose more than the amount they've invested in the corporation. The biggest drawback of corporations is the incredible amount of legal paperwork and number of procedures needed to maintain them.

Limited Liability Company

The *limited liability company* is a hybrid of partnerships and corporations. While the entity is still relatively new, it quickly has become the darling of small business advisors throughout the nation, and with good reason. This structure combines the primary advantages of partnerships (ease of formation and maintenance, and favorable taxation) with the key advantage of corporations (limited liability protection for all owners). This entity does have a downside, though. Its main drawback is its newness, since a lack of existing case law leaves some questions regarding the strength of liability protection. In addition, some types of businesses may be precluded from using the LLC structure, although this varies from state to state.

Things to Consider When Making a Choice

When you choose your business structure, there are many factors to consider—both business and personal. Too many business owners just look at one or two key business issues, and completely ignore their personal situations. But your financial situation, your life circumstances, and your long-term goals are also very important pieces of the puzzle. When looked at all together, these factors will point to the best entity choice for your business right now.

It's also a good idea to talk to a trusted business advisor, like your CPA or your attorney, before you take steps to actually form your business structure. Use their professional experience to avoid making common mistakes. You can bounce your ideas off of them to see if they agree with your choices. They may be able to shed some light on confusing issues (like the ever-changing tax regulations) and help bring potential drawbacks into focus.

> Too many business owners just look at one or two key business issues, and completely ignore their personal situations.

Don't Just Follow the Crowd

It's crucial that you devote some time and energy to choosing the backbone for your business. Too many would-be business owners get into trouble because they make quick decisions based on a single factor, like a friend's accountant's suggestion or a brother's successful business. Although you might look at similar businesses to see which route they've taken, remember that your combination of business and personal issues is unique. Just because your friend incorporated his bagel store doesn't mean you should incorporate your bakery. And just because the limited liability company is the structure *du jour* doesn't mean it's the right structure for you and your business.

They need not make the entity choice for you, but they can offer sound advice and strong support.

Take These Business Factors into Account

When you're choosing the structure for your business, there are a lot of financial, legal, and management factors to consider. The relative importance of each factor depends on the type of business you plan to start. But even those that may seem relatively insignificant right now may gain importance as your business takes off. The business factors you should consider (not necessarily in order of importance) when choosing your entity are:

Taxation—Different tax rules and different tax rates apply to different types of businesses, and this affects how much of the business income appears on your personal return. Tax laws can also affect the way you'll move money into and out of your business. Understanding the distinctions will help you choose the best entity, and can literally save you thousands of dollars in taxes.

Liability—Some forms of business lay the responsibility for unpaid business debts at your personal door; others completely separate business and personal obligations. If your business is in a high-risk industry, you should choose an entity with inherent personal liability protection

Start-up costs—Simpler business entities cost almost nothing to start; more complex structures can cost thousands of dollars in registrations, organizational expenses, and professional fees.

Ease of formation and maintenance—Paperwork rules some entities from formation on throughout their lives; others require very minimal formalities. Neglecting to stay on top of the paperwork requirements can void your entity choice, so make sure that if you form one of the more paper-intensive structures that you'll be able to follow the rules to a tee.

Financing—Money for your business comes in two forms: debt (you owe money to others) and equity (others own part of your business). Debt financing does not restrict what business entity you may choose, but equity financing is a different story. If you require outside equity financing to start or run your business, some structures will not be viable.

Audit risk—The IRS has a track record of intensively auditing some businesses simply by their structure, while other entities are practically untouched by the T-men. Although audits are uncomfortable and time-consuming, they won't have too much of an effect on your business if you've run it legally and followed all tax-reporting regulations. If you'd like to avoid hearing from the IRS, choose one of the overlooked entities for your business.

Legal restrictions—Certain types of companies, such as professional service providers, are legally excluded from using particular business structures. Also, the number of owners of a company may constrain which entities are allowable.

Ownership transfer options—Some entities are as easy to sell or gift as buying a loaf of bread; for these entities, ownership can change without having any impact on the business at all. Other entities will actually cease to exist when ownership changes hands.

Ease of dissolution—Oddly enough, the entities that are the easiest to transfer to others are the hardest to completely dissolve, requiring notifications, reams of paperwork, and sometimes even permission. By contrast, other entities can be dissolved overnight, no forms needed.

As you learn about each entity, you'll come to understand how these factors all come together to create a unique business structure. You'll see which types of businesses fit best with which entity types. And you'll gain a working knowledge of the effect each of these factors will have on your particular company. When you've looked into each business structure, you'll see that one clearly suits your current needs better than any of the others.

Remember, if you're unsure of how any of these factors applies to your particular business situation, consult a professional. He may cost you some money, but he can save you a lot of research time now and help you avoid future problems.

Don't Forget to Look at These Personal Factors

Are you just graduating from college or nearing retirement? Do you have no kids, or one toddler, or two teenagers? Do you have a lot of money socked away or are you living on a shoestring budget?

Only you can answer all of these questions. And you should consider them an important part of the decision-making process. For example, if you have a lot of personal assets, you may want to avoid any business structures that don't limit your personal liability for business debts. Or if you have children close to college age, you may need to be able to sell the business quickly if you need extra money for their tuition. If you're just starting out, you may be able to take more financial risks because you have more time left to recover from problems than someone close to retirement.

Business advisors look at business factors and provide business solutions. But your business is part of your life—and you need to make sure that the type of business you run and the entity you choose fit in with your life plan as well as your business plan.

The personal factors you should consider include:

- Your age and life stage
- Your marital status
- The number of children you have and their ages
- How much debt you have
- Your net worth
- How much monthly household income you need
- Your total annual household income including expected business income
- How much time you plan to devote to the business
- Whether you make better decisions alone or with a group

If you're married, you need to include your spouse's information when you evaluate each of the factors above. For example, net worth should take into account the assets and debts of both spouses.

> Make sure that the type of business you run and the entity you choose fit in with your life plan.

Knowing When to Make a Change

What should you do if you've already started your business and have already "chosen" an entity by default? First, relax. Then take a look at how the default structure works with your business—it could be the entity you would have chosen even after careful planning and research.

Most companies actually start out this way—because entrepreneurs tend to be a passionate group, often jumping in with both feet before they even check to see if the pool has water in it. People just get an idea, and go into business. It's not ideal, but it happens, and it can (and should) be fixed. Don't make the same mistake again, though—don't choose the structure you're changing the same way you chose the first; some entities are much harder to convert than others.

Basically, the two default structures (sole proprietorship and partnership) are also the easiest to transform into other entities. So even if the structure you've fallen into isn't really the best choice for your company, it's not so hard to make a change. In fact, if you switch to certain other structures (such as from general partnership to LLC, as you'll learn about later in this book), you won't even have to change the tax forms you file.

So don't fret that you're stuck lying in a bed of your own making. Read up, ask questions, consult a pro, and make sure you use the best business structure going forward. You can't change the past, but you can make sure that your company has a long and fruitful life.

Remember: All businesses change. Sometimes those changes come from the inside, like growth and expansion. Other times, outside forces will dictate change, like when new laws are written. And change can also be brought on by a combination of internal and external factors, like when you need to bring in outside investors or get a bank loan. If your business undergoes a transformation, reassessing your business structure is definitely called for.

These events (among others) could signal that it's time to reconsider the business entity you've chosen:

- You decide to hire employees.
- You're a sole proprietor and you want to bring on additional owners.
- Your personal responsibility for business liabilities becomes overwhelming.

- The tax law changes, making one form of business significantly more advantageous than another.

Of course, like with everything else, there are potential drawbacks to making such a significant change. For example, you may have to rename your business. You could face adverse tax consequences. And, it will probably cost you money for some administrative items, like retitling all of your major business assets.

Those disadvantages should not, however, stop you from changing your business structure when the time is right. Yes, it might cost some money and it might give you a temporary migraine. But when all is said and done, the need for such a change is usually brought about by success—and isn't that what you're here for?

► **Chapter 2**

Things You Need to Do for Any Structure

Part One

Part Two

Part Three

Part Four

Part Five

Part Six

No Business Without a Business Plan

The best time to write a business plan is *before* you start your business. Unfortunately, all too many entrepreneurs jump into business first, then have to backtrack to deal with unexpected events, events that could have been planned for or even prevented if the business owner had prepared a plan.

Writing a complete business plan before you start your business will considerably increase your chance of success. Most people put off their business plans until they need funding—and by that time, it's often too late. Having a blueprint for your business from the outset will not only help you anticipate when you might need financing, but it also forces you to look at myriad issues that unfailingly crop up for new businesses.

What a Business Plan Will Tell You

By simply following business plan basics, you'll be able to determine whether your proposed business has a good chance of succeeding. You'll be able to figure out how much money you'll really need to get started—and that includes the money you'll need to live on until your business starts bringing in money on its own. You'll start thinking about how to define your target markets, how to best market your company, how to analyze your competition and how to start generating profits as quickly as possible.

In addition to preplanning, going through the motions of a business plan will teach you about problems you could encounter. By knowing what sort of issues could come up, you have a chance to figure out solutions beforehand, allowing you to be proactive rather than reactive. For example, you might run through a scenario where your biggest supplier suddenly can't supply what you need when you need it. By thinking about this drawback beforehand, you can keep a small stable of contingency suppliers that could get you through a shortfall. Chances are, a supplier you've never dealt with before may not be inclined to help you through a crisis, at least not without charging you an arm and a leg.

Perhaps most important, a business plan forces you to do some number crunching. If you need to raise outside funds from the beginning, you'll have to give the bank solid financial information showing why they should take a gamble on your fledgling business. Any potential lender or investor will only

> Going through the motions of a business plan will teach you about problems you could encounter.

want to give you money if they can be fairly sure they'll get it back. And a well-prepared business plan, complete with financial analyses and projections, is the proof they're looking for. It shows you know what you're talking about, and that you have a plan that will lead to profits—and profits are what you will need to pay them back.

You Have to Crunch Some Numbers

If you're like most people, the thought of financial calculations and projections makes you squeamish. Those queasy feelings might lead you to just plug in some numbers, or to skip the financial portion of your business plan altogether. But good financial planning is crucial for the success of your business. So steel yourself and go put some numbers together.

What you need for planning purposes, and what potential investors and lenders want to see, is a realistic financial forecast. And even if you're not looking for outside capital right off the bat, you need to know for yourself how much all of this is going to cost you. You also need to know how long it will take you to start seeing profits and, more important, when you'll start generating a positive cash flow.

Typical information you should have in your plan includes:

Estimate of start-up costs—This covers all the money you'll need to spend before you open your doors for business; it includes things like rent, phone installation, decorating and displays, and legal fees.

Break-even analysis—This statement shows how much you need to earn to cover both your start-up and regular operating costs.

Profit and loss forecast—This statement shows your expected sales and expenses for at least your first year in business.

Cash flow forecast—This details the way you expect money to flow into and out of your business for at least your first year in business.

A word of caution: It's tempting to try to make the numbers "come out good," but that's not necessarily realistic. You are more likely to succeed and/or get funding if your numbers are based in reality as opposed to what you'd like to see happen. The truth is that, in your first year, you may sustain a loss and you may have more cash flowing out than in. That's okay—as long as you're prepared for it and know how to turn it around.

Where Do the Numbers Come From?

Once you've resigned yourself to write a plan, and to do it right, you need to find the numbers to use for your calculations. Some of them will be obvious, some you may have to dig around for, and some you really will have to "guesstimate."

The expense numbers are the easiest to determine. For example, to find out a typical monthly rental payment on the kind of space you need, call a realtor; to find out how much glass bottles cost (for example), call a bottle supplier. It helps to look at typical profit and loss statements for other businesses in your intended industry to get an idea of typical—and unusual—expenses you might incur. Although it may be hard to get a hold of real financial statements for competing businesses, you can find statements for sample companies pretty easily on the Internet.

The real brainwork is in projecting your sales. To do that, you first need to know what you'll be selling and the price at which you intend to offer it. Then you need to do some fancy footwork to figure out realistically how much you'll be able to sell. For example, if you're starting a cleaning service,

SCORE Some Help to Prepare Your Plan

Wish you had a mentor to help you with all of this? Help is available. The SCORE Association has more than 10,000 volunteers ready to help small businesses nationwide. This group of mentors is made up of both retired and still-working entrepreneurs, professionals, and executives who know the ropes and are ready to hand their knowledge down to the next generation of business owners. They offer face-to-face, confidential, free counseling to small business owners—including assistance preparing business plans. You can connect with one of these mentors simply by going to the SCORE Web site (✉ www.score.org) or by contacting their office in your area.

you're limited by time as to how much revenue you can bring in during any given period.

Your Plan Will Change as Your Business Does

Business plans are not carved in stone. They make good blueprints for you to follow initially, but as you gain experience and see what actually happens in your unique business, your plan will be subject to change.

Whether you need to prepare a new plan because your business is expanding, because you need additional funding, or just because your original ideas didn't pan out quite the way you expected, it will be easier because you've already done it.

Naming Your Business

The first thing people will learn about your business is its name, so it's important to make the name count. Although there are some restrictions involved in naming your company, you still have a great deal of latitude. When coming up with possible names for your business, keep these basic guidelines in mind:

1. Make it easy to say and remember—word of mouth can be your best advertisement, but it won't work if people can't pronounce or recall the name.
2. Choose a name that specifically describes your business— *Donna Smith Interior Design* says a lot more than *The Donna Smith Company*.
3. Make sure the name is available—two businesses operating in the same general geographic area can't legally use the same name, and you can't use an already trademarked name without potential legal consequences.
4. Try to choose a name that doesn't box you in—since you want your company to grow, and to stay around for a long time, pick a name that doesn't limit you. For example, calling your business *Donna's Red Culottes* isn't such a great name when culottes go out of style, or if you want to sell something blue.

Doing Business As . . .

While many entrepreneurs name their businesses after themselves, many make up names for their companies; these are referred to as "fictitious" names or "doing business as" (or DBA) names. These names are not the legal names of the companies.

The legal name for a business is the official name of its owner. So if you're the sole owner of a company, its legal name is your legal name. If the business is a general partnership, its legal name is either made up of the last names of all the partners (like Johnson, Smith, and Riley) or the chosen name spelled out in the partnership agreement (if one exists). For corporations, limited partnerships, and LLCs, their legal names are those that have been registered with their state filing offices. A company's legal name is the one that must be used on all government forms.

The DBA name for a business is its trade name—the one customers and suppliers know it by. Any time a business uses a name other than its exact legal name, it's using a DBA name. For example, if sole proprietor John Smith refers to his business as *J.S. Antiques*, he is using a DBA name. If you are planning to use a DBA name you'll have to register it as discussed below.

How to Find Out Whether the Name Is Available

As you just learned, you can't name your business the same as someone else's company. To make sure you don't do that inadvertently, you'll have to conduct a name and trademark search. Since there is no one central location holding a list of every business name, you'll have to do some homework.

As a first step, do a simple Internet search. Pick your favorite search engine, type in the name you want to use and see what happens. You'll find out in just a few minutes if someone on the Internet is using a similar name for a similar business. If that step doesn't turn up any matches, move on to step two. Check with the U.S. Patent and Trademark Office (USPTO) to see if the name you want to use is already registered to someone else. They keep a log of all registered names on their Web site at *www.uspto.gov.*

Because the large majority of small businesses don't officially register their names with the USPTO, your search won't end there. If that search did not turn up a hit, your next step is to check the list of unregistered trademarks.

You can do that by surfing over the largest known register of such names on the Internet at ✑ *www.thomasregister.com.*

Finally, check with the local county clerk's office. All businesses legally must register their DBA names in order to use them in conducting business. If your business will be a corporation, LLC, or limited partnership, the clerk will search the state filing office of registered names. Often the county clerk will direct you to your home state's database, which holds the names of even very small companies.

Your Form of Business Dictates Part of the Name

Particular wording may be required or prohibited for your name, depending on which form of business you choose. Although these rules vary from state to state, they largely follow these basic guidelines:

- Sole proprietorships and general partnerships cannot include the terms "Incorporated," "Corporation," or any standard abbreviation of those terms (like "Inc." or "Corp.") in their names.
- Corporations must include one of the following terms (or the appropriate abbreviation) in their names: "Corporation," Incorporated," or "Limited."
- The names of limited liability companies must include an abbreviation that clearly identifies the form of business. Acceptable abbreviations usually are "LLC," "LC," and "Ltd." The business name cannot include such prohibited terms as "Corporation" or "Inc."

Sometimes the Same Name Is Okay

The main purpose of the rules about business naming is to keep customers from being confused. For example, if you have a small soda shop that sells homemade lemon-lime soda, calling that shop *The Seven-Up Store* would lead consumers to believe they were getting 7Up—clearly confusing the customers. But if your shop sold small spiral staircases with seven steps each, calling your business The Seven-Up Store would be fine, since the actual business has nothing to do with the beverage company and consumers aren't likely to confuse soda with staircases.

Don't Operate Without a License

A lot of people start conducting business before they bother with any legalities. They moonlight to bring in some extra cash—then expand into full-blown businesses. Along the way, they get so involved in what they're doing that they don't realize they've formed a company.

Such is the tale of Julie, who used to cut my sister's hair. She worked in a salon, and also cut people's hair in her kitchen after hours. She ended up with so much after-hours work that she stopped working for the salon, and she only coiffed those clients that came to her house. She still maintained her individual operator's license—but never licensed her home salon. When the state found out, they shut down her home business, and suspended her operator's license for six months. A tale of woe, to be sure, but one that could have easily been prevented by obtaining the required license.

Registering Your Business Name

If you plan to use only your company's legal name when you conduct business, you won't need to take any additional steps to secure its name. For sole proprietors using their own personal legal names as business names, no filings of any kind are required. If your business is a corporation, limited partnership, or LLC, its legal name generally will be registered when you file your organization paperwork.

However, if you plan to use a DBA name for your business, you have to register that name with the appropriate government office, usually the local county clerk's office. (In some states, you may have to register with a state agency, typically the Secretary of State.) To find out the exact requirements of your area, contact the county clerk's office and they'll tell you what procedures to follow, what forms to fill out, and how much to write a check for.

Even though the exact requirements vary by county, they follow the same general pattern. First you have to ensure the name you want isn't already taken. Next, you get and fill out a registration form and mail it in with the stated fee (usually no more than $50). In some states, that ends the process; in others, you have one more step to take. Depending on the laws of your state, you may have to publish your DBA name in a local newspaper and hand in a "proof of publication" at the clerk's office.

Although local registration is all that's legally required to begin trading under the chosen name for your business, you may want to obtain trademark protection at the state or federal level. That may seem like overkill now—but what if your business grows beyond your wildest dreams and you haven't protected its name? If your business is strictly local, registering with your home state is probably protection enough. But if you will be engaging in interstate commerce, federal trademark protection is called for.

Register Your Domain Name ASAP

When you're choosing a name for your business, it's a good idea to choose a Web site name at the same time, even if you don't plan to do business over the Internet. Whether or not you'll be selling your products or services via the Web, having some sort of presence on the Internet is a good way to keep the customers coming. Potential clients can use your Web site to find out more about your shop, and even to contact you during off hours should they have questions or problems.

The problem is that there are more registered Web names than there are Web sites! In fact, you can't find a single word in the (English) dictionary that hasn't already been registered. How do you solve the problem? You can use the full name of your business as the site name (if it's not already taken), like JohnSmithPlumbing.com. You can add hyphens between the words, as in John-Smith-Plumbing.com. If that doesn't work, you can add more words to the name, as in JohnSmithPlumbingServices.com. You can make up some kind of abbreviated term, like JoPlumb. Or, you can come up with a nonsense word that has nothing to do with your business, like Jexikon—the drawback being that no one will know what it means.

Once you've found a name you like (or at least the best one you can think of that isn't already taken), you have to register it. The cost to register your domain name will range somewhere from $15 to $50 per year, depending on the service you use and the features you choose.

Business Fees, Licenses, and Permits

To operate a business legally, you have to follow all the rules. And that means getting all the necessary licenses and permits, and paying a lot of fees. Which ones apply to your business depend on where you are and what you'll be doing.

On the Federal Level

While most small businesses don't have to get federal permits and licenses, federal tax registrations may be necessary. If your business will be organized in any form other than sole proprietorship, you'll need to apply for a federal employer identification number (EIN) by filling out and filing Form SS-4. If you'll be forming a sole proprietorship, you can simply use your social security number as your EIN—unless you plan to hire employees or independent contractors. To pay wages or contractor fees, you will have to apply for a separate EIN. You can find Form SS-4 on the IRS Web site at ✒ *www.irs.gov.*

The other potential federal tax registration for small businesses only applies to S corporations. If you choose to form your business as an S corporation, you'll have to complete and submit Form 2553. (This form will be discussed in more detail in Part Four.)

Although most small businesses don't need federal licensing, some types of businesses may. If your business fits one of the descriptions below, contact the appropriate agency:

- Investment advisors should contact the Securities and Exchange Commission.
- Some ground transportation services, like common carrier trucking firms, should contact the Interstate Commerce Commission.
- Businesses producing drugs or preparing certain food products should contact the Food and Drug Administration.
- Businesses producing alcohol or tobacco products, or dealing with firearms must contact the Bureau of Alcohol, Tobacco, and Firearms.

On the State Level

Licensing requirements vary greatly from state to state. Many states require business licenses for companies that provide particular products. Most states require professional licensing for certain professions, like attorneys, barbers, and real estate agents. And most states require licensing for businesses regulated by state law, like establishments serving liquor or selling lottery tickets. To find out which permits or licenses you need to conduct business in your state, you'll have to contact the appropriate state agency (or agencies). To help bewildered new business owners, the U.S. Small Business Administration (SBA) has a contact list of state agencies on its Web site at ✒ *www.sba.gov.*

In addition to the more common permits mentioned above, you may have to get a sales tax certificate in order to collect and remit sales tax.

Almost every state requires retail businesses to collect sales tax; many also foist this requirement on service providers. To find out whether your business will have to collect sales tax, and to get the application process started, contact your state tax board.

Even if you won't be required to deal with sales tax, you'll probably have to pay some form of state income taxes. That means another registration, and possibly another ID number. To find out if your business will be liable for income taxes and which forms to fill out, contact your state's treasury department (sometimes called the Department of Revenue).

A Word about Retirement Plans

Almost everyone knows about (and has contributed to) some kind of retirement plan. Both employees and business owners are squirreling away money for the future in tax-deferred plans; that means no income taxes are due until they actually start receiving the money. Although you probably have at least some money in a retirement plan, you may not really understand how they work—especially when you're the business owner helping your employees save for retirement.

Essentially, all kinds of retirement plans allow people with earned income to put pretax dollars into special accounts. Pretax dollars means that the money you put into a retirement plan is not counted as income when figuring your annual tax bill. On top of that, all the money earned by your

Start Saving Now for Retirement

Retirement may seem very far off, almost not worth thinking about. You have bills to pay today, a business to get off the ground—you don't have the time or money to spare to open a retirement account. Do it anyway.

Without getting bogged down in the mathematics of the time value of money, we'll skip right to the point: You'll end up with more money if you contribute less today than if you contribute more in five or ten years. The more time your money has to grow, the more it will grow. So set aside even $10 per week of your bill money for a retirement account—in twenty years, you'll be glad you did.

retirement account is tax-deferred; that means no tax is due on any of the income produced by the account until the money is withdrawn.

There are a lot of retirement plan options for small businesses, but each fits into one of two basic categories: defined contribution plans or defined benefit plans. The big difference between these two groups is their focus. Defined contribution plans look at only how much gets added to the account each year, with no thought of the total final accumulation or distributions. Defined benefit plans work backward—they look to eventual annual distributions from each account, and work back to this year's contribution.

Defined Contribution Plans

With a defined contribution plan, you (as the employer) will spell out the amount you'll put into each employee's account each year. The contribution is typically defined as a percentage of salary, rather than a fixed dollar amount. Because this method focuses on what gets put in rather than what will get drawn out, there's no way to measure how big an account will be at retirement time. The account balance for each plan participant at his retirement age depends on three factors:

1. The amount contributed to the account
2. The timing of contributions
3. How much the account earns

For small business owners, defined contribution plans offer both simplicity and flexibility.

For small business owners, defined contribution plans offer both simplicity and flexibility. The contributions are easily determined—you just pick a percentage according to the current year's federal tax guidelines, then multiply it by each eligible employee's base salary. You are not required to make contributions in lean years, such as when the business is in a slight downturn or money is tight. And since you haven't promised a specific payout, the employee bears all the risk in regard to account earnings.

There are several types of defined contribution plans:

- 401(k) plans
- Simplified employee pensions (SEP)
- Profit-sharing plans

- Money-purchase plans
- Employee stock ownership plans (ESOP)
- SIMPLE plans

Defined contribution plans work best for relatively young business owners, who have plenty of time left until retirement (twenty years or so). They have time to add to their accounts and watch their savings grow.

Defined Benefit Plans

Defined benefit plans guarantee each participant's annual payout at retirement. To make sure the account will be able to make those payments as promised, the employer must make the contributions required by the plan. The annual contribution for each participant is figured out based on complex actuarial equations, which look at the following factors:

- How long until the participant will hit legal retirement age
- The expected earnings on the account's investments
- The current account balance
- The guaranteed payouts

Older business owners who want to make the largest possible deductible contributions to their own accounts should set up defined benefit plans. Since business owners closer to retirement have a limited amount of time left to contribute to their plans, the tax law allows deductible contributions large enough to cover the promised payouts.

Be aware: There are significant drawbacks to defined benefit plans. First, contributions have to be made regardless of profits and cash flow. Second, if an account isn't growing at the projected rate, the business has to make even bigger annual contributions—meaning that the business, and not the employee, is bearing all of the investment risk. Finally, if the account earns more than expected, the account will be "overfunded" and no (or low) contributions will be allowed until that situation changes.

How to Choose the Right Plan

With such a variety of plans available, you should take your time in choosing the one that best fits your situation. The plan should mesh with your retirement goals, first and foremost. If you're unsure of your cash flows and earnings, and you have a long time to go before you hit retirement, one of the defined contribution plans probably makes the most sense. If you have less time to fill your retirement piggy bank and no employees to worry about, a defined benefit plan may be ideal. But since your business wasn't made with a cookie cutter, the choice of retirement plan will likely require a more in-depth look.

To make sure you select the best retirement plan for your business, talk to a financial advisor. They know the unique advantages and drawbacks to each type of plan, and they can tailor any plan to your specific requirements.

If you have employees who will be involved in the plan, consulting with a professional is even more important. They'll help you perform a thorough cost-benefit analysis before you choose and implement a plan.

> **Chapter 3**

Get Professional Help Before You Start

Part One

Part Two

Part Three

Part Four

Part Five

Part Six

PART ONE   HOW TO GET STARTED IN BUSINESS

▦ CHAPTER 1 Choosing the Best Business Structure ▦ CHAPTER 2 Things You Need to Do for Any Structure
■ CHAPTER 3 Get Professional Help Before You Start

Why You Shouldn't Do It Yourself

Professional help is expensive. Attorneys charge upwards of $250 per hour. Accountants charge anywhere from $75 to $350 per hour. And the list of professionals goes on, and quickly adds up. So struggling entrepreneurs try to save some money and do things by themselves. They go online and read about do-it-yourself incorporation kits. Or they head to the stationery store and buy an "LLC in-a-box." While they're there they pick up some accounting software package that looks very easy to use—the box even says that you don't need to know anything about accounting to use the program.

Where else can they cut back? Marketing is often one of the first areas to head to the chopping block. New business owners often expect that their customer base will go solely by word of mouth. But the fastest way to go out of business is to have no customers—because no customers means no sales.

Since many businesses start up without employees, payroll services don't even come into question in the early stages. But once a company grows to the point that additional help is needed, the owner looks at the cost of paying the employees and balks at the extra cost of employing a payroll service. If you love filing forms and reams of paperwork, do it yourself—but keep in mind that mistakes are costly, as the IRS won't balk at charging interest and penalties if you do it wrong.

Yes, professional help will cost money. And that's the one thing most fledgling businesses never have enough of. However, in these cases, the benefits far outweigh the costs. If you want to cut corners, don't get Caller ID; buy the cheapest paper you can find for your copier and printer; and skip the cleaning service and do that yourself. But don't hold back on serious professional advice: It will cost money now (maybe even a lot), but it will save you money, time, and headaches in the long run.

Have an Attorney Draft Your Legal Documents

The number one reason to hire an attorney at the outset: You can't go backward, and if you have a problem, it's already too late. A good business attorney will help you prevent problems from ever occurring, or put in place methods to deal with anything that does crop up. But even the very best lawyer in the land can't help you if difficulties are already on your doorstep.

How to Choose Your Attorney

It's tempting to "use the guy who did Joe's shop" or to pick a name out of the phone book. But, hopefully, your business will be around for a long time—and you should plan to have just as long a relationship with your attorney.

Think of your business lawyer as a business partner, a colleague. Certainly during the start-up phase he should be an integral part of your team. You need to choose someone you're comfortable with, someone you're not afraid to question. You also need a lawyer with business start-up experience, preferably in your industry (or at least a related one).

Here are some points to consider when selecting your attorney:

Firm size—Small firms may not be able to handle every aspect of your business both now and in the future; large firms typically cost more, and smaller clients can get lost in the shuffle.

Experience—Make sure the lawyer has handled business start-ups before; you don't want to be his practice case.

Client list—Find out whether the attorney has other clients in your industry or at least a good deal of familiarity with it.

Communication style—Look for a lawyer who will help you learn about the legalities pertinent to your business in a way you can easily understand; he should be willing to discuss your concerns and answer your questions with more than one-word answers.

Location—Lawyers charge for travel time, and your time is precious, too; pick someone whose office is as close to home as possible, as you'll be going there a lot.

Chemistry—You're going to spend a lot of time with this person, especially during the stressful start-up period of your business, so make sure you choose someone you actually like.

> Think of your business lawyer as a business partner, a colleague.

What You Need a Lawyer to Do

Like most other professionals, lawyers are creating smaller and smaller niches, specializing in just one or two areas of law. You need a business lawyer, preferably one who specializes in start-ups. The guy who drew up your will and did the closing on your condo probably isn't the right guy to start your business with, no matter how much you like him. But he may just be able to refer you to a capable colleague.

You need an attorney who's competent in the following areas:

Business organization—Your attorney should be able to help you decide which is the best entity for your company, and do all the requisite set-up paperwork.

Taxes—While he won't be preparing the actual tax returns for your business, he probably will be the one who gets all the tax ID numbers your business will need; plus, he should be familiar with the tax implications of your entity choice and those of your industry's more standard transactions.

Licensing—Your business will be shut down if it doesn't have all the proper licenses and permits; your lawyer should know about and help you acquire all the licenses you'll need to operate.

Contracts—Your attorney must be able to draw up standard business contracts at the drop of a hat, and he should peruse contracts you receive (from customers or suppliers, for example) to make sure they're kosher before you sign them.

Those are the basic must-haves. And there are a few more areas that wouldn't hurt, like lease negotiation (if you plan on renting office or retail space) or intellectual property (if you'll be creating original products). One lawyer may not be able to do all of this—or at least not do all of it well. Don't be taken aback if he involves a second attorney, or farms some of the work out. You're better off with someone who knows what he can't do, then someone who thinks he can do it all.

When You Should Use an Accountant

Like attorneys, accountants tend to charge pretty steep fees. For some areas of your business finances, the cost is well worth it. For others, you may be able to do it on your own or use a lower-cost service.

At a minimum, you should use an accountant to do your business's tax return (for sole proprietors, this is the same as the personal return). By using a trained professional, you'll be able to take advantage of all possible deductions, ensuring your tax bill won't be higher than it needs to be. Also, tax accountants are up to speed on tax compliance, new regulations, and special tax treatment for particular businesses or transactions—ensuring that you follow all tax laws to a tee and file on time.

Although this is not as crucial as filing a fully compliant but not overly taxing tax return, setting up your accounting system is another function best done by professionals. Your accountant should be able to help you select, install, and set up most mass-market bookkeeping software (although they typically recommend the one that their office and most of their other small business clients use). He'll set up your accounting periods and your chart of accounts (another way of saying "numbered account list"). Then he'll show you how to enter common transactions, like customer invoicing and bill paying.

As for the day-to-day functions, your best bet is to use a professional bookkeeper. This is the function small business owners usually plan to do themselves during their "free" time, or rope a family member (like a spouse) into doing for them. But in most cases, it just doesn't get done on time, correctly, or sometimes even at all. This is another one of those circumstances where paying a little now will save you from paying a lot later on. If, at tax time your books aren't kept, or are kept incorrectly, paying the accountant to do a year's worth of bookkeeping at once or to fathom and fix the mistakes can cost you a pretty penny.

What Kind of Accounting Help Do You Need?

CPAs (certified public accountants) are accountants who have attained the required education level, passed comprehensive exams, and fulfilled experience requirements in order to obtain special state licensing. To maintain their licenses, CPAs must meet annual continuing education requirements, ensuring

A True Story

Just last April, a new client with a sole proprietorship handed me a grocery bag full of canceled checks, receipts, and deposit slips; he then asked how much it would cost to have his taxes done by the 15th. I asked to see his check register, any computer printouts, and his year-end credit card statements. It turned out that he didn't have any of those things. He had planned on doing the bookkeeping himself, but it just kept getting pushed back as he had customer issues to handle.

I sent him to a friend with a bookkeeping service who had more time for sifting through the bag. I also told him to buy a copy of QuickBooks and to apply for a business credit card. By mid-June, the client had hired my friend to enter his transactions into QuickBooks each week and was now recording all his checks and deposits in a register. When I did his return then, he was due a pretty large refund—which he would have gotten a lot sooner if he had hired help from the outset.

they'll always know the latest information that affects businesses. Some functions, like independent audits, require a CPA. CPAs can also handle other high-level accounting and finance tasks, including business and tax planning, tax return preparation, and financing proposals. Accountants who are not state-certified can help you with most of your accounting needs (except, of course, the ones that demand use of a CPA). Although they may have similar background and experience, non-CPA accountants usually charge lower rates than their certified counterparts. They can prepare tax returns, help you set up your accounting system, and even provide write-up services (another way to say "do your year-end bookkeeping and financial statements").

Bookkeepers are great for handling everyday transactions—and for much less money than an accountant doing the exact same thing. From balancing the checkbook to sending late-payment reminders to customers, bookkeepers can provide myriad services for small businesses. The most important function they will serve is keeping everything up to date. You need to know the balance in your checkbook, how close you are to the limit on your credit cards, how much you owe to your vendors (and when it's due), and how much your customers owe you. Without this crucial information—on time—you could find yourself running into a serious cash crunch. But a bookkeeper can keep on top of everything, more easily than you can with all the other positions you'll be filling as your business gains momentum.

Choosing Your Accounting Team

A new business owner should hire an accountant to set things up, oversee the financial status, prepare the tax returns, and assist with overall business and financial planning. But he should use a bookkeeper to handle the everyday transactions and bank account reconciliations.

Some accounting firms keep bookkeepers on staff—allowing the client to get the work done in-house but at lower bookkeeping rates. This mix is often the best fit for a start-up business, because it allows the accountant to keep an eye on the initial financial situation, and that often leads to enhanced planning opportunities. If you find an accountant you really like to work with but he doesn't have a bookkeeper on staff, consider splitting your business. Use the accountant for higher-level financial tasks, and hire an outside book-keeper for the rest. This arrangement will save you a lot of money.

As with attorneys, take some care in choosing your accounting team since you'll likely be working with them for quite some time. Try to find someone familiar with your business entity, industry, and business size: an accountant specializing in *Fortune* 500 companies listed on the New York Stock Exchange may have an impeccable pedigree, but how well will he really be able to serve a local restaurant owned and run by a sole proprietor?

Find someone you're comfortable with whose prices won't seriously impact your profit margin. Your accountant should be more than a numbers cruncher—he should be involved in helping your business to start and grow.

Don't Skimp on Marketing

It's a vicious cycle—you have to spend money to get customers, but without customers you don't have the money to spend. How can you break the cycle? With a marketing plan. You don't need to run to Madison Ave. and get ad time during the Super Bowl right out of the gate. But you do need to have a cohesive plan, and the best way to get it all done is with a professional. Even if you can't afford to hire out for every aspect, you should at least consult with someone who knows how to bring in customers.

Like all other service-oriented businesses, advertising and other marketing consulting agencies come in all shapes and sizes, with different areas of specialty. If you're working with a tight budget, look for a small, local firm who will still give you time and attention for your money. They'll come up with a marketing plan tailored to both your business and your budget.

Although it sounds backward, you should be spending more marketing dollars when business is slow, and even more when you're new and trying just to get your name out there. When cash is flowing like molasses, you need to promote your business more than at any other time. Don't plan to wait until you're in the black to start advertising, or you may never get there.

> You should be spending more marketing dollars when business is slow, and even more when you're new.

Consider Using a Payroll Service

Frankly, doing payroll is a pain in the neck. The number of calculations needed to prepare even a single payroll check can put even the most math-friendly business owner in a bad mood. Plus, tax rates and tax laws change *all the time*. Merely keeping up with the changes can be a full-time job in itself. Add to that all the paperwork, government filings, and payment deadlines and

Let Your Fingers Do the Walking

One of the best marketing tools for new small businesses is the local Yellow Pages. Listing your name there is great, and buying some ad space is even better. The cost varies by region, but the phone book is where a lot of potential clients turn to find what they need. Advertising in the phone book takes advance planning, as they typically only publish once or twice a year. Find out the schedule so you don't miss the current cutoff and have to wait six months to a year to get in.

you'll be ready to buy a year's supply of aspirin. The most important reason not to do this yourself? Interest and penalties: when you do payroll wrong or file the forms late, you have to pay more.

Enter the payroll service. Originally only for large companies with thousands of employees on the payroll, these companies now cater to small businesses. Even companies with two or three employees can benefit from using a payroll service.

Not only do payroll-processing companies prepare employee paychecks to your specifications, they also take care of all of your tax filings throughout the year. They make sure all the payroll taxes that need to be remitted are. They prepare W-2s for your employees at year-end. Some companies send reps out to see you during the year to make sure you're happy with the service.

Payroll service firms may also provide additional services. They'll hand deliver your weekly payroll, or handle your direct deposit checks. Some firms will even help set up and administer your company's retirement plan (like a 401(k) plan). A lot of payroll processing companies will also handle your worker's compensation claims or administer cafeteria plans (the IRS lingo for "pick-a-benefit" employee benefit plans).

They manage to provide all of this for a relatively modest sum. They also often have special pricing plans for smaller companies. Charges do vary widely by payroll company, region, and service level, so call around before you pick one. Unlike your accountant or attorney, it's very easy (and very common) to switch payroll companies.

Unless you are your only employee and you like doing mind-numbing paperwork, get a payroll service. Especially at tax time, you'll be glad you did.

> **Chapter 4**

The Easiest Business to Start

Part One

Part Two

Part Three

Part Four

Part Five

Part Six

Defining the Sole Proprietorship

A *sole proprietorship* is a business that is unincorporated and owned by only one person. For tax and legal purposes, there is no distinction between the business and the owner—they are considered to be one and the same. While a sole proprietorship cannot have more than one owner, it can have any number of employees. The exception: The owner can never be considered an employee of the business.

Almost all small businesses start as sole proprietorships, largely due to the fact that it is the simplest business entity to form. According to the most recently released IRS figures, a staggering 18,336,500 sole proprietors filed tax returns in 2002 (20,072,000 when you include farmers). Now compare that to a total of 8,010,700 for all other entities combined, and you'll see how popular a business form this really is. In fact, the IRS is projecting (based on returns already examined) 18,724,900 nonfarm sole proprietorships in 2003—that's almost an additional 400,000!

You May Already Be a Sole Proprietor

The only prerequisite to starting a sole proprietorship is to open for business, so many people become sole proprietors inadvertently. If you're an independent contractor or a freelancer, you already are a sole proprietor—whether you meant to be or not. If you've ever received an IRS Form 1099-MISC for nonemployee compensation, you are a sole proprietor.

An Overview of the Pros and Cons

Choosing to operate as a sole proprietorship will bring you some unique benefits:

- Simple administration
- Clear-cut accounting procedures
- Special tax breaks
- Freedom to move cash in and out of the business whenever and however you want
- Minimal legal paperwork

Keep in mind, though, that this apparently trouble-free business structure comes with some disadvantages, too. The biggest drawback is unlimited personal liability, followed by high taxes and difficulty in transferring ownership.

A Trial Run

Just because you start out as a sole proprietorship doesn't mean that you're locked into that choice for the entire life of your business. In fact, many businesses that begin their lives as sole proprietorships switch to more formal entities as they grow. But while you're still trying things out, this entity lets you focus on getting your company off the ground without having to worry about all the administrative headaches of the other forms of business.

In addition to avoiding paperwork, you'll also escape the myriad fees other business entities are subject to simply because of their form. Since profits can be hard to come by in the early years of a business, minimizing administrative expenses can help your company stay afloat.

As your business (and your confidence in its success) grows and your income stream stabilizes, you may want to start looking at the other entity choices. When your company has gained a solid foothold, a different form of business could enhance it.

Going It Alone

Entrepreneurs tend to take initiative and make decisions quickly. In some workplaces, these attributes are frowned upon; in a sole proprietorship, these attributes are vital. Since only one person owns the business, he controls every part of its existence. Whether deciding to run the shop or hire a manager, or figuring out how much cash he'll take home today, a sole proprietor just makes a choice and acts on it.

Don't Pay More Taxes Than You Have To

Anyone who pays someone more than $600 for services rendered has to send that person an IRS Form 1099. If you've received a 1099, you have to account for that income on your annual income tax return. Most people, not knowing that they do count as a business, just report the income, but don't deduct any legitimate business expenses against it.

Although you as a self-employed individual could simply include that income as "other income" on the first page of your annual 1040, why pay more taxes that you have to? Taking the easy way out actually prevents you from deducting your business expenses. So, to make sure you're getting all the tax breaks you deserve, consider yourself a business now, and take full advantage of all the deductions that come with that.

As a sole proprietor, you will have complete control over all aspects of your business. There are no committees to pitch to, no partners to vote with. This lack of red tape allows you to implement new ideas and strategies as you think of them—because every decision that's made ultimately comes from you. You will direct all of the business activities; even if you hire a manager to run the day-to-day operations, he'll still receive direction from you.

The Dark Side of Doing It Alone

In many start-up sole proprietorships, the owner not only controls the business—he manages it and works for it as well. And while many of these small companies eventually hire employees to take over those tasks, at the outset most go it alone. Sole proprietors (especially new ones) often work 24/7, with little time for family, friends, and relaxation. But once things get rolling, they typically turn the daily tasks over to salaried employees, and just stick around to oversee the direction of the business.

Limited free time is one drawback of going it alone—but it's not the biggest disadvantage of flying solo. All of the financial resources needed to bring the business to a point where it can support itself come from you: your

The SBA Can Be Your Best Friend

Imagine a government agency devoted to finding money for small business owners. Picture a group of government employees who cut through all the red tape and actually make things happen. Now try to visualize your new company, fully funded, and up and running—all thanks to the U.S. federal government.

It may sound like a lovely dream, but in fact it's a lovely reality. The SBA (Small Business Administration) really does exist to help small business get funding—and their streamlined operations and knowledgeable staff actually get things done. They even get things done fast.

If your small business needs some start-up cash and you're not sure where or how to get it, contact the SBA. Go to their Web site at ✑ *www.sba.gov*. Not only will you find a lot of handy information, you'll also find the phone number and address of the SBA office nearest you.

savings, your credit cards, your home equity loan. If you go to a bank for money, they'll ask to see your personal financial statements (if you're married, they'll want to see the same for your spouse). If you go to a private investor, he'll also take a magnifying glass to your personal financial situation. And if you're already overextended, because you've put everything you have into your "baby" business, it may be hard to find outside capital without paying very high interest rates.

Another point to keep in mind: The only loan interest that will be tax-deductible to the business is a business loan. The interest on personal debt you incur for the business will not be tax-deductible to the business, or to you for that matter. In fact, if you take out a personal loan for use in your business, the interest won't be deductible at all for tax purposes.

Back on the Bright Side

Back to the plus side of going it alone: You don't have to share your profits with anyone (except the IRS). That means when your business turns around and starts bringing in lots of cash, it's all yours. You can leave the money in the business, or take it out and spend it—it's totally up to you. Also, because you're the only owner, the rules for accounting are much easier to understand and apply. This often frees you from the need to hire an outside bookkeeper and spend precious cash (which you can put in your own pocket instead).

Best of all, you have no one to answer to except yourself. If you want to wear sweats and sneakers to work, that's your choice. If you choose to roll in at 11:00 and roll out at 2:00, it's fine with you. Being your own boss without any interference from other shareholders or partners allows you to run things your way at your pace. And, at the end of the day, isn't that really why you started your own business in the first place?

The Best Businesses for This Structure

Sole proprietorship is the simplest business form, and it's appropriate for the simplest types of businesses. This entity may be the best choice if:

- You have no employees.
- You work as a freelancer or independent contractor.

- You provide only services.
- Your business doesn't need inventory.
- The business will start small and possibly stay small.
- You don't need a lot of outside financing to get started.
- Clients/customers will not be coming to your place of business.
- Your business doesn't pose any inherent dangers to outsiders.
- You won't be working directly with children or animals.

In a nutshell, if you plan to run a small, service-oriented business that doesn't require a lot of face-to-face contact with customers and won't need employees to run (at least initially), a sole proprietorship is a good start-up choice. Suitable businesses would include such things as bookkeeping services, freelance writers and editors, research providers, mail order or catalog sales, and graphic designers.

Businesses That Should Not Be Sole Proprietorships

Look at the list above—if you take each point and turn it into the opposite, that would make up the list for businesses that should avoid this entity choice. Plus, other factors may make your business unsuitable for the sole proprietorship form. To spell it out, you probably should not form your business as a sole proprietorship if any of the following conditions are true:

- You have (or soon will have) employees.
- You sell physical goods.
- Your business requires inventory to meet customer demands.
- The business is large to begin with, or should soon be large.
- You need a lot of outside financing to get started.
- Clients/customers will be coming to your place of business.
- Your business poses inherent dangers to outsiders.
- You'll be working directly with children or animals.
- The product you sell is inherently dangerous.
- You (or your employees) will use a company vehicle to make deliveries.

If you're already in business as a sole proprietorship and do meet one or more of the above conditions, consider switching to one of the other entities available. If you haven't formed your business yet and any items on the "don't" list are true for your company, use one of the other business forms—don't use this entity just because it's the cheapest and easiest right now, because it might not be in the long run.

How to Get Started

One of the best features of operating a sole proprietorship is the utter lack of paperwork needed to set it up. You can literally roll out of bed one day and declare yourself in business. In fact, whenever a single-owner business starts up without incorporating or forming an LLC, the company is automatically considered a sole proprietorship for legal and tax purposes. And if you decide to change, sell, or discontinue your business, you can—no forms, no fees, no fuss.

Permits, Fees, and Tax IDs

Generally, you'll have no special organizational forms to file or fees to pay when you open your doors for business. However, most states require all businesses to obtain licenses and/or permits before beginning to trade. Depending on what your business is, you may have to file for things like zoning permits or tax registrations. So check with your county clerk (or other appropriate government office) to find out what you do need to file to legally start trading.

> Most states require all businesses to obtain licenses and/or permits before beginning to trade.

If you use your own name as the business name, you'll cut down on state paperwork. But if you'll be using a DBA name, you may have to register with your home state (or city or county, as required). In some states, including your legal name in the business name keeps it from being a DBA; for example, if your name is George Thomas and you do business as George Thomas Appraisals, you may not have to file a fictitious name certificate. Again, check with the county clerk (or whichever office your area uses). The fees for filing a DBA name usually run less than $100.

If your business doesn't have any employees, you can use your Social Security number as your tax ID number. When your business does have employees, you'll need to file for a federal EIN, and possibly a state ID number as well.

Simple Start-up Means No Legal Fees

Sole proprietorships don't need to write bylaws, file corporate charters, or keep a log of meeting minutes to satisfy federal and state regulations. You don't have to keep a roster of owners—there's only you. This reduced paperwork will save you lots of time, and lots of money. Since you don't have to file any legal paperwork, you don't need an attorney to help you form your business. No lawyer means no legal fees—and at a national average of $250 per hour, that's a lot of savings!

Get an EIN, Even If You Don't Need It

Even if you don't need to get an employer identification number (EIN), it can't hurt to apply—especially if you plan to hire employees soon. Plus, as silly as it may sound, your business may be taken more seriously if it has an "official" ID number assigned to it. Banks look at an EIN as a sign that you plan to be in business for a long time—and that may tip the scales in your favor when you're trying to get a loan. Suppliers may be more willing to extend more advantageous terms when they perceive your company's stability. And customers may be willing to pay higher rates to a "real" business than to "some guy" who says he's in business. Remember, perception is reality. And your reality is that you want your business to be taken seriously.

> **Chapter 5**

Keeping Good Records Is Crucial

Part One

Part Two

Part Three

Part Four

Part Five

Part Six

PART TWO   SOLE PROPRIETORSHIPS

■ CHAPTER 4 The Easiest Business to Start ■ CHAPTER 5 Keeping Good Records Is Crucial ■ CHAPTER 6 Dealing with Taxes Throughout the Year ■ CHAPTER 7 Protecting Your Assets ■ CHAPTER 8 Getting Out of Business

Separating Personal and Business Finances

The typical new business owner uses his personal savings, credit cards, and home equity loans to finance his company. And while this strategy can get your business started, it's not one you should keep in place. Relying on personal self-financing doesn't offer the benefits of business financing—like more flexible loan terms, establishment of a business credit line, and more tax-deductible interest.

One good reason to keep personal and business finances separate is to ease your bookkeeping burden. When you use one checking account, one credit card for both purposes, you have to analyze each check, deposit, or charge to determine its purpose. Doing this monthly is hard enough, but trying to separate a year's worth of finances at tax time is enough to drive anyone mad. In December, will you remember whether a check made out to the Postmaster in April was for business or personal expenses?

> One good reason to keep personal and business finances separate is to ease your bookkeeping burden.

Business Checking Accounts Establish Your Company

At the very least, you should open a business checking account. For numerous reasons, having this account will benefit both you and your business:

1. It establishes a business relationship with a bank, which can help when you later apply for a business loan.
2. It's easier to track business expenses: Everything running through this checkbook is business-related.
3. Business account statements typically close on the last day of the month (personal statements usually close mid-month), making it easier to do bank statement reconciliations, especially at year-end.
4. You'll be able to get larger and lower-interest overdraft protection than you would with a personal account.
5. All bank service fees will be fully deductible to the business, including charges for check printing, ATM card use, and balance inquiries.
6. An established business checking account can serve as proof that your business is not a "hobby." (See Chapter 6 for a discussion of this topic.)

Business Credit Cards Make Life Easier

In addition to your business checking account, it's smart to get company credit cards as well. Instead of maxing out your personal credit cards, you'll be able to put business charges on the company cards, leaving room for you to charge personal expenses. Although you're still personally responsible for paying off all balances—whether personal or business—you'll be glad of the extra flexibility during the lean start-up months before your company starts bringing in money. And you can always draw money from the business to pay down your personal credit card debt, no questions asked.

On top of the extra credit you'll get, obtaining business credit cards can actually help your business in a number of ways. First, credit card companies provide additional services for small businesses, like year-end expense summary statements (a great timesaver at year-end when you're running around trying to get all your receipts together for the accountant). Second, interest you pay on your business credit card is fully deductible to the business; interest you pay on your personal credit cards—even if for business purchases—isn't deductible anywhere on your tax return. Finally, having credit cards in the company name establishes credit for your business in its own name, making it easier to apply for business loans in the future.

Moving Money In and Out of the Business

One of the best features of the sole proprietorship entity is the unlimited ability to move cash between your business and you—and that's a two-way street. There are literally no tax implications to funneling every penny of profits into your personal account, or transferring your personal savings into the business. Since you and the sole proprietorship are one and the same, both legally and for tax purposes, the company's money is your money and vice versa.

Because transferring money into and out of the business triggers no taxable events, accounting remains simple. When you want to pay yourself, simply write yourself a check and record the draw on the books. If you want to put more of your personal money into the business, simply make a bank deposit into your business account and record the contribution as additional equity. There is no formal paperwork to fill out; in fact, you only have to keep track of cash transfers for yourself—or for anyone from whom you want to borrow money. As far as the IRS is concerned, these transactions just don't matter.

Dealing with Family

Not surprisingly, the lion's share of sole proprietorships are family businesses. Tell people you operate a sole proprietorship, and they instantly imagine a "mom and pop" shop, with children of all ages doing chores in the store: an eager five-year-old sweeping the aisle, a determined nine-year-old stocking shelves, a fresh-faced teenager at the register. Clearly, this scenario only applies to one sector of sole proprietorships, but the stereotype still exists.

Actually, there are some distinct advantages to employing your family in your business. And not just social and emotional benefits, but business and tax benefits as well. For example, there are special tax rules that apply only to the children of small business owners who work for their parents. And husband-and-wife businesses don't have to file complex partnership returns—unlike other two-owner businesses.

When Spouses Co-own a Sole Proprietorship

If you and your spouse own and run the business together, the dividing line between sole proprietorship and partnership can appear murky—but the distinction can be crucial at tax time.

By definition, a sole proprietorship can have only one owner. But by following some simple guidelines, a husband and wife together can actually own a business together without having to legally create a formal partnership. To work together but be counted as a sole proprietorship, just follow these two basic rules:

1. Only one of you can be named as the official owner.
2. You file a joint tax return, with a single Schedule C.

So even when both of you materially participate in the business as owners, you still can keep the "single-owner" status by filing a joint tax return. Basically, you file a single Schedule C as if only one of you owns the business; the other spouse has technically *donated* time and labor. This way you can both work at the business without either of you having to be considered an employee. And that can save you a lot of time and money: no payroll taxes to pay, no payroll tax returns to file, no tedious record keeping, no need for an EIN.

There can be a minor drawback to this strategy, though. Although as a couple you'll share the overall income tax liability when you file your joint return, the self-employment tax you pay will be applied only to the account of the spouse considered the official owner. This means that one of you will accumulate all of the Social Security dollars, while the other gets none.

To get around this Social Security inequality, you can have one spouse act as owner and the other function as an employee. Of course, that brings all the paperwork associated with maintaining a payroll into play. But if you already have other employees, or plan to in the near future, you're going to have to deal with payroll anyway. And just like all other paid employees, the salary you pay your spouse and all employment taxes you pay on his or her behalf are fully deductible to the business.

Getting Your Children Involved

When you bring your kids into the family business, you get the biggest benefit of all—spending time together. And thanks to a very family-friendly section of the tax code, you'll also enjoy some substantial financial benefits.

Community Property Laws May Come into Play

Due to community property laws in some states (currently Arizona, California, Idaho, Louisiana, Nevada, New Mexico, Texas, Washington, and Wisconsin), a sole proprietorship may be considered the property of both husband and wife automatically, regardless of the company's tax status. But if both spouses want to be formally recognized as owners of the business, a different entity choice must be made.

If the couple wants to show formal legal ownership by both partners, they would have to forgo using sole proprietorship as the business form and choose one of the more formal entities.

As with all tax benefits, you have to follow the rules to reap the rewards. Here the rules are pretty straightforward:

- Your kids must really work for the business.
- Their pay has to be appropriate for the work they actually do.
- You have to pay them with real payroll checks, complete with taxes taken out.

You can hire your children regardless of their ages, as long as the tasks you hire them for are age-appropriate (for example, a first-grader could not be hired as your bookkeeper). When your children work for your business, they aren't subject to standard labor laws so they can work any number of hours, any time of the day. On top of that, if you don't have any employees outside your immediate family, you can pay your kids any reasonable amount without worrying about the federal minimum wage laws.

Unlike the typical child's allowance, any wages paid to the kids are fully deductible to the business. The kids will have to pay some taxes on their income, but typically at a much lower rate than you'd have to pay. So by paying your children wages, you'll be shifting income from your higher tax rate (which would also include an additional 15.3 percent of self-employment tax) to your children's lower tax rate. It gets better: Because wages are counted as earned income, a portion of it is sheltered from taxes by the child's standard deduction. Best of all—your company can pay any amount of wages to your children that are under eighteen without owing any employer-based payroll taxes; this scores you an employee without incurring the extra payroll tax expense. And the children are also exempt from paying their employee portion of FICA, meaning more take-home pay for them.

> Any wages paid to the kids are fully deductible to the business.

More Family Tax Savings

To create even more tax-deductible expenses, you can gift business property (since legally it's considered to be owned by you anyway) to any of your children who are at least fourteen, then have the business lease that property back. This strategy works particularly well when your company has fully depreciated assets (which can be as early as year one, when you take advantage of special accelerated depreciation legislation) that no longer offer any tax benefits to the business. This new lease arrangement effectively creates an expense for the business—rent of business property. Although your child could owe some taxes on the income he will receive for leasing the property to your company, at least that income will be at his much lower income tax rate.

Your overall family tax savings can be calculated very easily, and you should do the math before you sign a formal lease agreement to make sure it works in your favor. The tax savings generally will equal the total annual lease payment times the difference between your income tax rate and your child's rate. For example, if for 2004 your child falls into the lowest tax bracket (which he probably will if he's still in high school), he'll be taxed at 10 percent. Even if your tax rate is in the next lowest bracket, 15 percent, you would still have a 5 percent tax savings. If the lease payments came to $10,000 per year, your total family tax savings for 2004 would be 5 percent of $10,000, or $500.

Be aware: There are actually times that this strategy will not benefit your family tax-wise. If your only income is from the business, and your business is currently running at a tax loss, this method will actually cost your family more in taxes. Also, if you fall into one of the lower tax brackets and your child's rate is higher due to investment income or securities sales (as often happens in the year the child will start college, when parents sell off investments in the child's "college account" to pay for his tuition), this strategy won't be beneficial.

Keeping Receipts and Mileage Logs

There are two important reasons to keep receipts and mileage logs:

1. To help you figure out your profit at year-end.
2. To act as proof of expenses in case you get audited by the IRS.

That's not to say you have to keep every single receipt for the entire life of your business. It's next to impossible to save every one—in fact, you can rest assured that some of your receipts will end up in the Twilight Zone, never to be seen again.

So how can you make sure that all of your expenses get accounted for? The easiest way to keep track of your expenditures is to pay for things with credit cards, especially business credit cards. Most business credit cards will provide, in addition to detailed monthly statements, summary information at year-end. These simple compilations are great for small business owners too tired to deal with hundreds of credit card receipts, and great to turn over to a bookkeeper or accountant who's trying to put some numbers together.

Paying by check from your business checking account is the next best way to keep expense tracking under control. For monthly bills and the occasional purchase, checks provide automatic receipts. To make sure you know what a disbursement was for (or that your accountant or bookkeeper can figure it out), it's a good idea to actually write a memo on the check itself or in the check register. That way you'll be able to tell even months later what you paid for—this is especially useful with vendors you use for more than one purpose, or vendors that you used only once or twice during the year.

Expenses Paid from Personal Accounts Are Harder to Track

When you use a business checking account and/or credit card, it's pretty safe to assume that all of the expenditures were for business purposes. But when you start mixing business expenses in with your personal ones, you're setting yourself up for a mind-numbing exercise at financial statement time.

If you're using your personal checking account to pay for business purchases and bills, you'll have to go line by line in your check register every month (or week, or year, depending upon how often you keep up with bookkeeping tasks) to determine what belongs where. Even worse, if you don't indicate in your check register which items are business expenditures, you may actually have to go back to the canceled checks to figure it out.

You may start out with a coding system—like marking all business-related checks with a red asterisk or starting the description line in the register with a "B." And even if you keep at it, you'll still have to play the separating game every time you enter payments into your accounting records. That's a pretty monotonous task, at best—and it's very easy to get lulled into a rhythm where you end up including every check, then have to backtrack to get rid of the ones that don't belong.

The same goes for expenses paid with personal credit cards—which don't, by the way, usually offer year-end summary analysis statements. You'll need to keep every statement for every card, and possibly every credit card slip, to evaluate whether a charge you made was personal or for the business.

Bottom line here: Save yourself (and your eyes) a lot of extra work. Use business accounts to pay your bills and make your purchases. It may seem annoying to have two sets of everything, especially at first when the payouts can be minimal. But in the long run it will make your life easier—and your bookkeeper's life, too.

Receipts for Cash Purchases

It's easy to say you'll pay for everything with the company credit card or checkbook. But in reality, many sole proprietors use the cash from their own pockets to make purchases on a fairly regular basis.

So when you buy something from the business with your personal cash, *get a receipt* and don't lose it. Carry an expense envelope around with you at all times. You can keep it in your glove box, in your purse, or in your backpack. But keep it and use it.

You don't have to go crazy here. Keeping a detailed written log of all paid-in-cash expenses is great, but overkill. It's enough to have the receipt itself, with a brief hand-written note on it if you won't be able to tell later on what it's for. Make sure the date and amount are clearly visible, and that the business purpose is obvious. For example, if you have a receipt for two ice cream cones, write the customer's name on the receipt and a three-to-five word description of the business reason for the get-together ("Mel Smith, discussing grain storage" would suffice).

When you buy something for the business with your personal cash, *get a receipt.*

Mileage Logs

Keeping a mileage log fulfills the two goals set out at the start of this section: easy expense tracking and proof for the IRS. If you don't keep a mileage log, you'll probably be cheating yourself out of legitimate business expenses at year-end. If you take a deduction for mileage without having kept a mileage log and the IRS calls you on it, you could lose the deduction.

A mileage log is particularly important if you use your personal car for business. When the use is split, keeping track of at least the business portion is crucial. The usage percentage (calculated by dividing business miles for

SAMPLE MILEAGE LOG

Date	Destination	Business Purpose	One-Way Mileage	Parking	Tolls
February 16	555 Main St., Centerville	Drop off presentation	67	$21.00	$5.00
March 11	222 River Rd., Northtown	Pick up client disk	45	$14.00	none
May 5	1234 Pleasant St., Westboro	Deliver proposal	33	none	none

the year by total miles driven for the year) is used on some year-end tax forms to determine allowable deductions.

Again—don't go crazy here. A simple log is all you need, but you do need to fill it out when you use an auto for business travel. Your mileage log should include such things as the date, destination, business purpose, and one-way mileage. You can also keep track of travel-related expenses like parking and tolls on this log; for parking, keep the receipt. The table above shows an example of what a typical simple mileage log looks like.

Most Sole Proprietorships Use Cash Basis Accounting

> Most small businesses use cash basis for their accounting systems.

To make financial chores as easy as possible, most small businesses use cash basis for their accounting systems. *Cash basis accounting* does pretty much what it says:Transactions count only when cash actually changes hands. If, for example, you get a delivery inventory today but don't pay for it until next month, you would not record the transaction today. Instead, you would wait until you actually write and send the check to put this entry on the books. The same holds true for sales: Under the cash method, your sales wouldn't go on the books until you had cash in hand.

Since everything is cash-driven, there's never a question as to when to record transactions. When customers send you full payment, you post a complete sale. When customers make partial payments, you only record the part they've paid for.

What counts as a cash transaction? More than you'd think:

- Cash (of course)
- Checks
- Money orders
- Credit cards
- Debit cards

So when a customer pays you with a credit card, you book the sale then—not when the credit card company puts the cash in your account. If he pays with a check, you post the sale when you get the check—not when it clears.

The Alternative Is Accrual Basis Accounting

The main difference between the cash and accrual basis accounting methods is timing. Under accrual basis accounting, transactions are recorded when they occur, regardless of whether money has changed hands. With the cash method, money determines the transaction date. So with the accrual method, the inventory delivery that came today but won't be paid for until next month gets recorded on the books today. The flip side applies to sales— when you make a sale, you record it, even if you won't be getting the cash any time soon.

Sometimes, though, using the accrual method can be a little confusing. Some transactions aren't quite so clear-cut as deliver today, check tomorrow. Some jobs take months to complete, and some equipment is shipped in pieces. So how do you know when to record a transaction that doesn't happen all at once?

Generally speaking, completion is the key. If you're performing a service for someone that takes two weeks, the day you finish is the day you record the sale.

Who Can Use the Cash Method?

As with everything that involves the IRS, there are a slew of guidelines involved. The IRS basically says that if your business has inventory, revenues over $10 million, or is formed as a C corporation you have to use the accrual method. If you're operating as a sole proprietorship, that last rule has no impact. But the inventory and revenue rules may come into play. Luckily, there are loopholes, and many sole proprietorships fit right in.

The rule that knocks a lot of companies out of the cash basis arena covers industries with inventory. Generally speaking, if you maintain inventory, you have to use the accrual accounting method. However, there are exceptions even to that (surprised?). If you keep an inventory of supplies

The Constructive Receipt Rule

Under IRS regulations, having the ability to receive cash counts as receiving it. And that means recording the sale. In IRS jargon, this is called *constructive receipt*.

So if you receive customer checks, you have to record the sale whether you make a deposit. If a customer says you can come pick up a check, it counts as if he gave it to you. Essentially, when the payment is *available* to you, it's considered received by you. And that means you have to report it now—and pay tax on it this year.

rather than an inventory of merchandise for resale, you can still use cash basis accounting. And if you have "incidental" inventory, meaning not very much in comparison to the rest of your business, you may be allowed to use the cash method. (Incidental inventory would come into play when you have a mainly service business that also sells some retail items, like a doctor who sells vitamins to his patients.)

The next cash-basis hurdle is revenues: If your business has less than $10 million in revenues even with some inventory sales (as long as more than half of your gross receipts can be traced to service-related sales), you can safely use cash basis accounting. If you aren't sure you meet the guidelines, consult your accountant.

Timing Is Everything

When you use the cash method, you have some leeway in determining in which year transactions will be recorded. Simply by delaying (or accelerating) a purchase or deferring (or hastening) a receipt, you can shift income between tax years.

So if you want to reduce your current-year profits, you can ask customers to pay you in January. Or you can prepay expenses—pay your January rent in December, for example. What if you want to incur some extra expenses but don't have cash on hand? Use your business credit card to make purchases; the transactions count in this year, but don't require a cash disbursement until next year (when you collect that extra income from customers who held payments for January).

Making a Switch

Unlike choosing and using an accounting method, switching to a different one can be complicated. In some cases, you actually need permission from the IRS to make a change. Since the IRS typically benefits from accrual basis accounting, they aren't fond of companies trying to make the change from the accrual method to the cash method. The IRS concern is that such companies could be seeking unfair tax advantages. To seek permission, you (preferably with the help of your accountant) must file IRS Form 3115, Application for Change in Accounting Method, before the end of the tax year.

If your business is undergoing a "fundamental change" (at least in IRS terms), you don't need their permission to make a switch. For example, if your business starts out as predominantly a service business, but moves into selling products that require you to maintain inventory, you can switch from cash basis to accrual basis, no questions asked. If you'll be switching in the other direction, and you're not quite sure what the IRS considers a fundamental change, consult a professional before you file anything.

Keep on Top of the Bookkeeping

You already know some very good reasons to keep on top of your bookkeeping, like an easier time at year-end and knowing your true current checking account balance. But underlying these reasons is one more fundamental: Proper and timely bookkeeping is crucial to both maintaining and expanding your business. If you're not on top of this, you run the risk of negative cash flow, a waste of precious funds, inventory shortages, and lost opportunities you didn't even know existed. Believe it or not, taking care of the books is taking care of the business.

Inventory Tracking

Businesses that focus on merchandise sales need to have the merchandise on hand or risk losing sales. Customers won't remain loyal for long if you are constantly out of what they're looking for. Suppliers will get tired of—and probably charge you more for—emergency on-demand shipments. If you're not tracking your stock, it's harder for them to track theirs.

To keep your business flowing smoothly, you must know what you have in stock, which items are selling and which are not, and what your customers are asking for. If you know both what you have and what you need, you'll be able to fine-tune your inventory levels. And that means keeping the least possible inventory on hand without running into shortages, taking advantage of supplier discounts and specials, and tracking customer buying trends so you can predict (with reasonable success) what new items they might be interested in.

When you account for your inventory, make sure to track at least the following: purchase date, purchase price, quantity purchased, sales date, sales price, and quantity sold. For example, you need to know if you bought seven blue bowls for $10 each in May, and sold two of them for $15 in August. Now you can make key decisions, like whether to lower the sales price on the blue bowls, whether you should purchase them in July next year since they didn't start to sell until August, or whether you want to just write off the whole "blue bowl debacle" and return them to the supplier.

Paying Your Vendors

In business, you don't typically pay as you go. Instead, you negotiate payment terms with your vendors and suppliers. The most common terms are "net 30," which simply means you have to pay the balance within thirty days from the invoice date.

Paying your vendors in full and on time goes a long way toward establishing good credit for your company. Staying on top of the bookkeeping includes setting up an Accounts Payable (the accounting phrase for what you owe to outsiders) calendar so you know what's due when and can budget accordingly. This helps improve your cash flow management, and helps ensure that your vendor invoices don't get overlooked.

The second benefit to good vendor relations is improved payment terms. For large, long-term, or good-paying clients, vendors often offer discount terms. For example, you may receive an invoice with terms that say "2/10, net 30." This means you have an alternative to paying in full in thirty

> Paying your vendors in full and on time goes a long way toward establishing good credit.

days—instead you can choose to pay within ten days and take 2 percent off your bill. It may not sound like much, but it does add up over time.

Getting Customers to Pay You

If you've been extending credit terms to your customers, you have what accountants call Accounts Receivable. Basically you've sold something, but haven't gotten paid yet. To keep your business in the green, you've got to make sure that you do get paid, hopefully before you have to pay your suppliers.

Good cash management requires that you know who owes you how much and when it's due. You also need to be realistic, and look at the accounts that may not be paid ever, or will probably be paid very late. Keeping up with the bookkeeping helps you keep track of your Accounts Receivable, so you can tell when customers are paying late before it's too late for your business to survive.

> **Chapter 6**

Dealing with Taxes Throughout the Year

Part One

Part Two

Part Three

Part Four

Part Five

Part Six

PART TWO   SOLE PROPRIETORSHIPS

■ CHAPTER 4 The Easiest Business to Start ■ CHAPTER 5 Keeping Good Records Is Crucial ■ **CHAPTER 6 Dealing with Taxes Throughout the Year** ■ CHAPTER 7 Protecting Your Assets ■ CHAPTER 8 Getting Out of Business

Paying Self-Employment Taxes

If you live and work in the United States, you have to pay into the Social Security and Medicare systems, like it or not. Most people meet this obligation through payroll withholding taxes. When there's an employer/employee relationship, each party foots the bill for half of the tax.

But sole proprietors count as both sides of the equation, since they are self-employed. Therefore, if you operate your business as a sole proprietorship, you'll be responsible for both sides of the tax—infamously known as self-employment tax. And this is no minor tax either. When you have to pay the full amount due to your Social Security and Medicare accounts, it comes to a stiff 15.3 percent on the first $87,900 of profits (for 2004) plus 2.9 percent for all additional profits. Believe it or not, your self-employment tax may actually exceed the income tax due on your profits.

Filing Quarterly Estimates

Since as a sole proprietor you won't have any payroll taxes withheld, you'll be responsible for remitting payments into your personal tax account every

Calculating Your Self-Employment Tax

IRS Schedule SE is a step-by-step form designed to walk you through the fairly simple calculation of figuring how much self-employment tax you owe. First, you'll multiply your net profit by 0.9235. If the result is less than $400 (as it may be during the lean start-up years), you won't owe any self-employment taxes. If it's greater than $400, that figure gets multiplied by 15.3 percent for the first $87,900 (in 2004); all profits above that get multiplied by 2.9 percent.

Let's assume you had a first-year net profit of $2,000. In step one, you'd multiply that $2,000 by 0.9235, ending up with $1,847. For step two, you'd multiply that number by 15.3 percent; the result would be an amount of $1,847 owed in self-employment tax.

When you file your tax return, you'll show that calculation on IRS Schedule SE. That form will be submitted each year you're in business as a sole proprietorship, along with your Form 1040 and your Schedule C.

quarter. These payments will be based on the total taxes you expect to owe at year-end, based on the profits you expect to make during the year.

There are no hard and fast rules for how you'll come up with these expectations, especially for your first year in business. But the IRS expects you to have some kind of idea of what you'll be earning, and pay estimated taxes accordingly. They expect you to pay four equal installments through-out the year, and sometimes charge penalties if you don't. They do under-stand, though, that it's hard to know what might happen when you've never done it before, so they typically give new business owners a break on the penalties.

Here are some ways you can help yourself come out ahead for your first year as a sole proprietor:

- Pay at least the same amount as your previous year's total tax bill, broken into four equal installments.
- If you (or your spouse) work for someone else and have payroll taxes withheld, you can increase your withholding later in the year when you have a better idea of your profits.
- File your tax return by February 1; the fourth quarterly estimate need not be made if you'll file by then and pay in full any tax due.

Remember: You only have to pay estimated taxes on your *profits*. If you expect to incur a loss, you don't have to worry about taxes.

Coming Up with Sales Numbers

To figure out your estimated tax liability, you have to first come up with your expected bottom line for the year. Although this seems a daunting prospect to new entrepreneurs, it's doable—especially if you break it down into smaller pieces.

Start with your sales expectations, and try to be as realistic as possible. The first thing to look at is time—if you started your business near the begin-ning of the year, you'll bring in more sales than if you had started in October.

Along the same lines, the seasonality of your business is a factor. If you sell beach balls, you'll make more money if you started your business in May than if you started in September. On the other hand, if you started up in January and posted sluggish sales through April, don't count on those to be typical of the whole year—your sales surge may be just around the corner.

Rules of thumb don't really apply here. Every business has different cycles, peaks, and valleys. But to make your first tax-estimating job a little easier, you can follow these general guidelines:

1. Look at one month's worth of sales and multiply that by the number of months left in the year for a nonseasonal business.
2. For seasonal businesses, look at a busy month's sales, and multiply that by the number of months in your peak cycle. Then divide the busy month's sales in half and multiply that by the number of months in your slow periods. Add the two together for the estimated tax total.
3. Use the first year's sales you projected in your business plan, prorated based on the month you actually opened your doors. (If you now think this number is totally unrealistic, don't use it.)

Expense Estimating Is Easier

Compared to projecting sales figures, estimating your expenses is actually pretty straightforward and simple. While you may have no idea how much money you'll be bringing in, you should have a pretty good idea of how much money you're paying out.

Start with your fixed expenses, the ones that stay the same every month. These include things like your rent, online charges, and equipment leases. Then look at your predictable expenses like loan interest, property tax payments, and newspaper advertising.

After you've finished totaling your foreseeable expenses, switch over to expenses you know you'll have, but the amount may be in question. This category is a little broader, including such items as phone bills, utilities, and office supplies.

Last, tackle the sales-based expenses. Sales-based expenses cover things like inventory costs, credit card fees, and salespersons' commissions. The easiest way to come up with a number here is to take your estimated sales figure and multiply it by a reasonable expense percentage. For example, if you know credit cards charge 2 percent per sale, you pay your salespeople

6 percent per sale, and your inventory cost is 30 percent of each sale, you would use 38 percent as your sales-based expense percentage.

The final step is adding all four categories of expenses together. Now you'll have a grand total of all of your expected expenses for the year.

The Estimated Profit and the Estimated Tax

This is the easy part—all the estimating is done, the rest is just basic math. To calculate your estimated net profit, simply subtract the number you came up with for total expenses from your projected sales. If the result is a positive number, it's a profit and you need to do some more calculations. A negative result means you're expecting a net loss for the year, and that means no estimated taxes and no more calculations.

Now that you've figured out your expected net profit, you can come up with your estimated tax payments. The self-employment tax portion is the easy part—just use the formula from the self-employment tax section. The income tax portion is a little harder to compute, so the IRS provides instructions to help you with the calculation. They even provide you with basic tax tables to help you with the math.

Once you've computed and added up your income taxes and self-employment taxes, divide the total by four. That result will be your payment each quarter. Make a check out for the full quarterly amount, payable to the "United States Treasury." Make sure to write your social security number (and your EIN, if you have one) on the check, along with the words "Form 1040-ES" and the

Estimated State Taxes

If you expect to owe estimated taxes on your profits to the federal government, you'll probably owe them to your state (and possibly local) government as well. To find out if you do need to make quarterly estimated tax payments to your home state—and to make sure you use the right remittance forms—contact your state department of taxation. Many of these agencies have helpful Web sites, which may include downloadable payment coupons. A lot of new entrepreneurs overlook the state when paying estimated taxes, and end up paying nondeductible penalties.

tax year. Include a completed Form 1040-ES payment coupon, also called an Individual Estimated Tax Voucher, with each payment to make sure you get proper credit for your payment. Estimated tax payments are due on April 15, June 15, September 15, and January 15.

Don't Mess Around with Payroll Taxes

Companies with employees have to withhold a variety of payroll taxes from those employees' paychecks, and they must send the withheld taxes on to the federal government. On top of that, there are also additional taxes employers have to pay on behalf of their employees. Along with those payroll taxes come a lot of forms to file and a lot of rules to follow.

Because of the complexity of federal and state withholding taxes, you'll do best to enlist a payroll service to deal with them for you. Yes, this costs money—somewhere from $50 per month on up, largely depending on the number of employees you have and the total dollar value of your payroll. On top of taking away a mass of red tape and paperwork, good payroll service companies also take responsibility for remitting payments, and for any penalties charged if payments are inadvertently late or missed. This is not the expense to skimp on; payroll services are well worth their monthly fees.

Handling Payroll on Your Own

If you only have one or two employees, you may decide to try your hand at payroll before turning to an outside service provider. The most important thing in dealing with payroll is the calendar. Government paperwork must be filed on particular dates, and payments must be made by specified dates—but these dates don't necessarily coincide.

Messing up payroll taxes can have very large consequences. So if you do decide to go it alone, you have to stay on top of the recordkeeping. You have to keep track of all the filing and remittance deadlines. And you absolutely must make payments on time.

There's a lot of software out there designed to help small business owners do their own payroll. The programs are largely the same, with minor differences in appearance and style. If you go this route, get the program that looks like the rest of the software that you work with. Many bookkeeping

> The most important thing in dealing with payroll is the calendar.

programs come with payroll already included, or as a fully compatible add-on module. Make sure that the software you select comes with free updates, as payroll requirements and tax rates are ever-changing.

It makes sense to use a proven program to calculate payroll and taxes for you. But you should know, at least basically, how the payroll taxes work so you can make sure your program is working properly before the IRS tells you it's not. Simple input errors can cause tax calculations to be off dramatically, but you won't see that if you have absolutely no idea what they should look like.

Forms 941 and 940

When you do your own payroll, you'll quickly get familiar with two federal tax forms: Form 941 (which reports federal income tax, Social Security, and Medicare, a.k.a., the withholding taxes) and Form 940 (which reports federal unemployment tax). Form 941 is filed quarterly and Form 940 is filed annually. Payments, however, may follow an entirely different schedule.

So when do you make these payroll tax payments? That depends on how much tax you withheld during the quarter. If the total withholding is less than $2,500 per quarter, you pay when you file the Form 941. When the withheld tax hits or exceeds $2,500 for a quarter, the tax has to be paid monthly by the middle of the following month. For example, if you will be withholding $2,500 for the first quarter of the year (January through March), you would have to remit the January payroll taxes by mid-February, the February payroll taxes by mid-March and the March payroll taxes by mid-April.

Federal unemployment tax (commonly called FUTA) is typically paid quarterly, even though Form 940 is filed only annually. Unlike Form 941 taxes, FUTA is not withheld from employee paychecks; it is solely the responsibility of the employer, creating an additional payroll expense over and above employee wages.

Big Penalties for Skipping Payments

Because you remit payroll taxes on behalf of your employees, with money you've already taken out of their paychecks, the government takes payment of these taxes very seriously. In fact, they wrote special legislation to cover payment of these taxes with very steep penalties for noncompliance.

This special law is called the Trust Fund Recovery Penalty Act (TFRP), so-named because you are technically holding your employees' money in trust for them until it's time to remit it to the federal government.

If you do not pay these taxes on time, the penalty is harsh—equal to the full amount of payroll taxes that were required to be collected and paid. And that's why it's called the "100 percent penalty." This civil punishment can be inflicted on you personally, and the IRS will keep coming until the amount is paid.

The TFRP charges can be assessed against anyone who is both responsible to collect and pay the tax and who willfully fails to collect or pay them. As a sole proprietor with employees, you are a responsible party. So if you fail to both collect and remit the taxes, you will charged for both the original taxes that would have been due and the 100 percent penalty.

It sounds easy to avoid this penalty—just pay the payroll taxes when they're due. But, unfortunately, a lot of small business owners have cash flow problems, especially in the first year. They may use every penny to pay suppliers, employees, and other creditors necessary to keep the doors open another day. Without even noticing, they'll run out of money to use for remitting payroll taxes. So they file late, or skip a few payments until their cash flow turns positive. But under the TFRP, skipping just a couple of payments can trigger the penalty, and paying other creditors with the trust fund tax money counts as willful negligence. So skip payments with your suppliers if you have to, but don't mess around with payroll taxes.

How to Get Ready for Year-End

The easiest way to prepare for year-end is to keep on top of your book-keeping, receipts, and bank statements throughout the year. That way, you won't have a mad rush at tax time trying to remember where you put the bill for the computer you bought way back in July.

Whether you keep on top of things or do the mad rush at tax time, you should have the following information ready when you sit down to figure your profit or loss for the year:

- All business bank statements
- Your business check register (and your personal register if you used it to pay business expenses)

- Credit card statements that include business expenses
- Receipts for any assets purchased during the year
- Receipts for any expenses paid with cash
- A mileage log for business travel by car
- A sales register for the year
- Inventory on hand at year-end
- An annual payroll summary

With the information you've collected, you'll be able to prepare a basic income statement. This statement will show your total sales, less any returns, and your total summarized expenses. The bottom line of the income statement shows whether you have a profit or loss for the year. Once you have a good income statement, you can either proceed to do your own taxes, or turn the report over to your accountant. If you decide to go it alone, you'll become quite familiar with IRS Schedule C.

Preparing Schedule C

For tax purposes, you and your business are one and the same. So all of your business income and expenses are reported on your personal tax return on Schedule C. You'll pay tax on the bottom line profit, regardless of how much money you've withdrawn from the business. If your business suffers a loss, it's directly deductible from the other income on the tax return (like salary and interest income).

> All of your business income and expenses are reported on your personal tax return.

Schedule C looks pretty much like an income statement. Administrative information, like your name, the name and address of the business (if they're different than yours), and your chosen accounting method, appears on the top of page one. Then comes the income statement information: You'll report income in Part I, expenses in Part II, and cost of goods sold (if applicable) in Part III. You can copy the numbers from the year-end income statement you prepared directly on to Schedule C.

Some sole proprietors can file a simplified version of Schedule C, called Schedule C-EZ. You can use this pared-down schedule if:

1. You have only one sole proprietorship.
2. Your bottom-line profit is less than $400, but not a loss.

3. Your total expenses are $2,500 or less.
4. You had no inventory at all throughout the year.
5. You had no employees.
6. You aren't claiming expenses for business use of your home.
7. You use cash-basis accounting.
8. You didn't acquire any depreciable assets during the year.

You should file Schedule C with the IRS even when your business has suffered a loss, even if you're not otherwise required to file a return. In addition to offsetting other current income, a reported loss can be carried forward to decrease profits in the future.

Using the Home Office Deduction

Most sole proprietors use at least a part of their homes for the business. Since self-employed people usually don't work the standard "9 to 5," doing some work at home is the norm. In fact, some sole proprietors don't do business anywhere else.

If you work out of your garage, store inventory in your shed, or do paperwork in a home office, you're using your home for business purposes. It doesn't matter whether you rent or own your house. Using your home for business purposes can score your company some additional deductible expenses—when you make sure to follow all of the IRS guidelines.

The Home-Business Deduction

The total deductible expense when you use your home for business purposes can't be greater than the net income of the business. It can bring your profit for the year down to zero, but it can't be the expense that causes a loss. So, of course, you have to figure it out last.

While you won't see a tax benefit this year if your company is already operating at (or close to) a loss, figure out the deduction you should have gotten anyway. You can take a partial deduction to reduce your income to zero, plus any leftover deduction can be brought forward to your tax return next year.

Qualifying for the Deduction

You have to follow some pretty strict guidelines to be allowed the home office deduction. First, according to IRS regulations, you can deduct the expenses that pertain to the business part of your home only if you use it *regularly <u>and</u> exclusively*. The IRS definition of "regularly" isn't really time-oriented; it really refers to the fact that you perform business tasks in that part of your house on a fairly frequent basis (weekly or every other week).

More people fail on the "exclusively" part of the rule. Basically, you can't use that space for anything else, at all, ever. If you have a desk in your guest room, only the part of the room with the desk counts as the business portion. If your kids use that desk to do their homework, it no longer counts as a business area. Using your kitchen table to pay your business bills doesn't count. To repeat: You can't ever use that space for anything but business, or it won't qualify.

Second, you must use that business-designated area in at least one of the following ways:

1. As your main place of business.
2. As a place where your customers (or clients, or patients, depending on your business) typically meet with you during normal course of business.
3. In any connection with the business when the area is a separate structure on the property (such as a detached garage).

As with all IRS rules, there are some exceptions to these hurdles, but they apply only to day-care facilities and inventory storage (including product samples). If you use your home for business under either of those circumstances, you can check out IRS Publication 587 (as with other IRS documents, it is available on their Web site at ✍ *www.irs.gov*).

Which Home Expenses Are Deductible?

Some expenses of your home are tax-deductible if you use your home for business, such as mortgage interest and property taxes. Other expenses, like utilities and homeowner's insurance, wouldn't be deductible at all if you weren't using your home for business activities. Essentially, any expenses you pay for your home that also benefits the portion that you use for business are at least partially deductible now.

The qualifying expenses are split into direct and indirect categories. Direct expenses are those that cover only the business portion of your home, like extra coverage on your homeowner's policy or a security system added to protect stored inventory. Indirect expenses cover the whole house, and need to be prorated based on square footage. Indirect expenses include things like rent (if you don't own your home), electricity, and heating oil. Some home expenses may not be deductible by the business. For example, if there is no running water in your office, you can't deduct a portion of your water bill as a business expense.

On top of regular expenses, home improvements that benefit your business now count as business expenses: a new roof, for example, or even installing central air. On top of that, if you own your home, the business portion is considered a depreciable asset—meaning you get even more deductions without shelling out any cash at all.

Filling Out Forms

To take the home office deduction, you must complete IRS Form 8829. This one-page schedule is separated into four sections:

- Square feet calculations
- Expense listing
- Home depreciation calculation (if you're a home owner)
- Expense carryovers (if you have more expense than income this year)

The first part helps you figure out the percentage of your home dedicated to business use. You need this number to help you compute the deductible portion of the indirect expenses. All you need here is the square footage of the part of your house used for business and the total square footage of your home (approximations are okay). For example, if the room you use for your office is 85 square feet and your entire home is 1000 square feet, your business percentage would be 8.5 percent.

Part two has two columns, one for direct expenses and one for indirect expenses. Direct expenses go on as is. Indirect expenses need to be prorated, based on the business percentage you calculated in part one. So if your total electric bill for the year came to $1,400, you would multiply that by 8.5 percent (as calculated above) to figure the indirect expense of $119 for your business.

Part three is for homeowners only. If you own your home, you'll need to know how much you paid for it and how much it's worth today—depreciation will be based on the lower of the two. You'll also need to know the approximate land value, because only the building counts for depreciation purposes. You'll figure out the depreciation for the whole house, then multiply that by your business percentage to get the allowable deduction.

The fourth part of Form 8829 only comes into play if the full home business deductions will cause a loss. Any excess expense gets reported in this section to be carried over to next year, when you'll have enough profits to absorb the additional expense.

Once you've completed Form 8829 and know the total allowable expense, you simply carry that number to your Schedule C. Both forms will be included when you send in your Form 1040.

Special Tax Issues for Sole Proprietors

Running your business as a sole proprietorship comes with tax advantages (like when you employ family members) and tax disadvantages (like self-employment taxes). The main tax advantage (when you've had a profit year) comes from above-the-line deductions that can seriously reduce your tax bill. The biggest drawback is the threat of reclassification as a hobby.

Benefit from Above-the-Line Deductions

Some of the biggest expenses you'll incur aren't deductible to your business. But they are deducted in the AGI section of

Bigger Benefits When Home Expenses Appear on Schedule C

Yes, your home mortgage interest and property taxes are always deductible on Schedule A when you itemize. But those itemized deductions come after your adjusted gross income (AGI) is calculated. And reducing AGI is the best way to decrease your tax bill.

By shifting these expenses to your business, you turn them into AGI-reducing deductions. Because they actually lower your company's profits, they also lower your AGI. And since some other personal deductions are linked to AGI (like medical expenses, which are only deductible when they exceed 7.5 percent of your AGI), shifting expenses here can actually help increase your remaining itemized deduction.

So apply the business portion of mortgage interest and property taxes to Schedule C, but don't forget to include the remaining expense on your Schedule A.

your 1040, informally called "above-the-line" deductions. These deductions will lower your AGI, which is used later in the return to figure out certain other deductions and credits. A lower AGI can mean bigger allowable itemized deductions and higher tax credits, such as child tax credit, that might otherwise be reduced if your AGI exceeds certain levels.

The business-related above-the-line deductions are:

- Half of your current self-employment tax
- 100 percent of health insurance premiums paid for you and your family
- Contributions to a qualified pension plan for yourself

Reclassification as a Hobby

Most sole proprietors are in business to make money. But a lot of them lose money for a year or two before profits start rolling in. Unfortunately, when a business loses money for the third consecutive year, the IRS may take a closer look.

What can the IRS do? They can reclassify your business as a hobby. That means your total business deductions can't exceed your total business income—and all of your previous net losses will be disallowed. This rule most often applies to businesses that seem "hobbylike," such as craft vendors, freelance photographers, and baseball card dealers, for example.

If the IRS tries to reclassify you, you can appeal their ruling. All you really have to do to prevail is show that you're running your company in a businesslike manner. Having a separate checking account, for example, goes a long way toward proving you take your business seriously.

Minimizing Audit Risk

The IRS is a dual-purpose agency. They exist primarily to collect revenues for the federal government, and they also attempt to help taxpayers comply with their tax obligations. The "new" IRS is more friendly and more helpful, but that doesn't mean they don't still perform audits.

Experience has shown the agency that the audits most likely to turn up additional revenue are of sole proprietors, especially those who use home offices and/or run cash-intensive businesses. This is not to say you should not take legitimate home office expenses, or that you shouldn't operate a cash-based business. But if your business does involve either or both of these facets, be prepared for a possible audit.

A lot of accountants advise clients to not include Form 8829 with their tax returns in order to minimize potential audit risk. But this means you'll have to exclude valuable tax-deductible expenses every year. Yes, this is traditionally a high audit area. But if you're following the guidelines and taking legitimate expenses, there's no need to worry.

The bottom line here is to operate your business honestly, to try to follow all the pertinent tax laws, and keep good records. This is the best defense against an audit—not cheating yourself out of legitimate expenses. Remember, simply getting audited doesn't necessarily mean you'll be paying more taxes.

Most Audits Are Just Correspondence

By far the most common method of audit is by letter. If you get an audit letter from the IRS, open it right away. These letters take care of themselves quickly when you handle them—but can cause ongoing problems if you ignore them.

Most of the time, these correspondence audits are just simple questions. For example, maybe they want to see a receipt for a large deduction. You probably have the paperwork to clear things up. So send it. If you made a mistake, you just have to pay a little more in taxes. If they're wrong, it's finished.

But if you just ignore the letter, they assume that you agree with whatever they're questioning. That means you agree to pay more taxes (they almost never say you owe *less* tax), and possibly some interest. The longer you wait to respond, the more interest adds up. So open the letter, answer it, and relax.

> **Chapter 7**

Protecting Your Assets

Part One

Part Two

Part Three

Part Four

Part Five

Part Six

PART TWO SOLE PROPRIETORSHIPS

■ CHAPTER 4 The Easiest Business to Start ■ CHAPTER 5 Keeping Good Records Is Crucial ■ CHAPTER 6 Dealing with Taxes Throughout the Year ■ CHAPTER 7 **Protecting Your Assets** ■ CHAPTER 8 Getting Out of Business

Understanding Liability

Having liabilities means that you owe something to someone. Although that something is usually cash, it could also be goods or services. The "someone" is most often a creditor, but it could also be someone who sues you and gets a judgment in their favor, a customer who pays in advance for something, or an employee or contractor who has done work for your business and expects to be paid.

Owing is not usually a business problem; most businesses wouldn't be able to operate without credit terms. Most new businesses get some kind of outside debt financing. It's practically unheard of to pay inventory suppliers C.O.D.—virtually all inventory-intensive businesses live by thirty-day terms.

When Regular Business Liabilities Turn into Problems

The problems come into play when you can't meet your obligations. If your business runs into some cash flow problems, its creditors may not get paid on time. If you do all the work for your company (as is often the case with sole proprietors), you could overbook and be unable to complete jobs as scheduled. Or you could owe a subcontractor for work on a job for which you haven't yet been paid.

The first step in dealing with these unpaid liabilities should be communication. If you don't let your suppliers know what's going on, they could cut you off—and that means you have nothing to deliver to your customers. If you don't pay your employees on Friday without letting them know the checks will be coming soon, they'll stop coming to work. By clearly communicating the problem and your expected solution, you can at least buy yourself some time.

But if your cash flow situation doesn't turn around, you may be facing bigger problems. Unpaid creditors can take you to court and go after any of your business or personal belongings. Your company can be liquidated and any assets sold. If that doesn't cover it, your personal belongings could be at risk.

Nothing Can Protect You from You

No business entity can ever protect you from liabilities born from your own errors, omissions, or negligence. On top of that, anything you do that causes injuries or property damage to others in the course of business will be your liability. So if you're a landscaper and you chop down someone's prize-winning orchids, you have to pay the damages. If you've neglected to get the roof replaced on your art gallery, and the leak ruins some paintings, you're fully responsible for restitution.

Insurance, like malpractice insurance, can absorb some of the payout. But you can be sure your rates will skyrocket with each and every claim. And, of course, you're always responsible for deductibles, co-payments, and liabilities exceeding insurance payout caps.

Unlimited Liability

When you operate as a sole proprietor, it's not just your business that owes—it's you. A sole proprietorship is considered legally to be the same as its owner. So every single business liability incurred exposes your personal assets completely. From your Christmas Club account to your cabin in the woods, everything is fair game in the event your business does not meet its obligations. On top of that, the opposite is also true: Your personal creditors can go after the assets and income of your business. In plain English, creditors can go after anything owned by you or your business.

When you're operating a sole proprietorship, its debts are your debts, and its losses are your losses. You stand to lose all the money you put into the business if it doesn't succeed. And you also could lose some or all of the

Unlimited Liability May Not Be a Deal Breaker

Unlimited liability sounds scary—and for some businesses it is. But your business may not have high liability potential. For example, you could be a freelance writer who doesn't need to operate on credit (like a retail business that needs inventory on hand). And freelance writers are not likely to pose a potential threat to their customers (as opposed to a delivery service, for example, which could drive into someone's garden). Plus, freelance writers don't usually have employees, and that cuts down potential damage risk even further. So if your business is an inherently safe one, don't worry about liability. It will probably never be a problem.

company's assets if the company is unable to make payments to creditors out of its regular earnings.

Unlimited personal liability is one of the biggest disadvantages of running your business as a sole proprietorship. Because when the worst happens, you stand to lose *everything*.

Points to Consider

If you answer yes to any of the following questions, operating as a sole proprietorship may not be the right choice for your business:

1. Will your business need a lot of outside debt funding to get started (like bank loans or maxed-out credit cards)?
2. Do the typical day-to-day operations require considerable indebtedness to creditors (like inventory suppliers)?
3. Will you be hiring employees (aside from family members)?
4. Will either you or your employees do things that could create liabilities (like driving company vehicles)?
5. Will your company be making products, which can expose you to product liability claims (like children's toys)?
6. Will your employees be doing things that could potentially harm them (such as heavy lifting)?

These questions are designed to make you think ahead. No one expects his company to go broke—or no one would ever start a business. But any one of the factors above could wipe out an unprepared small business, and its owner as well. The bottom line here is this: If your business is likely to either run up tremendous debt or faces a strong possibility of being sued, consider an entity choice other than sole proprietorship. Or at least take serious steps to mitigate your liability risk. Because when all is said and done, you will be the one forced to pay in the end.

Having Employees Is Inherently Risky

With more people around, there's always a greater chance of incurring liability. Employees, in particular, will greatly increase your risk level. Even if your business is typically a safe one (like a resume writing service), your liability potential shoots up with the mere presence of employees. They can get injured on the job and sue. They can injure customers, who will then sue. And there are a lot of other ways you can end up losing your shirt when employees are involved. From sexual harassment and wrongful termination suits to theft and embezzlement, your exposure increases with each new hire.

Understand Product Liability

Making products exposes you to a lot of potential liability. In order to make claims stick, the litigant has to prove both that the product is defective and that it was defective when it left the control of the manufacturer. And in addition to manufacturers, wholesalers and retailers can be named in product liability claims.

Basically, there are three types of product defects:

1. Design defects, which cover all units of a particular product that causes danger, like a child's toy that shatters easily into sharp pieces.
2. Manufacturing defects, which means that your product is different and inherently more dangerous than it would be if it were made correctly.
3. Inadequate warnings, which refers to labeling and product instructions; all possible dangers should be made clear to the user.

Although the general rule states that manufacturers are responsible for damages incurred during normal use of the product and where the litigant can show that the product could have been made more safely for about the same cost to the producer, there are exceptions. The two basic exceptions come into play when the product is obviously dangerous and can't really be made safer (like a knife) or when

It Could Happen to You

A sole proprietor client walked into my office in tears. Her longtime bookkeeper and friend had stolen most of her money, left her on the verge of bankruptcy, and disappeared. This bookkeeper had been skimming cash from deposits, making checks out to "suppliers" (in reality, to her and her boyfriend), and neglecting the company's creditors. But since she did all the deposits, bill paying, and bank statement reconciliation, only she knew what was happening.

My client was forced to sell her house, cash out her retirement plan, borrow from relatives to satisfy all the creditors, and eventually shut down the business. Although her financial picture is beginning to turn around, she'll never get back what she lost.

The lesson here: Don't trust anyone with 100 percent of the financial responsibility for your business. Carefully check out all employees before you hire them. And make sure to keep tabs on what your company owes to its creditors. After all, its debts are your debts.

the manufacturer really couldn't have foreseen this danger when he origi-nally made and marketed the product.

Product liability also includes things like:

Negligence—This is when someone produces a defective product because he didn't take proper care during the manufacturing process.

Implied warranties—Essentially, this covers the fact that consumers can legally expect a product to work the way it's supposed to (for example, a printer will print).

Explicit warranties—Manufacturers are liable for anything they explic-itly state their products will do—and that includes marketing claims; if the ad says a vacuum cleaner can pick up a bowling ball, it had better be able to.

How to Protect Yourself and Your Business

So, you've thought it through and you still want to start out as a sole propri-etor. That's fine—millions of people do it—but just make sure that you insti-tute at least some of the following strategies so you don't end up losing everything because someone slips in your store.

There are several things you can do proactively to protect your assets. Some of the best strategies are prevention—using independent contractors instead of employees, for example. Other strategies shield your assets, like asset protection trusts. The best approach combines the two methods, to both limit your risk and mitigate your personal liability.

Independent Contractors Mitigate Employee Risks

In addition to the significant tax savings involved in using contractors (since they're not employees, you're not required to pay employment taxes for them), you'll cut down your potential liability risk significantly. Unlike with employees, your business is not responsible for tortious acts (that is, those that may involve legally actionable damages) committed by indepen-dent contractors. For example, if your employee runs over a bicycle with the company van, you are ultimately responsible for replacing the bike. But if you've instead hired an independent contractor to make deliveries, and he runs over the bike with his van, he bears all responsibility for any and all liabilities arising from that tortious act.

Of course, there are exceptions to the general rule. In some specific circumstances, you can still be held accountable for acts of an independent contractor. These situations include:

- Legal duties that can't be passed off, such as the owner of a cab company who has the obligation to ensure the vehicles are maintained safely
- Being negligent when you hired the contractor, such as not making sure he's legally qualified and certified to perform the tasks you hired him to perform
- Unusually dangerous activities, such as using explosives in rock quarries

Asset Protection Trusts Can Preserve Personal Assets

The most important thing to know about asset protection trusts is that they can't be created after the fact. In order to shield your personal assets, you have to place them in trust before you have even a hint of a problem. If you wait until creditors are breathing down your neck, the trust will be overturned and the assets distributed.

The best time to form this type of trust is when you start your sole proprietorship, before you run into financial difficulties. Asset protection trusts work best when you (as the one making the trust, or the trustor) are not also the beneficiary (the one benefiting from the trust). However, if you do assume both roles, your trust can still work when:

1. It's irrevocable, meaning you can't terminate it.
2. It's run by an independent trustee.
3. All distributions are made at the discretion of the trustee.
4. It includes a spendthrift clause, meaning that you can't assign your current or future beneficiary rights to creditors.

Most states won't recognize a spendthrift clause when the trustor is also the beneficiary, thus invalidating the asset protection value of the trust.

> The most important thing to know about asset protection trusts is that they can't be created after the fact.

However, Alaska and Delaware currently do allow this provision. Regardless of your location or that of your business, an asset protection trust can be set up in Alaska or Delaware.

A properly formed asset protection trust will shield your personal assets from creditors. The key here is "properly formed," so make sure you have a qualified attorney set it up for you.

Business Insurance Basics

Because sole proprietors have so much to lose, insurance is a must. At the very least, you should purchase liability insurance, which covers damages to other people—especially in our extremely litigious society. Not only are more people suing, but more of those suits are returning ridiculous awards. A single verdict against your company has the potential to put you out of business, and put you in the poorhouse. So unless you will have virtually no personal contact with customers or anyone else, liability insurance is a must.

What kind of coverage can you get? These days, insurance companies are pretty creative and flexible when it comes to designing policies specifically for small businesses. Some things you should consider specifically insuring against (depending on what your company does) include:

- Accidents
- Errors and omissions
- Personal malpractice

In addition, you should be sure to get property insurance, which covers damages to your own property. Like liability insurance, this comes with both general and specialized coverage options.

Get an Umbrella Policy

An umbrella policy fills in the gaps in your insurance portfolio. Essentially, an umbrella policy covers liability above and beyond that covered by your other policies. And it can go a long way toward making sure it's not necessary to tap into your personal assets to settle claims. And because it offers supplementary insurance, umbrella policies typically cover a very wide

> Because sole proprietors have so much to lose, insurance is a must.

range of losses—from auto accidents to customer falls to libel. (Make sure you know exactly what is included, and what is specifically excluded from your policy.)

Since umbrella insurance picks up where other coverage leaves off, it's typically quite inexpensive to purchase. You can probably get about $1 million of protection for as little as $300 a year. To get such a policy, you have to prove you have other underlying insurance policies providing protection in the $250,000 to $500,000 range. Your underlying insurance counts as the deductible for your umbrella coverage.

Here's how it works. Suppose your business has been sued and lost. The settled-on payout is $1 million. Your business liability insurance kicks in $250,000, after you pay a $2,500 deductible. Your umbrella policy pays $747,500. And you go home. All you and your business were responsible for was your original $2,500 deductible.

Take Care to Insure Your Home-Based Business

Think your homeowner's policy will cover your home-based business? Think again. Most home policies explicitly exclude business coverage. So talk to your insurance agent, and make sure you get all the additional policies and riders you need to protect your business.

Here are some examples of common items people typically think are covered, but may not be:

- A client comes to your home office, falls down the stairs and sprains his ankle. Your basic homeowner's policy doesn't cover any injuries connected with business meetings.
- Your house is robbed and, among other things, your computer and everything that goes with it are stolen. Typically, lost business property is specifically excluded in homeowners' policies.
- Your house burns down. The insurance company says your fire coverage is null and void because you never told them you were using your home for business purposes.

The simple way around the lack of coverage is to tell your insurance agent what you're doing. It's typically pretty inexpensive to add the necessary bells and whistles to your existing homeowner's policy. And paying an extra $250 (or so) a year is a lot better than paying thousands of dollars for a new computer or a client's injuries.

Sole Proprietors Need Disability Coverage

You are your business; your business is you (to paraphrase Louis XIV). But what happens to your business if you become disabled? More important, what happens to your income?

If you're temporarily unable to work due to an extended illness or injury, you're going to need some coverage to get you through. Disability insurance keeps the cash flowing until you're back on your feet. If your business comes to a halt without you, you'll need these steady payments to keep you going, so you can get back to business.

When the business can be run without you (although it may not be run as well), disability overhead insurance can fill in the gaps. This kind of coverage takes care of some of the business's overhead expenses, like rent, giving your company a good chance at survival while you recover.

When you look into disability insurance, check out the following options:

Waiting period—How long does it take before benefits kick in?

Payment caps—The insurance company or the state may limit the total amount you can receive.

Disability defined—Will you get payments only if you can't do anything, or can you perform some functions and still collect?

> **Chapter 8**

Getting Out
of Business

Part One

Part Two

Part Three

Part Four

Part Five

Part Six

PART TWO   SOLE PROPRIETORSHIPS

■ CHAPTER 4 The Easiest Business to Start ■ CHAPTER 5 Keeping Good Records Is Crucial ■ CHAPTER 6 Dealing with Taxes Throughout the Year ■ CHAPTER 7 Protecting Your Assets ■ CHAPTER 8 Getting Out of Business

An Easy Business to Dissolve

In the same way that you can simply wake up one morning and declare yourself a sole proprietor, you can wake up and stop being a sole proprietor. Of course, actually winding up the business can take a little more effort than that, but you don't have to file any official paperwork to stop operating your business. Once you make the decision, you simply close the doors.

The flip side is that if *you* can no longer run the business (or just don't want to), your sole proprietorship will terminate. It can only exist as long as you are alive, capable, and willing to run it. So if you become disabled, or otherwise incapacitated to the point where you can't run the company, your sole proprietorship will cease to exist.

As soon as *you* stop being in business, so does your sole proprietorship. Although the day-to-day business might continue, the company no longer exists. So whether you pass your business on to a family member or sell it to a stranger, your sole proprietorship ends when you leave it. You can transfer your company's assets, but the company itself is not transferable.

Cleanup Tasks

For income tax purposes, there are no special "termination" forms that need to be filed. In fact, all you have to do is to check a single box on your Schedule C. For sales tax purposes, though, you may have to file some kind of notification that you're discontinuing operations, but this varies by state. Contact your state sales tax office to find out what and when you need to file, or you could end up facing nonfiling penalties.

As to business debts, you are still responsible for paying them. You should contact all vendors and suppliers to whom you still owe money and inform them that you have dissolved your business. If you can pay them right away, do so. Otherwise, try to negotiate reasonable payment plans; they'd rather get paid slowly than not at all.

Although you may not technically owe them money, you may have outstanding debts to your customers. You could have unfinished jobs that you promised to finish before you knew you were terminating—and you still have a legal obligation to perform those jobs if the customer demands it (or pay them back any deposits). Like vendors, you must notify your customers that you're closing up shop. They may rely on you, and they need to know they'll have to make alternate arrangements.

Exit Strategies

Your business is thriving, and it's more demanding than ever. You've enjoyed the gamble of start-up, loved watching your "baby" grow, and reveled in the positive cash flow all those naysayers said would never come. But now you're tired, and you want to retire to a tropical climate. Or maybe someone's made you an offer that you just can't—and don't want to—refuse. Maybe your kids are ready to take over, and you want to give them room to do so. Then again, maybe things have gone the other way. Maybe you're working harder and harder but the business just isn't doing as well as you'd like.

Most sole proprietorships follow the same exit path. First, they want to pass the business down to the kids or other family members. If that doesn't pan out, they sell the company as is. If they can't sell the business in whole, they chop it up, liquidate the business, and sell off the individual assets. In the last and worst-case scenario, they're mired in business debt and holding assets that just won't sell, so they turn to the bankruptcy courts.

As much as you may not want to think about this now, your sole proprietorship literally can't be around forever. Don't wait until the moment is upon you to figure out what to do. By thinking about your exit strategy now, you'll be better prepared to handle it when the time comes to get out. You'll be thinking with a calm head and an eye to the future instead of running around in a panic when time is already up. Planning ahead for the end phase of your business maximizes your chances to walk away with a light heart and a beneficial financial settlement.

> By thinking about your exit strategy now, you'll be better prepared to handle it when the time comes to get out.

How to Keep the Business in the Family

Though it sounds like the simplest solution, turning your business over to family members can be the toughest challenge you'll face. To make the transition successful, you'll have to take the company, your family members, ongoing personal finances, income tax issues, and estate and gift tax issues into account all at once.

You can't just decide one day that tomorrow you'll turn the reins over to your daughter or your nephew and head off to the beach. You must carefully plan this transition, include everyone who will be involved in the changeover, and keep the plan flexible—because things change.

Your plan should be split into two sections: transferring power (meaning control and management of the company and its assets) and transferring assets (meaning passing the actual wealth on to specified family members). The power and the assets need not end up in the same hands. If not, you'll need to take steps to insure that everything flows together cohesively.

> Your plan should be split into two sections: transferring power and transferring assets.

Transfer of Power

You'll need to consider a lot of factors when determining to whom you'll be handing over your company. The first factor (maybe the most important) is who actually wants to take over, followed closely by whether that person (or group) is capable. Also, with a family business, what affects the family also affects the business. And that includes things like health, marital status, education level, and interrelationships.

Chances are, you already have your eye on someone that you'd like to eventually take your place at the helm. Most of the time, the choice will be obvious: someone eager to join the business who's both qualified and experienced enough to do so. If there's no one family member who fits the bill, you can split ownership and management responsibilities. To keep the rest of the family from getting ruffled feathers, let them stay involved, even if just peripherally.

If your business has employees, let them in on the transfer before it's a done deal. They'll respond better to taking orders from someone who's been around than from someone who just walked in the door. This is especially important for key employees, because the business just may not survive without them.

The most important thing is to be clear. Your business won't stick around for long if the kids are fighting over who gets to place inventory orders and what color the new fliers should be. Management responsibility should be spelled out from the start, because time wasted quibbling could be better spent retaining customers and employees.

Transferring Assets

Passing along business assets is much more complicated than just giving Junior your office computer. You have to consider federal gift and estate taxes and business valuations. You will probably have to get professionals involved.

With a sole proprietorship, you actually own anything the company owns. And that takes at least one layer of complexity away from asset transfers. But you still need to plan carefully, or you (and your eventual heirs) can get hit with a nasty tax bill. You can transfer $1.5 million of assets estate-tax-free (for 2004, under current law). But if you use up the entire exemption on business assets, everything else you own will be subject to the tax instead. You can make completely tax-free gifts of up to $11,000 per year (for 2004) to anyone you want, though, and those never get reconsidered as part of the $1 million gift exemption. If your business has smaller assets, you can begin gifting them early on to your designated asset "transferees," and lease them back to the business. The leases will still be in effect when your control successor takes over; and if you choose the same person for both assets and control, he'll own the assets when he takes over the management functions.

What about Estate Taxes?

The Economic Growth and Tax Relief Act of 2001 made sweeping changes to rules governing federal estate tax. This rewrite even included a full (although possibly temporary) repeal of the burdensome tax. Under that law, federal estate taxes gradually decline until 2010 when they hit zero. And unless Congress takes steps by that time to maintain the repealed status, the federal estate tax law will revert to its status as of 2001—and that will be a pretty large blow to family businesses.

Estate tax law is especially important to sole proprietors because their business assets are considered to be their personal assets, and therefore will be fully included in their estates. If the business is asset-heavy, it could cause a sole proprietor's total net worth to exceed the federal estate tax exemption in the year of death (unless he dies in 2010), leaving his family stuck with a nasty estate tax bill.

Generally speaking, estate taxes must be paid in cash within nine months after death. And although the family business might be worth more than a million dollars on paper, it probably won't have enough cash on hand to pay the IRS in full all at once. Unfortunately, this has caused the families of many sole proprietors to lose their traditional livelihood when the heirs are compelled to have to sell the business assets for anything they can get in order to raise enough money to pay off their enormous tax bill.

SCHEDULE OF REMAINING ESTATE TAX PHASEOUT

Year	Unified Credit Exemption	Top Estate Tax Rate
2004	$1,500,000	48%
2005	$1,500,000	47%
2006	$2,000,000	46%
2007	$2,000,000	45%
2008	$2,000,000	45%
2009	$3,500,000	45%
2010	N/A	Repealed
2011*	$1,000,000	55%

Based on current law.

Most people think that estate taxes only affect the very wealthy. But times have changed, and the bulk of taxpayers that end up owing this tax would never consider themselves part of the rich elite.

These days it's not so hard to have $1,000,000—or even $2,000,000. A house, a retirement plan, a modest stock portfolio, and a family business can easily put you over the top here. And every penny over the exemption amount gets taxed, some of it possibly at close to 50 percent!

Because it's so easy to hit the limit, estate planning is especially important for sole proprietors. Since legally the business isn't a separate entity, you personally own every asset employed by your company. Plus, you also personally own the inherent value of the company, based on an independent appraisal, which could easily and greatly exceed the underlying value of the physical assets.

Small Business Valuation

In order to find out the value of your business for estate tax purposes, an appraisal will need to be performed. For your family's best interests, you should direct that a new appraisal be done upon your death. This will ensure that your heirs aren't locked in to an old appraisal that may bear no resemblance to current market values. A current valuation is important because your heirs will have to pay taxes based on what the appraiser says your business is worth—whether you can actually sell the business for that amount is a completely different story.

The appraisal will include such things as:

- Current market value of physical assets
- Inventory on hand (whether saleable or not)
- Cash and securities held in the name of the business
- Existing business debts

Selling Your Business to Outsiders

Whenever you're ready, you can sell off any and all of your company's assets. You can sell the company as a whole, or you can chop it up and sell it for parts. You are solely in control of this decision—it's 100 percent up to you how you want to go about it.

Of course, the business itself will largely dictate how it can be sold. A business with a lot of physical assets (like a landscaping company) is easy to sell in pieces. A shop, complete with inventory, will typically sell as a whole. A service-oriented business, like a bookkeeping firm, will involve selling your client list—and that's very different from selling machinery or teacups.

Who Will Buy Your Company?

Outside buyers for your business could come from anywhere. From suppliers to competitors, you have a pretty wide audience to sell to. Although you may be dreaming of some fancy Wall Street takeover, most small businesses sell somewhat close to home.

Wealthy Without Knowing It

A longtime client came to my office to talk about his company. As we did, some bells went off in my head. I asked him about his personal financial and estate planning—he said he didn't have any "fancy" planning, just a retirement plan.

We sat and added up his assets: the IRA, his home equity, the company's net worth, etc. Plus, he owned his own life insurance policy, meaning it would be included in his estate. When he saw the final figure, he was astonished. He knew that he had money here, money there—but he never thought about how much it came to all together.

To make a long story short, I sent him to a trusted colleague who specializes in estate planning for people with small businesses. It cost the client about $300 for the consultation, but potentially saved his children thousands of dollars in estate taxes.

You can basically characterize your potential buyers in two ways: those who want your cash flow and those who want to merge your company into theirs. Cash flow buyers typically own several diversified businesses, and act more like investors than business owners, although sometimes they are displaced professionals looking for an established company to run (all the rewards of entrepreneurship without the start-up risks). The buyers who want to subsume your company are usually already enmeshed in the same industry, although often in a different phase of it.

These strategy-oriented buyers can be:

- Mid- to large-size companies looking to expand into a new area
- Competitors looking to take over your share of the market
- Suppliers or customers looking to expand "vertically," such as a customer buying your company so he can own the manufacturing piece of the product he already sells

Before you put your business on the auction block, think about to whom you would like to sell it—and who you wouldn't like to see owning it. If it will make you cringe to see your former competitors take over your shop, scratch them off the list of potential buyers. If you have a great relationship with one of your customers, and you know he's looking to expand, pitch the idea of a vertical strategy to him. Try to find a buyer for whom your company is a good fit. Because the better your little company will fit into his, the more he'll want it and the more he'll pay for it.

Confidentiality Is Key

So, you found someone who wants to buy your company, and pay a pretty penny for it, too. He's seen your books, your inventory stockroom, even your client list. Everything is in place—and the deal falls through. Now you still have your business, but someone else has all the inside information—and that can hurt your future negotiations.

For starters, until you're sure someone is seriously interested in buying the business, give him only enough information to make him want to come back. If he does come back, and it seems like things are progressing, have him sign a confidentiality agreement—and still keep very sensitive information (like that client list) tucked away. This is for your own protection. If the deal does fall through, you may have just given someone enough information to start up as your competition. With enough of your inside information, he could do serious damage to your business. So tell him enough to clinch the sale, but don't give away everything until the deal is done.

Tax Consequences of Selling the Business

When you sell your business, you're really selling off each asset individually—at least for tax purposes. If you sell your landscaping business, the IRS acts as though you sold two lawn mowers, three weed whackers, two tree trimmers, and a truck. Because each asset included in the sale is treated separately, you have to compute individual gains (or losses) for each. For each asset, you'll need to know:

- The current book value
- The current fair market value (which counts as its individual sale price)
- How long you've had the asset
- Whether it qualifies for capital gains (loss) treatment

Qualifying for Capital Gains Treatment

Most business assets are eligible for capital gains treatment. The big exception here is inventory—or anything you held for resale in the normal course of business. So if a landscaping company sells a lawn mower, that counts as a capital asset; if a lawn mower retailer sells a lawn mower, it counts as an inventory sale, and therefore any profit (or loss) on the sale is treated as ordinary income.

Why does this classification matter? Because tax on capital gains, especially for assets held longer than one year, is typically lower than tax on ordinary income—sometimes significantly lower.

Under our current federal tax law, the maximum tax rate for long-term capital gains is significantly lower than that for ordinary income. Right now, sale of assets that have been held for longer than one year are taxed at a maximum capital gains rate of 15 percent (10 percent if you fall into the 15 percent bracket). The maximum tax rate for ordinary income (for the 2004

Tax on capital gains is typically lower than tax on ordinary income.

Installment Plans Questionable for Accrual Basis Taxpayers

Under current tax law, some accrual basis taxpayers may not be able to defer any of their tax liability even with an installment contract. So even if you sell your business using this method, you may have to report the full income from the sale in the year of the sale—and pay the full tax bill—even if you haven't been paid in full. And that means you'd be paying tax on a lot of money you haven't even seen yet. But, after all, that's how accrual basis accounting works.

The IRS jumped in and confused things even more. They said that since certain accrual-basis taxpayers could be using the cash method, they would be allowed to use the installment plan method of tax deferral.

The moral of the story? See a professional before you agree to sell your company with an installment plan.

tax year) is 35 percent. Because it's more beneficial tax-wise to have items classified as capital assets, you should try to allocate as much of the sales price to those assets as possible.

Regardless of the tax classification of its assets, you could end up facing a pretty hefty tax bill when you sell your business. In fact, unless you do some careful planning, you could end up sharing close to half of your sale proceeds with the government. Luckily, there are ways to lower, or at least to defer, some of the tax liability.

Defer Your Taxes with an Installment Sale

One way to delay at least a portion of your tax bill is to put off receiving the full purchase price at once. This method is called an installment sale, and when you use it taxes on the gains can be put off until whenever the money is actually received.

Selling a small business with an installment contract is a pretty common arrangement. Instead of getting the full price in cash when you sell, you get a down payment (typically somewhere between 15 percent and 40 percent) at the time of the sale, and the rest in equal installments over several years. This effectively makes you the lender for whoever buys your business—they make payments to you instead of to the bank. The installment payments include agreed-upon interest for the life of the loan.

So, for example, suppose you sell your business this year for $250,000. Instead of traditional bank financing, the buyer agrees to an installment plan with you. He'll pay you $50,000 now, and $40,000 a year plus 5 percent interest for the next five years. You pay ordinary income tax on the interest you receive, and capital gains tax on the profit portion of the sales price only when you receive it.

> **Chapter 9**

Understanding Partnerships

Part One

Part Two

Part Three

Part Four

Part Five

Part Six

What Is a Partnership?

By definition, a partnership is simply an unincorporated business owned by at least two individuals who will each share in the company's profits and losses. Each partner has to bring something of value to the business, in the form of money, property, or talent.

Partnerships are very easy to form. In fact, just like with sole proprietorships, many people form legal partnerships without even knowing it. Basically, any time two or more people (or other "individuals," as you'll see below) pool their assets, share services, and go into business together, they have formed a general partnership—even if they don't have any kind of formal partnership agreement in place. Any kind of profit-seeking undertaken by two or more parties together is considered a partnership, for both legal and tax purposes. For example, if you and your friend Joe buy a house together, rent it out to some tenants, and provide some typical landlord services to the tenants, like yard work or appliance repairs (even if through some kind of management company or agent), the two of you have created a legal partnership.

Types of Partnerships

Partnerships come in two basic tried-and-true setups, general and limited, plus one new addition, the *limited liability partnership (LLP)*. On top of that, a much-talked about form of limited partnership is one called the *family*

Partners vs. Co-owners

Merely owning property jointly does not count as a legal partnership by itself. Even if the property is leased or rented, the co-ownership alone does not constitute a legal partnership. However, when landlord-type services are provided, you automatically have a partnership under the law.

If you want to have a partnership to own property, you'll have to form a legal partnership first, then transfer title for the property to the partnership. On the flip side, if you want to co-own property with others but do not want to become a legal partnership, make sure to not to cross the service-providing line.

limited partnership, although there is no legal definition for it other than a regular limited partnership owned by a family. Finally, there's the *limited liability limited partnership*, or *LLLP*.

In a general partnership, you and all of your partners will each participate in the daily activities of the business, at least in some capacity. With a limited partnership, there will be two separate and distinct classes of partners: general and limited. The general partners have full responsibility for the business and the limited partners just provide and receive cash (or other assets). The LLP adds a limited twist to a general partnership to add some basic legal protections for its partners. And the LLLP adds some protection for the general partner of a limited partnership.

Although the differences may sound minimal, they're not. As you'll learn (repeatedly, because it is very important), the distinctions among partnership types exist mainly for liability protection purposes. And as a partner, the more insulation you have for your personal assets, the better off you'll be.

General Partnerships

General partnerships are very easygoing business structures. You won't have to follow all kinds of legal formalities, like having board meetings, recording minutes, or voting for officers. Plus, you don't have to have any kind of legal agreement to form a partnership, although it is *strongly* recommended. Just like with a sole proprietorship, you can simply wake up one morning, start a business (although you have to start it with someone else), and be a general partnership—no fuss, no muss.

But the simplicity does come with a serious drawback: All general partners are fully personally liable for all debts of the partnership. This all-encompassing liability is the reason that general partnerships are not recommended by most business advisors.

Although not popular among business experts, general partnerships are very common—however, as the new generation of entrepreneurs bones up on the topic, the number of new general partnerships may begin to wane. If you've already inadvertently formed a general partnership and would like to make a change, the sooner the better. If you think you want to form a general partnership, think again.

Limited Partnerships

Every *limited partnership* has to have at least one general partner to run the day-to-day business operations. Most partners in this structure, though, will be classified as limited. Limited partners have a very limited role in the business—as pocketbooks. They contribute only capital to the business, usually in the form of cash, and not time or management. The general partners run the business; the limited partners just invest and keep quiet—hence the phrase "silent partners."

Unlike their general partners, the limited partners don't face the burden of unlimited liability. In fact, they can't ever lose more than their total investment in the company. There is a caveat here: If a limited partner joins in actually running the business or making management-type decisions, he loses his limited partner status and the limited liability protection that goes along with it.

And there's the downside to this entity: The general partner is completely personally liable for all obligations of the business.

Family Limited Partnerships

First things first: There is no legally recognized business structure called a "family limited partnership" (FLP). It's just a name given to standard limited partnerships owned largely by a single family.

An FLP may be used appropriately for tax planning and asset protection for some families. When you create an FLP, your family assets can be held all together, instead of going here and there to various heirs—which may be desirable when the family assets are used in a business or make up some type of collection that means more as a whole than the sum of its parts.

In an FLP, when you want to change who has control over the assets, you would simply change the general partner. Another benefit: your family business enjoys all the other protections that come with standard limited partnership. And on top of the liability protection, your family may get substantial tax benefits (especially with gift and estate taxes) by forming an FLP. Finally, it's very easy to transfer small portions of the business to your children and grandchildren over time.

Limited Liability Limited Partnerships

The extra "L" in LLLP adds limited liability protection for general partners in limited partnerships. This structure is still very new—and largely untested in the courts. It's mainly been used so far to transform already existing limited partnerships, but it's beginning to open some eyes as a challenger for the very popular LLC (see Part Five for more information about LLCs).

So far, this entity isn't recognized in many states. The states that do allow LLLPs include Texas, North Carolina, Maryland, Georgia, Florida, Delaware, and Colorado.

Should this entity become more widely available and accepted, it will likely mean the end of the plain vanilla limited partnership. Who would want all the liability of the general partner if he could avoid it simply by adding an extra "L" to all the paperwork?

Limited Liability Partnerships

An LLP is really just a general partnership with some added bells and whistles, formed and regulated by state statute. The main difference between an LLP and a general partnership is crucial: LLPs will protect their partners from at least some of the personal liability that comes standard with partnerships. Under an LLP, you'll get some (possibly full) protection against financial obligations caused by the tortious acts of your partners.

Texas allowed the first LLP statute back in 1991. The new structure was designed to protect general partners from the potentially crippling personal financial liability they would normally suffer for a different partner's negligence, errors and omissions, incompetence, and malfeasance. Within a few years, more than twenty states plus the District of Columbia wrote some form of LLP statute. Today, every state formally recognizes the entity—although the statutes themselves vary widely. To cut out some of the interstate confusion and provide a little

Beware of FLP Promoters

Although they've lost momentum due to changing estate tax legislation, some less than scrupulous business promoters are still touting the wonders of the FLP. And since most people don't really understand estate taxes, how they work, or how they are changing, they get taken in by seemingly well-meaning business advisors who explain that without an FLP (set up for just a few thousand dollars) their heirs may get to keep next to nothing after the "evil" taxman takes his cut.

I'm not saying that everyone who advises his clients to set up FLPs is disreputable. But there really aren't very many cases where an FLP is the best thing for a family to do. On top of that, because FLPs have usually been used primarily for tax avoidance, the IRS tends to look at them very closely.

standard guidance, a Uniform LLP Amendment to the Uniform Partnership Act was created in 1996. More and more states are now conforming to this standard, so the fifty-one LLP statutes will begin to be more consistent—this is especially important if your business will span more than one state.

Just as the LLLP could mean curtains for the limited partnership, the LLP may spell doom for the general partnership—at least in states where anyone can form them.

Suitable Businesses for Partnerships

Almost any business can be a partnership, but there are some particularly suited to this laidback entity. In addition, some other entities may bar certain business types, leaving partnerships as the best option. If you're looking for a simple setup and beneficial taxation, a partnership can be a good fit.

Limited partnerships work especially well when you want to take on an infusion of capital without taking on a lot of debt, but you want to be in sole control of the business. Although limited partnerships require more paperwork than their general counterparts, they are much simpler to maintain than corporations. Of course, if you're in a state that allows LLLPs, you (as the general partner) are much better off starting out with the promise of personal protection.

Professional practices have traditionally been formed as partnerships, mainly because in the past that was the only entity they were allowed to form. Today's professional practices should look to form LLPs, where allowed, for the added liability protection.

> If you're looking for a simple setup and beneficial taxation, a partnership can be a good fit.

The Dangers of General Partnerships

Although almost any business can be formed as a partnership, there are some that should definitely shy away from the general partnership entity. Three business types that are definitely not suitable to be formed as general partnerships include those that need significant levels of inventory, substantial debt financing, or are high liability industries by nature. The general partnership in particular can be very dangerous from a personal liability point of view. As you'll learn more thoroughly in Chapter 12, this business entity will provide the most exposure for your personal assets—even more than they'd be exposed under a sole proprietorship.

Who Can Be a Partner?

Both legally speaking and for federal tax purposes, literally any person or entity can be a partner in either a general or a limited partnership. This extensive list includes:

- People (possibly including your spouse, depending on your home state laws)
- Other partnerships
- Corporations
- Trusts
- Estates
- Foreign individuals, partnerships, corporations, trusts, and estates

Restrictions really only begin to apply to professional partnerships, like accounting firms, law firms, and medical practices. In fact, some states forbid members of particular professions (such as CPAs) to form anything other than general partnerships or LLPs (for companies with more than one owner). These types of partnerships typically, under state law, require that all partners be licensed in the named profession of the group. So, if you are a CPA and you want to take on a partner and call your company a CPA firm, the new partner has to be a licensed CPA as well—and in your company's home state.

For LLPs, the constraints may be greater, although they do vary from state to state. For example, some states (like New York and California) only allow specific professionals to form LLPs, and general businesses don't fit the bill. Most states, though, allow pretty much anyone to use this structure.

The only other restriction on partners is quantity. While there is no limit on the number of partners you can have, there is an obvious minimum—two. There must be at least two partners—or you have a sole proprietorship.

It's Important to Know Your General Partners Well

Choosing your partners—especially when you will be general partners—is possibly the most important factor in starting up a partnership. Although this is a very easy business form to start, it can be difficult to get out of, especially when the reason you want out is trouble with a partner.

The most common general partnerships start with friends and/or family members. And you may think you know them well; maybe you've known them for years. But take the quiz below anyway to make sure you know whether they have what it takes to be a good business partner.

1. Do you know your partner's true personal financial picture? A partner with limited financial resources will not be able to pay his fair share of partnership obligations, and you could be left holding the bag. No matter how much you like your partner, ask to see some independently corroborated personal financial statements.

2. Is your partner a team player or more of a loner? If your partner acts alone in the name of the partnership (and he absolutely can), you (and all other general partners) will be individually and personally responsible for everything he does.

3. How committed is your partner to this business? If one partner leaves for any reason, your partnership will no longer exist. Find out what your potential partner's long-range plans and goals are, and whether they include sticking around for the long haul.

4. Is this a person you can see yourself working with for years to come, and spending the majority of your waking hours with? If you doubt you'll be able to stand being with this partner almost all the time, reconsider. You can't sell (or otherwise transfer) your interest in the partnership without the consent of all the other partners; and you can only get rid of him by buying him out.

5. What skills and talents will he bring to the partnership? Complementary skills and talents will serve the business better than ones you share.

Questions one and two are the most important to your personal financial health. Not only will you be personally liable for any and all business transactions made by your partner, you could also end up dealing with his personal debts. Plus, he can file personal bankruptcy to avoid paying his share of partnership obligations.

It's crucial to find out all of this information before you actually start your business. Partnerships have started more family feuds and ended more friendships than practically anything else. In fact, general partnerships historically generate the highest percentage of internal lawsuits of all the different business structures.

Traits to Look for in Your Partner(s)

You know your strong and not-so-strong points. The best kind of partner is one who possesses traits you don't, one who can compensate for your weak spots. If creativity is your bailiwick but paperwork makes your head spin, look for a partner who shines in the office management area. If you're a great numbers cruncher but a lousy salesperson, get an outgoing partner who could sell ice to Alaskans.

By finding a partner (or partners) whose strong skills complement rather than duplicate yours, you'll be able to better manage your bottom line. How? Instead of hiring employees or professionals to take over tasks you either don't like or aren't good at, your partner can handle them. This is especially helpful during the early years, when cash flow can make or break the business. Any talents you have in-house are talents you don't need to seek out—and pay for.

Another way to keep cash in the business is to find a partner with a strong personal financial picture. Not only will this person be able to bring unencumbered capital into the business, he will also drain less cash out of it to cover his personal expenses. A partner who's already bad with money or in the middle of a financial meltdown can be very dangerous to your company's cash flow.

> The best kind of partner is one who can compensate for your weak spots.

How to Assess Your Prospective Partner(s)

Chances are your potential partner is someone you already know—probably a close friend or a relative. But that doesn't mean that you shouldn't look at his financial picture, take a talent and skills assessment, and find out his long-term plans and life goals; in fact, you should provide the same information to him about yourself. Keep in mind: Some people prickle when you ask them for this type of information. But anyone who's serious about starting and growing a business should want (if not welcome) this open exchange. If your prospective partner isn't forthcoming, or avoids answering questions, you may want to reconsider locking yourself into a business with him.

Start with the goals and plans—it's the easiest way to begin sharing this sometimes sensitive information. Ideally, your long-range plan should mesh with your partner's. For example, if you want to settle in and put down some roots, you might want a partner who's looking for similar stability. Someone who wants to work for a year, then spend time kicking around Europe would not be a good choice for a hands-on partner, but might make a great silent partner.

Next comes the skills assessment. This test is crucial for general partners, but not for limited partners, whose role is limited to cash provider anyway. You don't have to make this a formal "exam," but can make it more like a brainstorming session. What you want to focus on is individual strengths; try to figure out who can do what and what is important to your company's success that neither of you brings to the table.

Finally, each of you should prepare some basic personal financial statements. The two most important are a statement of net worth and a cash flows statement. The statement of net worth is really just a listing of what you own and what you owe; the difference between the two is your net worth. Don't get crazy with this statement—only include cash and substantial assets (like your house, your car), not how many pairs of running shoes you have. Include everything that you owe, from your mortgage to your credit cards to your checking account overdraft protection.

The cash flows statement has two main sections: cash in and cash out. For cash in, include your total family income, interest and dividends, rents you receive, etc. The cash out section is a modified budget. This shows things like your mortgage or rent payments, grocery bills, car expenses, and home utilities. The statement of cash flows should cover at least a three-month period, but not longer than a single year. If you're not sure how much you spend, use your check register for reference.

> **Chapter 10**

Start-up Procedures for Partnerships

Part One

Part Two

Part Three

Part Four

Part Five

Part Six

Why a Partnership Agreement Is Essential

Although a general partnership can be started without any kind of formal agreement (written or oral), it is not a good idea. There's not a single state law that requires a written partnership agreement, but common sense dictates you'll be much better off with one, preferably one that's drafted by an attorney.

Can you get away without one? Absolutely, but it's not recommended. If you don't have an agreement that mirrors your wishes, your company's home state regulations will take charge, quite likely in ways that don't match your intentions. Partnerships are governed by their home state statutes, most of which follow the Uniform Partnership Act (UPA) and the Revised Uniform Limited Partnership Act (RULPA). LLP regulations, for the most part, still vary pretty widely.

> If you don't have an agreement that mirrors your wishes, your company's home state regulations will take charge.

So you can see why a written agreement is pretty important for the ultimate success of your partnership. Regardless of your company's financial success, if you don't plan ahead for possible problems down the road, disagreement can rise up among you and your partners—maybe even causing your partnership to dissolve. No matter who your partners are, whatever the outside-of-business relationships, hire an experienced lawyer to draw up a written partnership agreement. Figuring out solutions in advance for problems that may arise can only help you and your business in the long run. A little preplanning now can help you avoid costly and nasty litigation if any troubles arise.

What Should You Include in the Agreement?

Partnership agreements are pretty standard fare these days. But that doesn't mean you should use a prefab, cookie-cutter form. Although there are some standard points to include (as you'll see below), you, your partner(s), and your business are unique. So your agreement should cover any issues that pertain particularly to your set of circumstances.

The following list includes typical items that should be addressed in any partnership agreement. Issues lending themselves to a more in-depth look are discussed in detail later in this chapter. A basic agreement should include at least:

- The name of each partner and his contact information
- The name, main address, nature, and scope of the business

- When and how the company will be funded initially, and how additional capital will be raised
- How much time each partner will spend working at the business, and what his duties and responsibilities will be
- How profits and losses will be allocated, and when distributions will be made
- Legal authorizations of each partner to act on behalf of the partnership (called *actual authority*)
- Whether partners can participate in other businesses, especially those in direct competition with this partnership
- Steps to follow when a partner leaves the business
- Restrictions on how partnership interests can be transferred (called *buy-sell provisions*)
- How conflicts will be resolved, such as through using an arbitrator

When a Partner Wants Out

No one likes to think about breaking up in the new stage of a relationship—especially when you're excited about embarking upon a new adventure. And when you will be starting your business with a friend or family member, it's even harder to imagine that someday you may want to split up.

Even if everything goes perfectly—you work together well, maintain a close friendship outside the business, the company is successful—things outside your control can end the partnership. A partner's spouse can get transferred out of state, causing the entire family to move and your partnership to become impractical. Or one partner could get seriously ill or disabled, and be incapable of participating in the business.

Many common occurrences can affect your partnership. Change is inevitable, and it's best to plan for these kinds of changes in your partnership agreement. If you wait until the event is upon you, emotions and immediacy can impact the situation. But when you figure out the answers when everything is fine, when you're not under the gun, you'll be able to come up with the fairest, most beneficial solutions for everyone.

The two most important factors when a partner exits are the financial arrangements and to whom he can sell his share of the business. These issues are covered in the buy-sell provisions of the partnership agreement, explained in more detail below. Other items to include in your agreement are noncompete covenants (for when a departing partner wants to start a similar business), what will happen to the business (including its name) if a partner leaves, and how to handle a partner who stops participating in the business but maintains some ownership.

Buy-Sell Provisions

Many events can force the dissolution of a partnership, if they are not prepared for in advance. But when you include buy-sell provisions in your partnership agreement, you'll save time, money, friendships, and your business.

Buy-sell provisions deal with things like what events can trigger a buyout (the personal bankruptcy of one of the partners, for example), the amount and timing of payments to a partner for his share of the company, and to whom his interest can be sold (typically this is limited to the existing partners). Most partnership agreements specify that the other partners get first dibs on the departing partner's interest before it can be offered to an outsider, called the right of first refusal.

Funding the Business

All partners have to contribute something to the partnership, whether it's money, property, or services. In exchange for that, he gets his partnership interest. Each partner will have a capital account, which represents his percentage of ownership of the business. Once you contribute capital to the company, you can't take it back unless you completely withdraw from the partnership, sell off at least some of your partnership interest, or end the partnership.

When you put money into the partnership as your capital contribution, deposit it directly into the partnership's bank account, not a joint bank account in the names of the individual partners. If you contribute property to the business, you need to retitle the property in the name of the partnership to make it official.

When your partnership is formed, funding comes from the founding (original) partners. But once your business is up and running, you'll have more options available to supplement the cash balance. Your options fall into two categories: equity and debt.

Equity financing comes from owners. You can have all the existing partners make either additional proportional contributions or additional disproportionate capital contributions; disproportionate contributions mean you'll have to recompute each partner's new relative ownership interest. The other equity option is to bring on new partners, which usually requires total agreement of the existing partners (depending on what it says in your partnership agreement).

Debt financing usually comes from the bank. Just as for sole proprietorships, the credit standing of each partner affects the overall credit rating of the partnership, and that could make loans harder to get if even one partner has bad credit.

Getting an Employer Identification Number

Even though you don't need an employer identification number (EIN) to get started in business, your partnership has to get one before filing its first tax return (whether income or payroll tax) or making its first tax deposit. To get an EIN from the IRS, you have to fill out Form SS-4 (Application for Employer Identification Number) for the partnership.

This is definitely one form you don't need a professional to fill out for you. The very simple, one-page form asks only for basic information, like the name and address of the company, business structure, and when the business was started. You can expedite the whole process by applying directly online (go to *www.irs.gov* for the secure application), or by calling the automatic phone line assigned to your state (the phone number list is available at the IRS Web site also). If you use the IRS fax-back service, it takes about a week to get your EIN; if you do it all by mail, expect to wait four to five weeks for a response. If the partnership must file a tax return before the EIN is received, simply write "Applied for" and the application date on the EIN line; do not use your social security number.

Once an EIN is assigned to your company, it becomes the permanent tax ID for the partnership until it is terminated. If you merely change the name or address of the partnership, you can continue to use your original EIN. However, if you change the business entity—even if nothing else about the business will change—you may need to apply for a new EIN.

> To get an EIN from the IRS, you have to fill out Form SS-4 (Application for Employer Identification Number) for the partnership.

In most cases, your federal EIN will also be used for your home state tax ID number. But some states (like New Jersey) do require businesses to obtain a separate state EIN for tax purposes. Check with your home state tax authority to find out which ID number you should use on their forms.

Special Procedures for Limited Partnerships

Limited partnerships have two levels of partners: general and limited, and they must have at least one of each. A general partner is personally liable for all business obligations; a limited partner has limited liability and can never lose more than his total investment. Strict legal guidelines have to be followed to keep your partnership from being considered a general partnership, so have a lawyer help you during start up.

> Strict legal guidelines have to be followed to keep your partnership from being considered a general partnership.

You'll have to do all the things you need to do to form a general partnership, plus some extra paperwork. Limited partnerships typically must file a certificate of limited partnership with the applicable state office (usually the Secretary of State). The certificate will include things like the type of business, a basic description of the company's financial structure, and the names of all partners designated as either general or limited.

The name of your limited partnership will probably have to include the words "limited partnership." The name typically can't include the names of the limited partners. But the naming rules vary by state, so check with your state before you register the official name.

Most states have adapted their limited partnerships laws to conform to the Revised Uniform Limited Partnership Act (RULPA), but subtle differences still may exist. To make sure you'll get to keep your company's limited partnership status, you'll have to strictly follow the home-state statutes. If you don't, the partnership could be reclassified as a general partnership and all partners will be treated as general partners.

Special Procedures for LLPs

Limited liability partnerships (LLPs) are created under state law by filing an application with the appropriate state office and paying all of the required fees. In some states, such as Texas, the fees are assessed on a per-partner basis—which essentially means that the more partners you have, the more money you'll have to pay in fees.

The registration form (sometimes called a Certificate of Qualification or a Statement of Qualification) will typically include things like the name and purpose of the partnership, the registered agent and registered office, and the names and addresses of each general partner. Additional information requirements depend on state regulations. Most states allow you to complete and submit these registrations online via their secure Web sites, and you can easily surf your way to the requirements page. (Appendix 2 of this book contains a list of contact information for state business development offices, which are good sources for information on regulations and links to appropriate state sites.)

Many states will require that your LLP purchase sufficient liability insurance or keep a reserve of sufficient liquid assets to cover potential liability claims before your company can qualify for LLP status. For example, in Texas an LLP must maintain a minimum $100,000 "errors and omissions" insurance policy at all times to ensure that any obligations will be satisfied. Failing to maintain the coverage can result in loss of LLP status, downgrading your company to a regular general partnership.

Naming Requirements

The company name must clearly identify it as an LLP. Allowable terms differ a bit from state to state, but most permit a choice of the words "Limited Liability Partnership," "Registered Limited Liability Partnership," LLP, or RLLP. So, for example, if your company was to be called Smith and Jones Designs, you would have to add on one of the acceptable qualifiers, making the official name Smith and Jones Designs, LLP.

These state naming requirements serve a very important function: to inform the general public that your company limits the liability of its owners, at least to some extent. That's important for the protection of the general public. If an unfortunate incident occurs, the injured party has a right to know who can and can't be named in a lawsuit. Make sure you follow your home state's naming guidelines to a tee. If you don't, and if your LLP doesn't use its precise name in all business dealings, your partnership could lose its

Registered Agents

Most states require LLPs to authorize a registered agent who will keep a registered office within the state. All the registered agent really does is accept official documents and deliveries for the LLP, essentially ensuring that there is an actual person maintaining a legal presence within the state.

The registered agent and the registered office both appear in public records, so anyone can find out who and where they are. The address of the registered office has to be a physical location—it can't be a post office box.

Smaller LLPs usually appoint one of the partners to act as the registered agent, with the main place of business as the registered address. If your company will be registered in more than one state, you can hire registered agents to cover anywhere you maintain a business presence.

protective status, and leave you in the same position—complete personal liability—as plain old general partners.

Doing Business in More than One State

If your company will be doing business only in its home state, you only have one set of regulations to contend with. However, to carry on business outside the home state, your business will have to register as a "foreign" LLP in every other state you intend to trade in—and, of course, pay all of the appropriate filing fees and follow all the naming and insurance guidelines for each state. If you don't register your LLP in each state where you'll be conducting business, your company will end up being treated as a general partnership in those states.

On top of that, not every state recognizes LLPs from other jurisdictions. So if your company is operating in such a state, your LLP will be treated as a general partnership there.

Before you decide to expand your operations across state lines, find out what you're in for. If you need to take out a little extra insurance, or use a slightly modified DBA name in the non–home state, do it. If you'll be transacting business in a state that won't even recognize your LLP, it's better to know that before you have any problems.

Choosing an Accounting Method

There are two basic accounting methods that may be used for business and tax purposes: cash and accrual. The main difference between the two methods is timing. The cash method recognizes transactions only when money changes hands; the accrual method recognizes transactions when they occur, regardless of whether cash is involved. Although in the long run everything will come out equal, the difference from one year to the next can be significant. Because cash movement is the easiest factor to control, the cash method is usually preferred by business owners.

In most cases, all forms of partnerships can use cash basis accounting. But there are two exceptions. The first involves partnerships with corporate partners. If one partner is a C corporation and the partnership had annual gross receipts exceeding $5 million for the preceding three tax years, the cash method can't be used by the partnership. The other exception is for limited partnerships that qualify as "tax shelters," and that means limited partnerships that have tax losses and pass more than 35 percent of those losses through to limited partners.

The Basics of Basis and Capital Accounts

Basis and *capital* refer to partners' equity. Basis is essentially a partner's equity for tax purposes, and capital tracks equity for book purposes. For both, equity is a combination of what the partner puts into the business, what he takes out, and his share of the company's profits and losses. Basis is a pretty complicated subject, with its intricacies best left to accounting professionals. You should understand how it works in general, but you can leave the mind-boggling details to your CPA.

Tracking Equity Matters at Tax Time

Even though moving money in and out of the business won't trigger any taxable events, the cash trail still makes a difference at tax time. The IRS doesn't care when you take money out or throw more money into the partnership—but they do care how much equity you have at the end of the tax year. To make sure the year-end balance is correct, make sure to adjust each partner's capital account every time money (or other assets) is contributed or withdrawn.

If it has no direct impact on taxes, why do the partners' equity accounts matter to the IRS? Because when the partnership suffers losses, those losses get passed through to the personal tax returns of the individual partners (as you'll learn in Chapter 11). But the losses allocated to any partner are only deductible up to the amount of his current basis in the partnership. If his share of losses is $1,000 but his year-end basis is only $800, he can only deduct $800 of losses against his other income for that tax year.

Your original basis in the partnership, commonly called the *outside basis*, is equal to the amount you invested in the business. If you just put up money, the dollar amount you contributed is your basis. If you transferred some property to the partnership, you would use the "adjusted basis" of the property for your basis in the partnership. (Adjusted basis is an accounting equation that figures out the current book value of an asset, a calculation best left to the accountants.) Property transfers can cause an inequality in basis and capital when the value of the asset on the books (based on its original cost) doesn't equal its current fair market value; basis looks at book value, while capital (measuring your ownership percentage) is typically linked to market value.

Basis can also be affected by debt. If you take on partnership debt, your basis may be increased; but if the partnership assumes some of your debt (like if your capital contribution is a piece of land with a mortgage attached to it), your basis could be decreased.

Other factors that can affect your basis include partnership income (or losses), distributions you get from the company, new loans taken out or old loans paid off, and some other obscure tax-related items (like depletion of an oil well).

Special Allocations Among Partners

If you want to allocate profits and losses differently, you need to spell that out in your partnership agreement.

Unless you agree to something else in writing, all profits and losses will be allocated to the partners proportionally, based on their shares of ownership. If you want to allocate profits and losses differently, you need to spell that out in your partnership agreement. These special allocations are usually made when the amount of work a partner does for the company is out of proportion to his ownership percentage.

Generally, the IRS has no interest in how partners allocate their profits. But if the IRS decides that the special allocation has no "substantial economic effect" (as you'll read about below), they can force the partners to reallocate the profits proportionally.

Special Allocations Can Even Things Out

A lot of partnerships use special allocations when actual contributions of the partners are not reflected in their ownership percentages. In the real-life, everyday workflow, you and your partner(s) probably won't put in the same amount of time, energy, and dedication exactly matching your shares of the business. So special allocations can even out the differences between ownership on paper and the true contributions you make to your partnership in sweat every day.

Here's an example of how special allocations really work. Let's say you and your partner, Jim, own and run a coffee shop. You put up $10,000 cash and devote eighty hours a week to the business. Jim, on the other hand, contributed $30,000 cash to the business but only puts in about twenty hours of work each week. If you and Jim split the profits strictly in proportion to your original contributions, you would only get 25 percent and Jim would get 75 percent. If the two of you divvied up the profits based on actual work done, you'd be taking home 80 percent of the profits. What's really fair here? Probably something in the middle. But unless you explicitly put a special profit allocation into your partnership agreement, you'll only be allowed your proportional 25 percent.

Substantial Economic Effect

The IRS usually leaves partnerships and their allocations alone. But if they think a partnership allocation has been set up for the sole purpose of tax avoidance, they may disallow the allocation, reverting division of profits and losses to the default method—in proportion to each partner's share of ownership.

For the IRS to leave your allocation alone, you may have to show them a substantial economic effect. What does this mean in regular language? The actual size of the economic benefit to the partnership has to jibe with the actual value of the tax effect, created by the special allocation, for the individual partner. For example, it wouldn't make sense for a partner who contributed only 15 percent of the partnership's capital to deduct 90 percent of the partnership losses. However, if that same partner performed 75 percent of all the work for the partnership, a substantial economic effect could be shown.

Transactions Between the Partnership and a Partner

Sometimes one or more partners will have on-the-side businesses. These partners may provide goods or services to the partnership that fall outside his scope as a partner. For example, if you and a friend start a plumbing business, and you also own a plumbing supply store, your store could supply your service business with parts. Your role as supplier would be completely separate from your role as a partner in the plumbing business, at least for accounting and tax purposes.

When you do outside business transactions with your partnership, all of the transactions are treated as though they took place between the partnership and an unrelated third party. These extracurricular transactions could also include such things as loans, property sales, and providing services in a nonpartner capacity.

There is, however, one unique issue for partner-partnership transactions, different than the treatment of transactions with outside parties. The time when the partnership can take the business expense deduction depends on the accounting methods (for tax purposes) of both the partner and the business. If both use the cash method of accounting, the transaction will be recorded by both parties when the money changes hands. If both use the accrual method of accounting, the transaction gets recorded when the expense is incurred and revenue earned—regardless of when money changes hands. But when the partnership uses the accrual method and the partner uses the cash method (a very common scenario), the partnership has to wait until the expense is paid before it can be deducted.

A Real World Example

Donna is a general partner in a bookstore. When she's not working at the store, Donna creates one-of-a-kind sculptures of famous literary characters. The partners decide that they want to display some of Donna's sculptures to draw more attention to their classic literature section.

Donna sells three of her sculptures to the partnership at fair market value. The money she receives is taxable to her as ordinary income on her annual personal tax return. The partnership deducts the payment for the artwork as an ordinary business expense.

Guaranteed Payments to Partners

No matter how much work you do, as a partner you can never be considered an employee of the business. You can pay yourself a special kind of salary, called a guaranteed payment. This payment is above and beyond regular profit distributions. In fact, guaranteed payments are paid regardless of partnership income. And that's the whole point of the *guaranteed* payment—you get it no matter what.

When the partnership income is calculated income for both accounting and tax purposes, guaranteed payments are treated as though they were made to outsiders. They are usually deductible to the partnership and always income to you (in contrast to profit distributions, which do not count as additional income). However, because you are not an employee, no regular payroll taxes will be withheld from your payments.

Any guaranteed payments that will be made to partners must be spelled out explicitly in your partnership agreement. And the payments don't have to be just for day-to-day work done for the business, either. The partnership agreement can specify that set payments will be made for things like work done while organizing the partnership, loans that one partner made to the partnership over and above the capital contribution he was required to make, and even for medical insurance coverage for the partners and their families.

When you get guaranteed payments from the partnership, you have to report them on your personal tax return as income subject to self-employment tax. You also report separately any income or loss passed through to you by the partnership. In years that the partnership has suffered losses, you still have to report the full guaranteed payment; you can't deduct your portion of partnership losses from it.

> **Chapter 11**

Taxes and Partnerships

Part One

Part Two

Part Three

Part Four

Part Five

Part Six

Partnerships Are Pass-Through Entities

When you form your business as a partnership, your company won't pay any income taxes. Instead, every item relating to income and losses shows up on the personal tax returns of each of the partners as if he himself had earned the income (or sustained the loss). This phenomenon is called *pass-through taxation*, where all the tax effects pass through the partnership directly to its owners.

Even though the partnership doesn't pay any income taxes itself, all of the decisions about how income will be computed is made at the partnership level—and not by the individual partners. These accounting and tax decisions typically include things like depreciation methods, how inventory will be valued, and how specific items (like start-up expenses) will be accounted for.

Regardless of their personal tax situations, all of the partners have to deal with partnership items in exactly the same way they were treated on the partnership's tax return when they prepare their individual returns. For example, if the partnership declines to use accelerated depreciation for its new assets this year because it already has losses, you can't decide to take a bigger depreciation deduction on your tax return because you have a lot of other income.

For income tax purposes, the partnership is invisible to the IRS. It only really files a tax return for informational purposes. You and your partners are the ones who have to deal with the tax benefits or burdens generated by your company. And the tax benefits may be very helpful in the early years, when companies are more likely to suffer losses: pass-through taxation lets you use those losses to offset some or all of your other taxable income, which can considerably reduce your personal tax bill.

Tax Issues for Partners

On top of paying taxes on partnership income at the personal level, partners also have a lot of other tax issues to deal with. These issues include: which partner will actually deal with the IRS; making individual estimated tax payments; and how exactly to deduct partnership losses on their personal tax returns. Some of these issues are pretty simple, others downright complicated. By the end of this chapter, you'll likely know more about partnership taxation than you ever wanted to.

The first, and easiest, thing you'll need to do in regard to taxes is to designate an official "tax matters partner" (TMP). Even though your partnership counts as a separate entity for tax and audit purposes, it can't actually speak for itself where the IRS is concerned. So you and your partners will get together and select a TMP to represent the partnership in all tax matters. The one limitation is that only a general partner can be designated as the TMP.

It sounds a little scary, almost like picking a partner to go into the lion's den. But it's really rather harmless, more like a designated hitter. You need one partner to sign off on tax returns, answer IRS questions, apply for the EIN, and other paperwork-related tasks. If you're the TMP and some serious IRS issues come up, call your CPA—that's why he's there.

Paying Your Estimated Taxes

Since partners don't count as employees—no matter how much work they do—they don't have any taxes taken out of payments they get from the partnership. Instead, each individual partner has to make income tax payments into the system for himself on a quarterly basis. You and all of your partners will have to set aside some money to pay your income taxes in installments throughout the year. These tax installments are calculated based on the amount of profit you expect the partnership to have for the year.

Basically, you and each of your partners have to figure out your own total household income for the year, including your share of the expected profits or losses of the partnership. The income taxes due by each partner are based on all of his annual income. (The IRS Web site has worksheets available online to help you come up with your expected income tax due.) Added to that income tax will be the applicable self-employment taxes due on his share of partnership profits.

The IRS counts partners as among the ranks of the self-employed. When you are your own boss, you have to pay twice the Social Security and Medicare tax of people who just work as employees for someone else—you end up paying both the employee tax (like would normally come out of your paycheck) plus the employer expense portion (or the matching contribution). So you and all the partners who work for or help manage the business will have to pay these self-employment taxes on your portions of the partnership profits. If you don't participate in the business at all, even if you're a

> Each individual partner has to make income tax payments into the system for himself on a quarterly basis.

general partner, you may be able to get out of paying self-employment taxes; check with your accountant to be sure.

Computing your estimated self-employment taxes is just a matter of a little math. Your first $87,900 of profits gets multiplied by 15.3 percent (for 2004), and any profits over that hurdle are multiplied by 2.9 percent. If you have other businesses or work as an employee for someone else, include those salaries and profits in that initial $87,900 number—it's per person per year, not per job.

When you've calculated your total expected income and self-employment tax bill, you can break it down into quarterly chunks. Simply divide your annual estimated tax total by four. Each quarter, you'll send an equal installment to the government along with the IRS payment coupon, Form 1040-ES (also called Individual Estimated Tax Vouchers). Don't send a payment without a voucher or your account may not be credited properly. You'll make the checks out to "United States Treasury." Make sure to write "Form 1040-ES" and your social security number on your checks.

Business Expenses and Deductions

Partners pay partnership expenses out of their own pockets all the time. Accountants may advise them to pay for all partnership items with the company checkbook. The IRS may make deducting partner-paid expenses harder to put on a tax return. But it happens, all the time, in every business—especially small companies.

Most of the time, the IRS won't let you deduct partnership expenses that you paid for with your own money. These payments usually are considered to be partnership expenses, incurred by and deductible to the business itself. But just like almost all IRS regulations, there's an exception to the general rule. If your partnership agreement explicitly requires you to directly pay certain expenses with your own money, you will be allowed to take a business expense deduction on your personal tax return. For example, your agreement may require you to pay a temp to cover your partnership duties when you go on vacation. Those payments would be deductible on your personal tax return and wouldn't be counted as deductions for the partnership.

You can deduct all of your allowed out-of-pocket expenses on Schedule E, Part II of your individual income tax return. Those deductible expenses will reduce your share of partnership income for both regular and self-employment tax purposes.

The company can reimburse you for any business expenses that you pay with your own money. When you have the right to be reimbursed for your out-of-pocket expenditures, you can't deduct any amounts you paid for partnership expenses, even if you didn't get reimbursed.

Fringe Benefits

One small disadvantage of partnerships (at least when compared to C corporations) is the way certain fringe benefits are treated for the individual partners. Some benefits paid by the partnership are considered to be guaranteed payments to the partners, and that makes them includable in the partners' taxable income. Although that sounds like a major drawback, think of it this way: The tax you have to pay on the "income" is guaranteed to be less than the income itself. It's better for your personal cash flow to pay tax on $1,000 than to actually pay out a full $1,000.

The items listed below will be considered guaranteed payments to the partners when paid for by the partnership:

- Health insurance premiums
- The first $50,000 of group term life insurance coverage
- Dependent care assistance
- Disability insurance coverage
- Cafeteria benefit plans
- Meals or lodging provided for the convenience of the partnership

Fortunately, like all other self-employed individuals, partners can deduct 100 percent of their health insurance premiums directly on their annual Form 1040, canceling out their inclusion as income. This makes health insurance, at least, effectively a tax-free fringe benefit.

Like all other self-employed individuals, partners can deduct 100 percent of their health insurance premiums.

Limits on Deductible Tax Losses

If your partnership suffers a loss for the year, there's a silver lining to that cloud. You and each of your partners will gain a deductible loss for tax purposes. Nothing tax-related is ever simple, though, and restrictions apply here as well. If your adjusted basis isn't large enough, at least a portion of your loss deduction will be disallowed for the current tax year. That lost deduction can be carried forward to later tax years and used when your basis rises above zero. The other main restriction (talked about more below) applies to what the IRS calls "passive activities."

If you get any kind of distribution (whether it's cash or property) in the same year that your company sustains a loss, your distribution will be taken into account before your allowable loss deduction is calculated.

For example, let's say that you're a 50 percent general partner of Country Cooking Castle. At the beginning of the year, your basis in the partnership was $1,200. During the year, you got total cash distributions of $1,000. At the end of the year, the accountant calculated a $800 loss for the business. Being a 50 percent partner, your share of that loss comes to $400. Your tax-deductible loss for the year would come to only $200 (your starting basis of $1,200 minus the $1,000 distributions). The leftover loss of $200 will carry forward until you have enough basis available to deduct it.

Passive Activities and Tax Losses

The tax code defines a passive activity as one where the taxpayer in question did not materially participate. Material participation (defined in detail in the following section) refers to how much work you did for the business. So limited partners, who aren't allowed to participate in the business, are always considered passive for income tax purposes. And some general partners who can't clear the material participation hurdles could also be classified as passive. Why is being considered "passive" such a negative thing for tax purposes? Because passive activity losses are only deductible under specific circumstances.

When you're involved in a passive activity that suffers losses, you usually can't use those losses to offset your nonpassive income (like salary, interest, and self-employment, for example). Passive losses can, however, be deducted against income from other passive activities. The only time your passive activity losses can be used to reduce your nonpassive income is when you get rid of your entire interest in the activity.

If you do get stuck with passive activity losses, you have to fill out an extra form when you pay your taxes—IRS Form 8582 (Passive Activity Loss

Limitations). This form acts like a worksheet for all of your passive activities. You use it to add up all of your passive income and subtract out all of your passive losses. If the net result is positive, that income is fully taxable in the current year. If the net result is negative, it can't be deducted in the current tax year; your net passive losses will keep carrying forward until you either earn some passive income or you dispose of the activity.

How and Why the IRS Classifies Partners

You already know that there are two main classifications of partners: general and limited. The IRS splits general partners further, counting them as either active or passive. As you learned above, this crucial distinction controls how you're allowed to report your share of income and losses on your personal tax return.

It's pretty easy to figure out on which side of the line you fall. If you work for the business rarely or not at all, you're a passive partner. If you're a limited partner, your participation is passive by definition. Most other partners fall into the active category. Under IRS guidelines, you'll be considered an active partner if you materially participate in the everyday partnership activities on a fairly regular and continuous basis. Some partners land in the gray zone: not totally passive but not devoting heart, soul, and 24/7 to the business. If those partners don't materially participate (by IRS definition), they will default to passive status.

Each classification has a good side and a bad side, both tax-related. Active partners have to pay self-employment taxes on their shares of partnership income, but they can also deduct their full share of partnership losses to offset other income no matter what. Passive partners are bound by pretty strict loss-limitation rules, such as only using their passive activity losses to offset passive income. But passive partners don't have to pay those high self-employment taxes on any of their partnership income.

What Constitutes Material Participation?

Most people think that working for their business in any capacity gains them the right to deduct their full share of business losses. The IRS feels differently, and they usually prevail. To that end, the IRS puts out explicit (and

> If you work for the business rarely or not at all, you're a passive partner.

strict) guidelines that define what counts as material participation. (But, of course, some of these rules may be subject to interpretation—check with your business advisor if you're not sure whether you materially participate in your partnership.)

Any general partner can meet the material participation requirements by:

1. Participating in the business for more than 500 hours during the year (that translates to about ten hours per week).
2. Working for the company for at least 100 hours during the year, as long as no one else (and that really means *no one*) worked more than 100 hours during the year.
3. Being the only person who participates in the activity (that "only" includes everyone, not just owners).
4. Meeting any of the first three hurdles in a personal service activity for three years (and after that you'd be considered a material participant for life).
5. Participating in the business regularly, continuously, and on a substantial basis during the year (here's the rule with the wiggle room).

To make sure that everyone who wants to be an active partner actually meets the material participation requirements, your partnership agreement can actually specify minimum participation hours. You can assign particular functions and duties to each partner, like "Joe will write up all customer estimates; John will handle all supplier invoices." For married partners, the participation of both spouses counts toward meeting the above tests.

> Your partnership agreement can actually specify minimum participation hours.

A Look at Partnership Tax Forms

Even though partnerships are pass-through entities and never have to pay federal income taxes on their profits, they still have to file tax returns. Your partnership will have to file its own informational tax return on IRS Form 1065 (U.S. Partnership Return of Income). Along with that, the company has to prepare a Schedule K-1 for each partner. If your partnership has more than ten partners (and therefore more than ten Schedules K-1), it has to also file a Schedule K along with the rest of its return.

A Schedule K-1 lists one partner's share of all partnership items. Everything shown on that form will be transferred to his personal tax return. Remember, the partnership itself is invisible for federal tax purposes, so the treatment of each taxable item is determined as if the partner himself earned the income. For example, dividends received by the partnership is treated as dividend income on the partner's tax return. His share of ordinary partnership income will be reported in a special place in his overall Form 1040 package—on page 2 of Schedule E. Whether that ordinary partnership income is treated as active or passive determines exactly where on Schedule E it will be listed.

Partnership tax returns, and the Schedules K-1 that go to each partner, are pretty complicated. Since filling them out affects you and your partners personally, this is definitely a job for the professionals. As for your personal return, the K-1 you get will come with specific instructions that tell you where to put on your tax forms each item of partnership income. If the business is complicated, requiring you to transfer a lot of numbers onto a lot of different forms, you may want the accountant to prepare your personal return, too. (A lot of tax preparers have special software that electronically transfers information directly from the partnership's file to the partners' files.)

When it comes to state income taxes for partnerships and partners, most states follow the federal treatment. Generally, the partnership will file an informational return and pay no income tax—although filing and/or report fees may be assessed. And the partners merely report their shares of partnership income items on the personal state tax returns.

Separate Tax Treatment for Certain Items

You probably have a completely different personal tax situation than any of your partners—and this disparity is the norm in small U.S. partnerships. The differences among partners' tax positions can make a difference in how they are affected by partnership income. Various partnership items will have a different tax effect on each partner, depending on his other sources of income.

For that reason, certain partnership transactions are reported separately in Form K-1 as opposed to being lumped together with all of the general partnership income and deductions. And this separation follows all the way through. On each partner's personal income tax return, he'll report his share of these items separately.

Some of the items that merit this special separate treatment are:

- Gains (losses) from the sale or exchange of capital assets
- Meal, entertainment, and travel expenses for a partner that were paid for by the partnership
- Charitable contributions

All of these tax items could change an individual partner's personal income tax liability if they were considered separately (as opposed to combined with other income items). Therefore, they must be reported separately on each partner's Schedule K-1. For example, if you itemize your deductions on Schedule A of your tax return, your portion of the partnership's charitable contributions will be an additional deduction. But for partners who just take the standard deduction, the charitable contributions have no effect on their personal tax returns.

Tax Advantages to Partnerships

One reason partnerships have been such popular business forms are the significant tax benefits available to the partners. You've already learned about pass-through taxation, and how that can benefit your tax bill during years the partnership has losses. But you may not know that there a couple of other ways you can reap some serious tax benefits from your business—such as when you contribute appreciated property to increase your basis, or buy into an already successful partnership. Plus, partnerships are the least audited business entities (very comforting to those whose skin crawls when they just read the word "audit").

Tax-Free Transfers of Appreciated Property

Under a special passage in the tax code, which is casually referred to as the *nonrecognition rule*, any partner can contribute appreciated property to the partnership at any time without recognizing a taxable gain. That's a mouthful—and a very important concept. In translation, that means you get more equity than you really paid for—with no current tax consequence. And the flip side of this is also true (under a different code section). Your partnership can give you appreciated assets without anyone recognizing, or paying taxes on, any capital gains.

There are absolutely no restrictions on the type of property that you can put into the partnership. In fact, the only requirement is that you can easily determine the property's fair market when you make the transfer to the partnership. This very beneficial treatment is based on the theory that, technically speaking, you still really own the property, just through your partnership interest instead of personally (or vice versa, if the transfer went the other way).

This freedom from current tax consequences gives you, your partners, and your business the flexibility to transfer appreciated property whenever it's advantageous. The only time taxes will come into place is if the property is eventually disposed of; gain (or loss) will be recognized at that time, with the appropriate effect on income taxes.

Now you're waiting for the exceptions to the rule. You're right, there are exceptions (this is a part of the tax code, after all). Under some circumstances, there may be a tax consequence when appreciated property changes

What's So Great about These Tax-Free Transfers?

Suppose you want to increase your equity in the partnership, and you know the business could use some new office furniture. You happen to have two beautiful antique mahogany desks that you bought at an auction for $100 each a few years ago. You've painstakingly refinished and repaired them, and now they're worth over $1,000 each. You could sell them for a nice chunk of change, but then you'd have to pay capital gains tax on your profits—and the company would still need new office furniture.

The tax code provides you with a great solution here. Instead of selling them, you simply contribute the desks directly to the partnership. Since they're actually worth $1,000 each, your capital investment increases by a full $2,000. Now you and your partner have some really nice office furniture, you have increased your stake in the partnership, no one pays taxes on your theoretical $1,800 gain (the $2,000 equity you got for the $200 you put out), and everyone is happy.

hands. The first exception applies when one partner contributes appreciated property, and that property is immediately distributed to another partner—which is really an elaborate way of just transferring property from one partner to another. Exception number two deals with stocks, bonds, and the like, causing tax consequences when marketable securities are distributed to a partner. Finally, taxes may come into play when a partner contributes appreciated property to the partnership and then receives a distribution of different property (sort of like the partner is trading property with the partnership, and you can bet that the partner usually gets the better end of the deal).

Buying into an Existing Partnership

If you buy an interest in an existing partnership, the tax basis of your share of appreciated partnership assets can be increased to reflect the price you actually paid for your share—if the partnership makes a special election (under IRS section 754). Plus, your share of the deductions that go along with the asset (like depreciation) will be calculated using your higher basis. What does that mean and why is it good for you? An example can help you understand one of the greatest tax advantages of partnerships.

Suppose John, Joe, and Jim each own a one-third interest in Triple J, a general partnership. The company's only asset is a piece of machinery that is being depreciated over seven years. The original cost of the machinery is $150,000 and so far they've depreciated it by $30,000. That makes its current book value $120,000. The machine has a fair market value of $180,000.

You buy Joe's interest in the partnership for $60,000, and the partnership makes the special election. Now your basis in the machine is $60,000, but it would have been only $40,000 (one-third of its book value) without the election. The basis of the other partners doesn't change, leaving theirs at $40,000 each. If Triple J sells the machine for its current fair market value of $180,000, you would have no taxable gain (your third is worth $60,000, so the sale nets to zero for you). But the other partners would have to pay taxes on gains of $20,000 each (a $60,000 share of the sale price minus the $40,000 share of book value). Neat trick.

Minimal IRS Audit Risk—Always a Plus

The job of the IRS is to collect taxes due. To maximize their efficiency, they usually audit those most likely to have underpaid their taxes. But partnerships can't underpay their taxes—they don't owe any. So partnerships rank pretty low on the list as good audit candidates. In fact, partnerships are the least audited business entity. Only 5,070 partnership returns were looked at by agents in 2001 out of the more than two million filed during tax year 2000.

The audit of partners, however, is an entirely different matter. In the past, the IRS has typically left taxpayers with K-1 income alone, mostly because the information shows up all over the place on the partner's tax return—and not necessarily in the same manner it appears. For example, if you have personal interest income and partnership interest income that only total $100 together, you wouldn't have to report the two sources separately on your tax return.

The IRS relies on "matching" technology to catch taxpayer mistakes by using their computer system to compare information from different forms. Their program matches third-party information (like W-2s) with the amounts reported on Form 1040. While developing a similar program to track Schedules K-1, they hit a snag in that, so far, that schedule isn't standardized.

So, for the time being, partnerships and partners usually remain unaudited. But even if your partnership is one of the 0.25 percent that does get selected, don't panic. An audit doesn't always mean a bigger tax bill—it just means you have to answer some questions, maybe show some receipts. When you run your business according to the law, audit's not a four-letter word.

> Partnerships rank pretty low on the list as good audit candidates.

Tax Drawbacks for Partnerships

Most of the tax drawbacks for the partnership entity come up for limited or inactive partners and passive activity losses. But there is one pretty big potential disadvantage that could hit any partner at any time. This nasty phenomenon is called "phantom income," and it really is a monster when it comes out.

The underlying rule here is that all income that gets reported on the partnership's Form 1065 is taxable to the partners in whatever proportions they've agreed on, whether the income is distributed. So you and your partners will be taxed on your distributive shares of partnership income even if you don't see even one thin dime. And that's your phantom income: profits that you pay tax on, but don't receive.

How can this happen? The simplest version involves a decision made by the partners to forgo distributions, instead using the profits as funding for growth. Another possibility: profits on paper, but no cash on hand. This is a very common occurrence with new small businesses with poor cash flow management, and also those that use accrual basis accounting. Regardless of the reason, taxes must still be paid on the profits earned.

Special Considerations for Limited Partnerships and LLPs

Limited partnerships need to pay close attention to the IRS rules that define the differences between corporations and partnerships—or risk losing their favorable partnership tax treatment. If they cross the line, the federal government will treat them as corporations, and that means double taxation (as you'll learn in Chapter 16). So, on top of filing a certificate of limited partnership in your home state, your limited partnership has to have at least two of the following traits to keep its tax status:

1. Unlimited personal liability for at least one of the owners for all partnership debts.
2. Lack of centralized management.
3. A time limit on its existence.
4. Some restrictions on transfers of ownership.

LLPs are automatically treated as partnerships by the IRS, but they can elect to be treated as corporations under federal tax regulations (although tax classification is rarely used). The real difference in LLP taxation comes (possibly) at the state level. While most states treat LLPs just like regular partnerships, some states do require LLPs to pay income taxes on top of those paid by the partners. Some states, like California, charge LLPs annual franchise taxes or renewal fees, although general partnerships in those states pay no such tax.

> **Chapter 12**

Keeping Your Personal Assets Protected

Unlimited Liability for General Partners

Unlimited liability is by far the worst entity feature for general partners. Scary as it sounds, it's really even scarier than you think. Not only are you (yes, just you personally) liable for 100 percent of the partnership's regular debts and obligations, you are also responsible for business debts taken on by your partner(s) without your knowledge, and possibly even for the personal debts of your partner(s). If that doesn't scare you, it should.

Here's how it works, legally speaking: All general partners are *jointly and separately* liable for the all of the debts of the business. This means that all of the partners are personally liable as a group and that each one is also 100 percent individually liable for all partnership obligations. Any creditor of the partnership can sue a single partner for the entire amount due to him, and leave that partner stuck with the problem of collecting reimbursement from the other partners.

As a general partner, your potential liability is enormous. If the business can't manage its debt load, you have to pay up. If you don't have that kind of cash on hand, and your partners don't either, you could be forced into personal bankruptcy, losing everything—including the business you've worked so hard to build. Because of this overwhelming risk, you must demand full financial disclosure from your prospective partners. If you're going to be left holding the bag, you need to know, from the start, just how big that bag is.

If your potential partner is already in a not-so-great financial position, seriously reconsider forming your company as a general partnership. Because not only can your partner run up business debts for which you'll be personally liable, his personal debts can become partnership problems—even causing the dissolution of the company (see the section about charging orders below).

Liability for Your Partners' Acts

In addition to regular partnership debts (like supplier invoices), each partner is also personally financially responsible for any and all acts of any other partner. So if your partner commits a negligent act but doesn't have enough money to settle the claims against him, you (and any or all of your other partners) can be personally sued to settle the claims. You will be responsible for any partnership debt or obligation partnership caused by any other partner's errors and omissions, negligence, or malpractice.

On top of that, you or any other of your general partners can legally bind the partnership—and that can also expose the partners to increased personal liability. Under the law, all general partners can carry out any business on the partnership's behalf, including signing binding contracts. Even if you address this issue in your partnership agreement, specifically limiting this type of rights for a partner, you may not be protected. A clause in an agreement won't shield you or your other partners if one partner, acting with *apparent* authority, makes an agreement with an innocent third party for what looks like ordinary partnership business. The only possible defense for you and the other partners comes up if the third party reasonably should have known that the "signing" partner had no right to make the agreement or enter into the contract.

Some Real World Examples

You and Victoria are both active partners of your general partnership, a flower shop. Your partnership agreement explicitly bars any partner from acting alone to enter into transactions where the partnership will owe more than $5,000. Victoria decides she wants to buy a new delivery van. She goes out and buys a $35,000 new vehicle in the name of the partnership, and uses a partnership check to pay the $5,000 down payment. This contract will be legally binding on the partnership for two reasons. First, it will stand up because the transaction appeared to be in the ordinary course of business. Second, the car dealer would have had no way to know about the restriction in the partnership agreement.

Now suppose the same circumstances as the previous example, except that Victoria buys a $60,000 speedboat in the name of the partnership. She makes a down payment of $5,000 with a partnership check, and agrees to payments of nearly $1,000 per month for the next five years. This contract

Put an Indemnity Clause in Your Partnership Agreement

Cases where one partner ends up footing the bill for the acts of another are very common. And many times, that's where the story ends—along with the partnership, the business relationship, and the friendship. But it doesn't necessarily have to turn out all bad.

Because this scenario occurs frequently in the world of small companies, a lot of partnership agreements specifically address the issue. To protect the partner with more personal assets to lose, an indemnity clause can be added into your agreement. What does that mean? Simply that if one partner has to pay more than his fair share of partnership debt, the other partners agree to pay him back down the line. A few short paragraphs can go a long way toward protecting both your personal assets and your friendships.

probably will not be binding on the partnership. Even though the boat dealer has no way of knowing what's in the partnership agreement, a speedboat clearly isn't a purchase made in the normal course of business for a florist.

The next example has Victoria contacting one of the partnership's regular vendors, who usually works only with you as the partner in charge of ordering inventory. This vendor has been working with you for three years, and knows that you do all the ordering. Victoria calls the flower vendor and insists on ordering 200 African violets (because she read somewhere that they're the next big trend). Your vendor knows that you would never order even twenty of the same plant in a single order, but agrees to fill Victoria's demand anyway. In this case, your partnership (and therefore you) will probably not be bound by the deal. This vendor knows that he always deals with you and that you haven't told him about a change in this, plus the order is drastically different from the orders you normally place.

Now suppose Victoria is out making a delivery and causes an accident with the company's van. The company, and both you and Victoria personally are financially liable for any damages or injuries caused by the accident. If the partnership's insurance coverage isn't enough—or if there are deductibles to be paid—you could end up footing the bill. This scenario also holds true if Victoria had been using her own car to carry on partnership business.

Limited Liability for Limited Partners

Limited partners are limited in two ways: Their personal financial risk is limited to their investment in the company, and they play only a very limited role in the business—strictly as investors. As long as they stay inactive in the partnership, they can never lose more money than they put in.

The reverse is also true: The partnership can't be held liable for the debts of any limited partner, unlike the debts of general partners. When you have a well-drafted limited partnership agreement, none of the limited partners' creditors will be entitled to any assets of the business. Instead, those creditors will get only charging orders (more information on these later in this chapter) allowing them to receive that partner's distributions. And if your limited partnership agreement has been drafted by a savvy attorney, the creditors may never actually get any distributions, but would still have to pay taxes on the phantom income.

> The partnership can't be held liable for the debts of any limited partner, unlike the debts of general partners.

A word of caution: Any limited partner who starts to participate in the partnership's business could be reclassified as a general partner. If that happens, he'll be subject to the same liability risk as any general partner. So all of the limited partnership interests should given only to individuals who want to be true silent partners, making purely financial investments in the business without any participation in the management of the business.

LLPs Can Provide Some Liability Protection

In an LLP, limited liability applies to the partners but not to the LLP itself. Due to the wide variations in state laws, this liability protection can be pretty thorough or almost negligible. In most states, though, the limited liability protection keeps partners' personal assets safe from malpractice (and possibly other tortious acts) claims made against other partners.

Even this nod to shielding partners from the acts of other partners can help you—especially if your business is a professional practice. Where in a regular general partnership you could be held responsible if your co-owner committed malpractice, in an LLP you'd almost always remain obligation-free if it came down to a lawsuit. Beware, though, because in some states even that protection comes with strings attached. If you were technically supervising the partner in question, or were aware that he was doing something wrong, you could be held liable for the claims made against him.

Some Examples of LLP Liability

You are a partner in an LLP, formed by a group of doctors. When the business started up, your capital contribution was $20,000; your current personal net worth is $125,000. Ed LaPlata, one of your partners, has also put in $20,000 of capital, but his personal net worth only comes to $40,000. During the year, Ed is sued for malpractice and loses. The jury awards the plaintiff $400,000. Ed's malpractice insurance policy pays out $250,000, and his personal assets cover an additional $40,000. The LLP can be sued for the $110,000 balance of the judgment. But under the LLP statutes of almost every state, you can't be personally sued to satisfy the claim against Ed. So the biggest loss you could possibly sustain in this case is limited to your $20,000 investment in the business.

Suppose the same case exists as in the example above, but that you were Ed's supervisor—although not personally involved in this particular case. The mere fact that you did serve as Ed's supervisor can allow you to be named in the lawsuit. If you were found responsible, you could be held liable for the $110,000 balance due to the plaintiff. But you would have a good case to recover at least some of the money you had to put up from Ed, or other involved partners—especially if your partnership agreement includes an indemnity clause.

Other Protections Under LLP Statutes

LLP partners also may be protected against the general business obligations of the partnership, depending in which state the LLP was formed. Under some state statutes (like in Colorado, Delaware, Iowa, and Nevada) an LLP owner can get liability protection even for the regular contractual debts of the business that are greater than his investment in the partnership. That gives the partner liability protection nearing that of LLCs or corporations. But in all cases, every partner's investment in the business is always fully at risk, and so are all the assets owned by the business.

But even in the states that do offer true general limited liability to LLP partners, there are still circumstances for which they will always be held personally responsible. These circumstances include things like personally guaranteed loans when the company subsequently defaults (such as when the company can't get a loan on its own and one of the partners cosigns). Plus, even the strongest limited liability protection will never protect any LLP partner from responsibility for debts that come about because of his own professional malpractice or negligence.

States Offering Only Limited Protection for LLP Partners

Alaska	Louisiana	Ohio
Arkansas	Maine	Pennsylvania
District of Columbia	Michigan	South Carolina
Hawaii	Nevada	Tennessee
Illinois	New Hampshire	Texas
Kansas	New Jersey	Utah
Kentucky	North Carolina	West Virginia

Understanding Charging Orders

When partnership creditors aren't getting paid, they can sue both the partnership and the general partners to get their money back. But when an individual partner isn't paying his own personal debts, his creditors can get what's called a *charging order*. A charging order basically lets the creditor stand in the shoes of the partner in question—at least as far as distributions are concerned (although in some cases, it can be even more).

Under the law, the personal creditor of a partner gets assigned the partner's interest in the company. How far that interest reaches depends on the classification and actual role of the partner. Typically, the creditor will own an interest in the partnership, but not the underlying assets of the partnership (unlike a regular partner). Whether he can actually force the dissolution of the partnership to collect his money depends on the particular facts and circumstances of the case, and the setup of the company.

Charging Orders for General Partnerships

Under the Uniform Partnership Act (UPA), most of the time the law allows liquidation to satisfy the creditor of an individual partner. This means that when any partner's personal creditor gets a charging order from the court, he can actually foreclose on that partner's interest in the partnership—if the creditor can demonstrate that it would be unfair to let the partner carry on with the business while leaving the creditor a mere assignee of the business interest. That's a lot of legal talk, but what it really means is that if the creditor proves that getting income distributions from the ongoing business isn't really a fair way to settle the personal debt, he can get the courts to force the liquidation of the partnership. Unfortunately, this is usually pretty easy for the creditor to prove when a small business is involved.

> Most of the time the law allows liquidation to satisfy the creditor of an individual partner.

The court will compare the total debt to the size of the business. It will also look at how the other partners would be affected by a liquidation of the business. The judge then weighs those factors, and decides whether to force the creditor to accept distributions over time to satisfy the debt or to force the partnership to close up and sell off assets to pay the creditor in one big lump. With larger businesses and companies with a lot of partners, the courts typically don't liquidate, instead acting as a debtor-partner. But for small or closely held businesses, the typical court solution is complete liquidation of the partnership.

Regardless of the distribution-or-dissolution decision of the court, a creditor can't be made a full partner in the business. That's because partnership law in all states understands that the relationship among partners is a personal one. Therefore, a creditor can never become a partner unless the other partners unanimously vote him in as one (which rarely, if ever, happens). So even with a charging order in hand, the creditor can't take part in any part of the management of the business—or in partnership votes.

Charging Orders for Limited Partnerships

Limited partnership law goes much further to protect the company than the UPA does. The laws that govern limited partnerships (called the RULPA) specifically state that a partner's creditor with a charging order can't force a liquidation to satisfy the debt. Instead, the creditor is strictly limited, entitling him only to receive distributions made in the normal course of business. The only jurisdictions that currently don't adhere to this are Louisiana and the District of Columbia, and they may follow the liquidation plan that usually applies to general partnerships.

Since the creditor doesn't have the right to act as a partner, he can't even force the partnership to distribute any income or assets beyond what it would normally do—or at all. In fact, the remaining partners can simply stop

The Court as Debtor-Partner

The Uniform Partnership Act (UPA) gives the courts extremely broad powers to do anything necessary in order to make sure that the personal creditor of a partner gets paid. So the court is authorized to act in the role of debtor-partner, based on the actual facts and circumstances of the case. So in its role as debtor-partner, the court can participate in company votes, join in management decisions, even sell that partner's interest to a third party. In the worst-case scenario, the court can even force the partnership to liquidate to settle the partner's personal debt.

making distributions, and seriously hinder the intents of the creditor. It gets even worse for the creditor: He'll have to pay income taxes on his share of the partnership income even if he doesn't get any distributions. Because of the obvious downside here (like paying taxes on money you may never see), most creditors don't really want charging orders for limited partnerships.

Charging Orders for LLPs

LLPs protect partners in varying degrees from personal responsibility for partnership obligations. But nothing in the laws regulating LLPs protects the LLP from the personal debts of individual partners. So while registering your partnership as an LLP can protect your personal assets, it won't do much in the way of shielding the business from a forced liquidation in the event a charging order is granted to a partner's creditors.

Unlike a limited partnership, the LLP will be subject to the UPA regulations for these purposes, just as if it were a no-frills general partnership. So any owner's personal creditors can get a charging order and then seek to have the business liquidated to satisfy the debt. Whether the creditor will be successful depends on the circumstances of the case, the same as if it were a general partnership.

Using Insurance to Mitigate Risk

For every small business, insurance should be a component of the asset protection plan. This coverage is even more important in high-risk businesses and those where malpractice suits are commonly filed.

For general partners, business insurance coverage can mean the difference between personal security and bankruptcy. Any partnership debts not covered by either company assets or insurance become the personal liabilities of the partners. The more you can get the insurance company to pay, the less you'll have to cough up.

At a very minimum, your company should have basic liability and property insurance policies. Liability insurance covers you for property damage and injuries of other people. Property insurance covers your company's property in the event of loss or damage. But in addition to the basics, it's a good idea to get umbrella coverage to supplement all of your other policies.

Typically, umbrella policies step in to cover claims over and above your other insurance. And since they are strictly supplemental coverage, they can usually be purchased quite inexpensively.

With a professional practice formed as a partnership, you can require all of your partners to carry a set minimum amount of malpractice insurance as part of your partnership agreement. This may lead to grumbling, as malpractice insurance premiums can be quite costly. But—and this is a fact—the premiums will surely be less than a judgment. A judgment could literally wipe out a partnership, and possibly even the partners—even those not responsible for the malpractice.

If your business is inherently hazardous, purchase as much specific insurance coverage as possible. For example, if your company is a delivery service with several vehicles on the road, more than minimal auto insurance coverage is in order. Don't go for the least expensive, state-requirement-meeting policies; get coverage that can approximate your true potential liability. Again, it may cost a little more now (or a lot more), but it can save your business and your personal assets in the long run.

> **Chapter 13**

Getting Out of Partnerships

Part One

Part Two

Part Three

Part Four

Part Five

Part Six

PART THREE   PARTNERSHIPS

▩ CHAPTER 9 Understanding Partnerships ▩ CHAPTER 10 Start-up Procedures for Partnerships ▩ CHAPTER 11 Taxes and Partnerships ▩ CHAPTER 12 Keeping Your Personal Assets Protected ■ CHAPTER 13 Getting out of Partnerships

General Partners Can't Just Leave or Sell

An ownership interest in a partnership cannot be transferred freely. Restrictions on the transfer of partnership interests are usually included in partnership agreements. Absent such provisions, the Uniform Partnership Act (UPA) rules. Under the UPA, a unanimous vote by existing partners is required to admit any new partner to the firm.

Your partnership agreement should spell out the circumstances under which any partner can voluntarily get out of the partnership. In addition to the limitations on potential buyers, you should also include things like timetables (such as the minimum notice needed to withdraw) and name changes (meaning can you still use the same name for the company even once a founding partner has left). Typically, a partnership agreement will also have provisions under which the partnership would be required to purchase the ownership interest; otherwise, you could be stuck with a partnership interest that you couldn't get rid of (for example, if the other partners refused to admit anyone interested in buying you out).

In addition to those basic provisions, your agreement should also talk about what happens when the partnership itself buys out the departing partner. This should absolutely include a specific strategy for making payments, since the withdrawing partner will probably want cash right away but the partnership may want to pay over time to prevent operating difficulties. The reality is that most small businesses don't have enough liquid assets on hand to give withdrawing partners large lump sum payments. So your partnership agreement should definitely provide for an installment payment plan.

Changing Partners Creates a New Partnership

When a partner leaves your partnership for any reason, the original partnership simply ceases to exist. The remaining partners (as long as there are at least two) can elect to carry on the partnership, but that continuation technically will be a different partnership.

Voting in New Partners Protects You from Undesirable Co-Owners

The unanimous vote required by the UPA to admit a new partner is based on the theory that partnerships are personal relationships. The rule exists primarily to protect the remaining partners from being forced to work with someone they don't like or don't trust.

Without this safeguard, an exiting partner could sell his share of the business to absolutely anyone. And if the separation is a bitter one, he could purposely choose someone that you wouldn't want to work with. So although it sounds convoluted and restrictive (especially when you're the one trying to sell), the rule really exists to preserve the personal nature of the partnership.

Protect Your Partnership

Since the ongoing existence of your company could be threatened when one partner leaves (whether voluntarily or as the result of unfortunate circumstances), the partnership should take some practical measures to protect itself and the remaining partners.

For the first layer of protection, make sure to include buy-sell provisions in your partnership agreement. Setting up definite procedures to follow when a partner withdraws before it actually happens will serve to minimize potential disagreements over myriad issues. Likely bones of contention include valuation of the partnership interest and payment schedules (both very important when the partnership itself is the buyer).

The second layer of protection applies more to involuntary withdrawal. Those unfortunate circumstances include such things as the death or disability of a partner who was active in the business. For these occurrences, the partnership can purchase key man life insurance policies for any or all partners; at the very least, it should purchase policies covering the most active partners. Basically, having proper insurance in place can provide the partnership with cash upon the death of a vital member of the organization. You can then use the proceeds both to keep the business going in the departed partner's absence and to buy out his interests pursuant to the buy-sell provisions.

The Partnership Name Game

The legal name of a partnership is either a combination of the last names of all existing partners or another name spelled out in the partnership agreement. When the makeup of the partnership changes, its legal name may change as well—particularly when it's based on partners' names. This can cause a whole host of problems, from preprinted letterhead to customer recognition.

To keep your company from having to change names when partners come and go, you can include a provision in your partnership agreement that allows the partnership to keep its original name as its new official DBA name. For example, if your partnership starts out as Smith, Jones, and Carter and then Carter leaves the business, the new legal name of the partnership would be Smith and Jones. If the agreement allows, the remaining two partners could elect to use the DBA name of Smith, Jones, and Carter.

Make Sure All Business Contacts Are Aware of the Change

No matter how friendly the change in the makeup of your partnership is, you still must take steps to protect yourself against additional liabilities. To do that, the remaining partners should notify outside parties about the withdrawal of a partner. This step is crucial, because even though withdrawing from the company ends the partner's actual authority to legally bind the partnership, he may still have apparent authority with respect to third parties who don't know about the change. Therefore, the partnership could be held liable for actions taken by the ex-partner that involve innocent third parties. So, for example, if he entered into a contract to buy a vehicle in the name of the partnership after his withdrawal, the partnership could be forced to honor the terms of that contract.

Another True Story (But Not a Bad One)

Jason, Jordan, and Kristin formed a partnership to run their computer repair service. Each partner was well-versed in hardware and software—among the three of them, they could fix virtually any computer problem.

After almost four years of working together, Jason decided to leave the partnership and strike out on his own. He packed up all his belongings, sold his share of the partnership to Jordan and Kristin (in accordance with the terms set out in their partnership agreement), and moved out to Albuquerque. When he got to his new home/office, Jason called up a main supplier of the partnership and ordered some equipment. Since the vendor didn't know about Jason's withdrawal from the partnership, he billed it for the equipment.

When Jordan and Kristin received the invoice, they were understandably angry. They called the vendor and told him they weren't responsible so would not pay the bill. He told them they had to pay it or he would take them to court. Jordan checked with the partnership's attorney—and he agreed with the vendor. Since no one had notified the supplier of the change in ownership, he had no reason to know that supplies and equipment ordered by Jason would no longer be paid for by the partnership. Much to their dismay, Jordan and Kristin learned that they were indeed liable to pay for the equipment.

In a bit of a huff, the two remaining partners called Jason and blasted him for charging his equipment to them. Jason said that he had no idea what they were talking about. He had ordered some things, but he had expected to pay for them himself. When everyone calmed down, they realized it was a misunderstanding—the vendor hadn't bothered to ask Jason where to send the invoice, and Jason had forgotten to tell him of the big change in all his excitement to start over.

The happy ending: Jason paid for his own equipment, and set up his own account with the supplier. Jordan and Kristin made amends with the vendor (over a nice dinner). And everyone lived happily ever after.

Selling Limited Partnership Interests

Technically speaking, a limited partnership interest is considered to be a security. The key reason for this is that the limited partner is usually merely an investor in the company (in fact, acting in any other capacity can cause reclassification of that status). He invests money into a business, and expects some kind of financial return on his investment based on the efforts (and hopefully successes) of the general partner(s).

But whether your "security" will be subjected to federal or state securities law is the big question. From a federal standpoint, most small business owners—even limited partners—won't need to worry about securities laws when they sell off their shares of a business. These laws really apply to public offerings, and not to private sales. So if you offer your shares to fewer than ten people who all live in your state, and you discuss the offering only when you're face-to-face, you can forget about federal securities laws. That means no general offerings over the phone, through the mail, or on the Internet.

As you can imagine, the state laws vary somewhat—although most at least vaguely follow the recommendations of the federal statutes. If your limited partnership is considered a security under state law, make sure to conform to all requirements.

If you're concerned about correctly sticking to the rules like glue when you're ready to sell your limited partnership interest, consult with your attorney before you start making overtures to potential buyers. That way you're sure to be in compliance. (Plus, he may have clients who'd be interested in purchasing what you have to offer.)

Dissolving the Whole Partnership

Partnerships can remain in existence for as long as its original owners are alive and willing to run it. However, more than any other business form, partnerships often fall victim to disputes among the owners. But even without a bitter ending, partnerships will all end naturally—whether through a partner's retirement or eventual death. And there are many instances where the underlying business continues, but the entity housing it changes (as when a general partnership evolves into an LLC). Also, a partnership agreement may contain a dissolution provision, calling for the termination of the partnership on a fixed date, after a specified length of existence, or after the occurrence of a particular event.

A general partnership can terminate voluntarily by simply discontinuing all parts of its business and financial operations. Limited partnerships, on the other hand, may have to file certificates of dissolution in accordance with state law in order to officially terminate.

Dissolution Events

All of the following circumstances (with regard to any partner) are considered to legally dissolve a partnership:

- Retirement
- Disability
- Death
- Resignation
- Expulsion
- Bankruptcy

The listed dissolution events only apply to general partners. The withdrawal of a limited partner will not cause the dissolution of a limited partnership, regardless of his percentage of ownership.

When any of these events triggers a dissolution of either a general or limited partnership, the remaining partners can vote to continue, but the continuing partnership will be considered a new legal entity. Even though the legal existence of the original partnership is over, it continues to exist for federal tax purposes; these dissolution events do not cause the end of the tax year for the partnership.

Limit Your Unlimited Liability

Believe it or not, your full personal liability as a general partner may not go away just because you end your partnership. To make sure you are fully protected, you'll need to take some basic steps to let everyone know that the partnership no longer exists. Otherwise, you could end up being sued for things that happened after you thought the partnership was over and done with.

Although it may not technically be required by state law, find out whether your state will accept a statement of dissolution for the partnership (they may charge a fee for this, but it's usually nominal). This paperwork serves as formal notification to everyone that one or more partners are no longer responsible for any debts incurred by the others. In California, for example, outside parties are deemed to have full knowledge of the changes—and that means the end of even apparent authority to act for the partnership—ninety days after the forms are filed.

Sending out individual notices to customers and suppliers is another good way to notify third parties that the partnership makeup has changed. If you're the partner who's walking away, you should be the one to send out notices of dissolution to those your company does business with. You should also look through existing contracts to see if they explicitly continue your liability even after withdrawal.

And What about Taxes?

Here's the good news: There are usually no unusual tax consequences for general partners when their partnership

Big Changes Can Lead to a Technical Termination

As you now know, the withdrawal of a partner legally dissolves a partnership. You also know that the remaining partners (as long as there are at least two) can usually elect to continue the partnership without a lot of fuss. However, this is not always allowed. The exception occurs when any dissolution event causes a 50 percent or more change of ownership interest in either capital or profits within a twelve-month period. This event is called a *technical termination* under the Internal Revenue Code—and it causes the end of the partnership's tax year. That means all partners will have to report their share of profits up to the termination date.

Of course, as with most IRS regulations there is an exception to the 50 percent rule: A gift of a partnership interest or the bequest of the interest upon the death of a partner won't trigger a technical termination.

General Partners Go to the Back of the Line

The rules for liquidating limited partnerships are somewhat different than those for general partnerships (where all partners have essentially equal footing). In a limited partnership, the general partners must take a back seat to everyone else, receiving their final share of partnership assets last. Limited partners have the right to recover their interests before general partners receive anything—and that includes both loan paybacks (for any loans they personally made to the business) and their shares of capital and profits.

interest is dissolved. Most of the time, the exchange of a partnership interest is treated like a capital asset, and results in a capital gain or loss. That means gains gets taxed at favorable (read: lower) capital gains rates.

The exception comes into play when the partnership holds appreciated assets or "hot" assets. These are pretty tricky tax concepts—so you'll definitely want to have an accountant deal with this for you. Here you'll learn the basic concept behind this complicated IRS idea. The bottom line is that if your partnership has either of these types of assets, you may end up paying taxes on your final distribution.

When your partnership has what the IRS calls hot assets, at least some of your distribution will be treated as ordinary income, subject to regular income tax rates. The hot assets category includes unrealized receivables (the outstanding accounts receivable for which no payment has yet been received) and inventory (items held for resale). The portion of your partnership interest attributable to these assets counts as ordinary income to the selling partner. Basically, you're treated as if you sold off the individual assets rather than your partnership interest as a whole.

The hot asset rules are more convoluted than they seem. And any sale of a partnership interest that involves hot assets requires special forms to be filed with the IRS. For these reasons (and to save yourself a lot of headaches), consult with an accountant when you dispose of your partnership interest.

Winding Up the Business

When the partnership does actually dissolve, either because of provisions in the partnership agreement or because the partners elect to discontinue all business operations, various administrative tasks must be seen to.

Many states have public notification requirements to inform parties who transact business with the partnership of its impending dissolution. Limited partnerships may have to file certificates of dissolution in some states.

In addition to satisfying specific state requirements, your partnership has to wind up its regular business affairs. This means that all of the fixed assets have to be sold, all creditors must be paid, and any remaining assets must be distributed to the partners in order to liquidate their partnership interests.

Who Gets What When It's All Over

In the final analysis, you've been in business to make money. Sure, you got some personal satisfaction, you got to be your own boss, and you learned some invaluable business lessons along the way. But underneath it all, you wanted to increase the size of your nest egg.

Hopefully, you're dissolving your partnership to go on to bigger and better things. Maybe you've decided to branch out on your own so you no longer have to share profits. Or maybe, unfortunately, this business didn't turn out to be as successful as you had hoped. Whatever your reasons for disbanding the partnership, you want to walk away with something—and so do your partners.

Like the end of any relationship, dissolving a partnership can be stressful. There will be quibbling over who gets what, and who's responsible for cleaning up any outstanding business. In the worst-case scenario, attorneys will become involved. But there is a simple way to avoid any rancor when your business folds: plan ahead.

Spell Out Liquidation Procedures in Your Partnership Agreement

You can easily prevent quarrels over final distributions by actually listing how and when they will be made, and to whom, right in your original partnership agreement. There you can define all the assets (or asset classes such as property, equipment, and cash) to be used by the company, and how they will be disposed of at the end.

There are a few different ways to go with asset distribution. Your choices depend on the types of assets used by the partnership and what you plan to do after the partnership is dissolved. For example, if your company does consulting work, you won't have a lot of heavy machinery and equipment to deal with. On the other hand, if you have a landscaping business, the partnership probably will own a lot of equipment. Add to that your future plans. If you are simply retiring, you most likely want a big lump of cash. If you plan to continue the business in a different form (as a sole proprietorship, for example, or with a different partner), you may want to take equipment with you.

Dealing with cash is easy. First you pay off all the partnership debts, then you split the remaining cash in proportion to your ownership interests (or by following the partnership agreement, if different). When all the money is paid out, close the partnership bank accounts and go on your merry way.

Noncash but still liquid assets are also pretty simple to deal with. This category includes things like stocks and mutual funds (some successful companies park their extra cash in these types of investments to fund future expansions instead of making distributions to partners). You can either sell these at the listed market price and split the cash, or simply distribute the securities (remember, these will have to be retitled in the names of the individual partners—your broker or fund manager can help you with that). Illiquid assets, like furniture and lawn mowers, call for different strategies. How you split them up depends on your next move, and the way you've chosen to value them according to your partnership agreement.

Dealing with Illiquid Assets

Liquidating distributions become more complicated when illiquid assets, like real property and large machinery, are involved. To make sure your partnership finishes up smoothly, your partnership agreement should clearly state whether illiquid assets will be held until they are sold so that the partners can receive cash distributions, or be distributed to partners as is (meaning that a partner or group of partners would get title to the actual assets instead of cash). In addition, the agreement should spell out the valuation method for illiquid assets in order to make sure that every partner receives a fair and correct liquidating distribution.

If you've decided to sell everything, then split the cash, valuation is less of an issue. The value of your assets in this case will be whatever the market will pay. The resulting cash is easy to divide. But should some (or all) partners want physical assets, correct valuation becomes more important.

The valuation methods you'll use depend on the types of assets you have. For some assets, the fair market value is easily determined—used vehicles, for example. For others, figuring out a fair value can be more difficult—like old but serviceable office furniture. For very valuable or highly appreciated assets—like artwork—you'll want to call in an independent appraiser or two.

Once the assets are all valued, then the fun begins. It's highly unlikely that things will work out exactly evenly here, so some personal cash may have to change hands to keep things fair. Again, this can be a touchy area, so make sure to really spell things out in your operating agreement—that way no one can quibble about who valued the assets, or refuse to add in some cash to even things out.

An Example with Numbers

Joan, Jeff, Holly, and Brian were all equal partners in the general partnership for their small bookkeeping firm. After many successful years in business, they decided to end their association. Joan, Jeff, and Holly wanted to retire; Brian (who was a few years younger than the rest) wanted to strike out on his own.

Brian wanted to keep all the office furniture and equipment for his business; all the others wanted cash. According to their partnership agreement, an independent appraiser had to be called in should any partner want to receive physical assets

Don't Forget to Divvy Up the Debt

Sometimes partnerships fold because of financial difficulties. If this is your situation, you'll be splitting up shares of debts to be paid instead of assets to be received. Generally, debts will get divided in a manner similar to how assets would be. If you have a well-prepared partnership agreement, debt distribution will be spelled out along with everything else. Otherwise, apportioning the debt by ownership percentage is the fairest way to go.

This scenario can get especially uncomfortable when you and your partner(s) have disparate personal financial situations. If he can't pay his fair share of debt, it will fall on your better-off shoulders. The way to circumvent this potential problem is to include an indemnity clause in your partnership agreement. This clause will say that if any partner ends up paying more than his fair share of partnership debts, the other partner(s) will reimburse him for the difference.

as his liquidating distribution; the appraisal fee would be paid by the partner who prompted the appraisal. It also stated that in case the asset valuation resulted in an inequitable distribution, the partners receiving more than their fair share would have to pay the other partners the difference in cash within thirty days.

The four partners voted on an appraiser out of the choices in the phone book. He came to their office, and valued each asset as instructed by the partners. His final fee came to $150.

The appraiser valued the office furniture at $9,000. In addition to the physical assets, the firm had $21,000 in the bank. So the total assets for the company came to $30,000. Each partner's share of the total came to $7,500.

Brian got the $9,000 of assets. Joan, Jeff, and Holly each got $7,000 from the cash account. Within thirty days, Brian paid each of the other partners $500, and he paid the appraiser his $150 fee.

> **Chapter 14**

The ABCs of Corporations

Part One

Part Two

Part Three

Part Four

Part Five

Part Six

A Corporation Is Its Own Person

A corporation is a business structure where the business itself is its own independent legal entity, completely separate from its owners. Corporations literally count as legal "persons," able to open their own bank accounts, enter into contracts, and conduct business on their own. They can do all of this without any input from their owners (although they do need some human assistance). This is in complete contrast to sole proprietorships and partnerships, where the lives of the owners and their businesses are completely interrelated.

In addition to their legal independence, corporations have perpetual lives independent of the lives of their owners. They don't dissolve when ownership merely changes hands. They "survive" indefinitely, regardless of who owns them.

Fifty Sets of Laws to Follow

Corporations are created and regulated according to state law. That means there are fifty different sets of rules governing corporate entities. Although many states use Delaware's corporate statutes as models, there are still little variations unique to each. If you decide to use a corporate entity for your business, you must make sure to follow the laws of the state in which you incorporate. If you don't follow all the legal intricacies exactly, you run the risk of having your corporation terminated.

On top of following the rules in your company's home state, you have to make sure to follow all of the applicable statutes in every other state where your company will conduct business. So if you do business in New York and New Jersey, you have to comply with all the regulations in both states; if you do business in ten states, you have ten sets of rules to follow. Again, the consequence of not strictly sticking to the laws in every state in which your company trades is the termination of your corporate status.

How Is a Corporation Born?

When you and your company's co-owners originally form your corporation, you'll earn the title of *incorporators*. Incorporators do all the groundwork needed to create a corporation. The common tasks performed by incorporators include:

- Preparing and filing the articles of incorporation
- Selecting the first board of directors
- Adopting the corporate by-laws
- Bringing together all the necessary people and funding (typically for larger corporations)

Every state allows more than one person to take on the role of incorporator and sign the articles of incorporation. Most states require only one to get this done, except for Arizona, which requires at least two incorporators.

Once your corporation is officially born, you'll need three groups of people to make up the organization's structure: shareholders, directors, and officers. Shareholders are the owners of the corporation, but they do not directly manage the business in that role. The board of directors manages direction of the corporation by making all major decisions. The corporate officers are the ones responsible for the daily operations and management of the firm. Although you need three groups, you don't necessarily need a lot of people. One person can hold more than one role in the corporate structure. For example, shareholders can be directors and/or officers of the corporation. In a small business, one person wearing many hats is pretty typical. In the following sections, you'll learn more about each of these roles.

> One person can hold more than one role in the corporate structure.

What's a Shareholder?

A *shareholder* is an owner of a corporation. So anything that benefits the corporation effectively benefits the shareholders. Even though in their ownership roles shareholders don't take on corporate management responsibilities, they still have quite a bit of control over the corporation's business affairs.

The rights, responsibilities, and duties of shareholders will be specified in your corporate bylaws (fully discussed in Chapter 15). The most important right given to shareholders is the right to vote. Typically, the ownership percentage is directly linked to the number of votes a shareholder gets, but that's not always the case. There is some variation among the states, but typically shareholders have the right to vote on things like choosing and removing

In a Small Corporation, Be Aware of Your Shareholders

You came up with a great business idea. You needed a little extra financial backing, and, rather than deal with partners, you decided to form a corporation and trade some people stock for money. You may think the transaction ends there, but it doesn't necessarily.

Although shareholders don't have the right to participate in running the corporation, they do have some rights that can allow them to control the company. So if you're inviting Aunt Maribel into your business as a shareholder thinking she'll just give you cash and go away, think again. As a shareholder—no matter what percentage of shares she holds—she has some basic rights that could just conflict with your plans for the company. So pay attention to the people you get money from; they may want a say in how you spend it.

members of the board of directors, selecting the corporate president, and top-level corporate changes.

Top-level corporate changes cover things like:

- Changing the company's name or main address
- Changing the nature of the business
- Adopting additional bylaws
- Amending existing bylaws
- Amending the articles of incorporation
- Changing the size or members of the board of directors
- The sale of all (or substantially all) of the corporation's assets
- Dissolving, selling, or merging the corporation

When a corporation has more than one owner, the shareholders have to act together as a group. All major business decisions have to be voted on at shareholders' meetings. Almost every state requires shareholders to meet at least once a year. And, contrary to what you may have seen on TV, all shareholders must receive advance notice of meetings. That advance notice must also include a meeting agenda, so the shareholders have time to think about the issues they'll be voting on. Your corporation's specific notification procedures can be included in your articles of incorporation.

Shareholders can vote either in person or by proxy (which means having another person vote in his place). In most cases, votes are decided by number of shares, not by number of shareholders. So if you have one hundred shares and your co-owner has only fifty, your vote will be the winning vote. Whenever shareholders have a meeting, minutes of the meeting must be recorded (sort of like a shareholder's diary). When shareholders are far away from each other and meetings aren't really convenient, some states do allow "consent actions," which are really just documents signed by all shareholders instead of formal meetings.

Meet the Board of Directors

The board of directors of a corporation acts like its centralized upper management. The board of directors has many essential duties to fulfill. Some of the responsibilities of the directors are establishing overall business policies, picking the corporate officers (who will be the ones actually running the company every day), and approving any major business activities (like large bank loans). The leader of the board of directors is called the chairman of the board.

The directors have to act as a unit for their decisions to be valid. So they may hold votes and initiate actions only at meetings of the board of directors—and these meetings require certain formalities. For example, all of the directors must be notified of an upcoming meeting (similar to shareholder notification) in a specially defined way, such as two weeks ahead of time in writing. Sometimes, though, either the corporate bylaws or the articles of incorporation allow waivers of the formal notification.

How Many Directors Will There Be?

When they create the corporation, the incorporators or shareholders can choose how many directors the corporation will have, as long as they follow their state guidelines. The number they pick gets recorded in either the articles of incorporation or the corporate bylaws, and that's how many directors are required for the entire life of the corporation.

Most states explicitly allow a corporation to have only one director, but others at least three directors. In those states, though, they make an exception for very small corporations with less than three shareholders. In those circumstances, there have to be as many directors as there are shareholders. So a corporation with only one shareholder could have only one director.

A Look at Board Meetings

To make your board meeting official, there must be a certain number of directors present (as decided in the articles of incorporation or the bylaws). To decide a matter for the record, a *quorum* must be present. Most of the time a quorum is just a simple majority, but your corporate bylaws can specify a different percentage or minimum number of participants. If you don't have a quorum at the meeting, it doesn't count.

The board of directors has to meet regularly, at least once a year. Of course, they can meet more often than that, even calling special meetings whenever necessary. The most important meeting of the board of directors is its initial meeting. At that meeting, the directors adopt the corporate bylaws, they choose the corporate seal, and they begin the recording books.

Each director has a fiduciary responsibility to the corporation, so the board must document all of its actions and decisions. The directors also have to show that their actions and decisions were reasonable, made according to the laws currently in place, and in the best interests of the corporation. This responsibility is especially important for small, closely held corporations to follow in order to avoid losing their corporate status. If a creditor can prove that decisions were made in the best interests of the shareholders or directors, and not in the best interests of the company, the corporate veil could be pierced, and the shareholders would become personally responsible for the debt. (See Chapter 17 for a thorough discussion of corporate liability protection.)

To make sure you get to keep the personal liability protection offered by forming your corporation, the board (even if it has only one director) has to be able to justify all its actions and be able to explain why they were truly in the company's best interests. Especially when the directors' decisions involve compensation, dividends, and other related-party transactions, this step is crucial. For example, if the corporation is consistently losing money, and the directors (you and your brothers) give you a huge raise in salary, a creditor could argue that the raise is not in the best interests of the company—and he'd probably win.

Corporate Officers

When it comes to corporate officers, there are four types, each with its own functions and responsibilities. As you'd expect, the requirements for corporate officers vary from state to state—but most states require corporations have two: a president and a secretary (although both parts can be played by the same person). Regardless of how many officers you do end up with, most states permit the same person to act in all four roles. If you do that, your responsibilities would change as you took on each of the different officer roles. For example, if you're acting as the secretary, you'd keep the minutes of any meetings (yes, you'd still have to hold official meetings, even if you're just meeting with yourself).

The four corporate officers are president, vice president, treasurer, and secretary. In addition to those four main roles, your corporation can have supplemental officers—like multiple vice presidents, assistant secretaries, and assistant treasurers. There can, however, only be one president.

The President

The president of your corporation will be selected by the board of directors. Basically, the president is the chief executive officer, commonly called the CEO. The CEO is the captain of the corporate ship. He has the overall responsibility for running and managing the corporation, and he's completely responsible for carrying out any orders enacted by the board of directors. He has to keep employees motivated, make deals with vendors, and develop the overall strategies for keeping the corporation competitive.

The Vice President

The vice president of a corporation carries out the executive orders of the president. In his role as chief operating officer (or COO), the vice president oversees corporate operations and staff. The COO will often be in charge of hiring and firing, managing a distinct portion of the business, and making sure that the daily operations of the corporation run smoothly.

The Treasurer

The treasurer is the chief financial officer (CFO) of the corporation. The CFO is typically in charge of maintaining the corporate financial records, implementing accounting procedures, and dealing with the company's cash. In most corporations, the CFO is the one signing the checks. And although the overall financial policies of the corporation are decided by the board of directors, the treasurer is the one who really holds the corporate purse strings.

The Secretary

The corporate secretary has a more clearly defined role than those of the other officers. This role, though it sounds the least important, can be the most crucial role. The secretary is responsible for making sure the corporation is always in compliance with current state laws, and for maintaining the corporate records. In addition to keeping minutes, the secretary must stay abreast of corporate filings and confirm that all required corporate formalities are observed.

C Corporations

C corporations, also known as regular corporations, are perhaps the most frequently heard of business entity. Everyone has heard of the stock market—in fact, almost everyone of working age in the United States has participated in the market, even if just through an employer's 401(k) plan. When people think of these corporations, they think New York Stock Exchange, IBM, Microsoft—they think "big." But corporations can also be an excellent choice for very small businesses, and they've recently begun to gain favor in this small market.

The biggest difference between C corporations and every other business entity is that this form of corporation pays its own taxes on its own income. For tax purposes, the C corporation is its own person, individually responsible to the IRS to file its own annual tax return and pay any balance due.

There are a number of benefits to using the C corporation for your small business. In addition to ironclad personal liability protection, the company can fully deduct all fringe benefits (like deferred compensation and group term life insurance) without any taxable income to you as the owner—and no other entity can offer that. Also, corporate tax rates have historically been lower than personal tax rates, making this structure more beneficial when the business has significant profits. (Yes, personal income tax rates are relatively low right now, but it's really only a matter of time before they inch their way up again.) And C corporations offer the most options for income-shifting and income tax planning of all the currently available entity choices.

As with all business structures, there are drawbacks to the C corporation. First, the big one, double taxation: with this entity, the corporation pays tax on its income, then you pay tax on all the dividends you receive—so the same income gets taxed twice. (Again, current tax law makes this less of an issue, but tax laws are always subject to change.) The other big drawback applies to corporations in general—the massive amounts of paperwork, meetings, and formalities required to keep the entity in existence. Any lapse in meeting these requirements can result in loss of the corporate structure. And along with all the paperwork comes cash outlay, as corporations are usually the most expensive entities to form and maintain.

S Corporations

S corporations start out as C corporations then make a special election with the IRS. The distinction is mainly based on tax treatment, but there are also a lot more restrictions on S corporations than on C corporations. Differences aside, S corporations do have a lot in common with regular corporations. Both have to follow the same corporate formalities, both are governed by state law, and both can exist perpetually as independent legal entities.

For decades, the S corporation was the entity of choice for small business owners. This special entity gives its owners the proven liability protection of a regular corporation plus the benefits of pass-through taxation (like that enjoyed by partnerships). And although LLCs (the new darlings of business advisors) offer basically the same features, they don't offer the excellent track record of S corporations when it comes to lawsuits. This well-established personal liability shield combined with easy ownership transfers that have no effect on the company still make the S corporation a great choice for many small business owners.

With the benefits, however, come some strings. The second big difference between S and C corporations is the long list of limitations on ownership. Pretty much any individual or entity can own a C corporation, but serious restrictions come into play regarding those who may own S corporation shares. If a "forbidden" entity or individual owns even one S corporation share for just one day, the corporation will lose its S status, and revert to being a C corporation.

> Any individual or entity can own a C corporation, but restrictions come into play regarding those who may own S corporation shares.

Other Types of Corporations

In addition to the two big categories of corporations (C and S), there are also a couple of minor—but very important—variations on the original theme. For groups of professionals, there are personal service corporations. These corporate entities are mainly used to protect professionals from malpractice claims made against their associates. The other corporate form (available in some states) is the close corporation, designed especially for small businesses. The main benefit of close corporations is a reduced paperwork burden without loss of the protective corporate status.

Professional Corporations

Professional corporations, commonly referred to as *personal service corporations (PSCs)*, can be created only by members of certain professions. The principal activity of the PSC is performing personal services, mainly done by the employee-owners of the company. *Employee-owner* means just what it sounds like: any professional who is both a shareholder of the corporation and on the payroll as one of its employees. And although not all shareholders have to be employees of the corporation, they do all have to be professionals. The main benefit of organizing your professional company as a PSC is to insulate yourself against the malpractice liabilities of the other employee-owners.

For the purposes of forming a PSC, these professions are considered to be personal services:

> Although not all shareholders have to be employees of the corporation, they do all have to be professionals.

- Accounting
- Actuarial science
- Architecture
- Consulting

- Engineering
- Health
- Law
- Performing arts

A PSC can offer only one personal service. So, for example, if you had a firm of accountants and some of them were also actuaries, they couldn't provide actuarial services through the accounting firm.

To maintain the PSC status, there are a few very technical hoops that the company must jump through. For example, in order for the personal service to count as the principal activity of the corporation, more than half of the company's revenues have to come from those personal services. There are a couple of other tests the corporation would have to meet, some involving the percentage of employee-owners, some based on time and tax years. To see if your group of professionals qualifies to form a PSC, check with your business advisor.

Close Corporations

A *close corporation* is a regular corporation with one big difference: Its stock is not traded on any exchange. But some states' laws take the close corporations one step further, allowing them to be set up and regulated under special laws that add more to the state's regular corporation laws. In those states, these corporations are called *statutory close corporations*, and they're formed with distinct language in their articles of organization.

When some states realized that small, closely held corporations were being drowned in a sea of paperwork, they decided to throw these companies a lifeline. The extra legal language governing statutory close corporations were created specifically to help small corporations by reducing the amount of formalities typically required of corporations. The specific statutes for each state are different, but some points are commonly covered. For example, a statutory close corporation usually doesn't have to have a board of directors; they don't have to appoint any officers; shareholder meetings don't have to be held; the shareholders can agree to use a one shareholder–one vote system instead of the normal one vote per share method; and often, the shareholder can be run using a simple shareholder agreement.

The point of these modified rules is to ease the paperwork burdens for very small corporations, which are often family businesses. By significantly reducing the formalities required of corporations, these special laws can help protect the owners' personal assets. Because if a corporation falls behind in any of the official procedures typically required by law, it will be more vulnerable to adverse court decisions that can pierce the veil of limited liability.

States Allowing Statutory Close Corporations:

Alabama	Kansas	South Carolina
Arizona	Maryland	Texas
Delaware	Missouri	Vermont
District of Columbia	Montana	Wisconsin
Georgia	Nevada	Wyoming
Illinois	Pennsylvania	

The key to qualifying as a statutory close corporation is the number of shareholders your corporation will have. The maximum number is strictly limited: Some states set the bar at less than thirty shareholders, others allow a larger group as long as there are less than fifty. In addition, there are transfer restrictions on the shares, and those have to be printed right on the actual stock certificates.

Which Businesses Should Incorporate

When you need serious personal liability protection, form your business as a corporation. There is no stronger, more reliable protection out there—corporations have been shielding the personal assets of their owners for a very long time.

So if your company will be inherently prone to lawsuits, a corporation is probably the best entity to choose. If you'll be dealing with hazardous materials, food and/or alcohol service to the general public, employees, or other potential dangers, your corporation can protect you in the event of disaster or a lawsuit.

Another type of business well suited to the corporate form is one that will require a lot of outside capital. With a corporation, you can have as many owners as you like (as long as you adhere to the statutes that govern whichever type of corporation you form). That means you can raise a lot of outside funds without incurring outside debt. Plus, since shareholders don't really directly control the business, you can run your company as you see fit. So if you will need a large outlay of cash to get your business up and running (you need a lot of special, expensive equipment, for example), this entity can help you raise money without giving up a lot of control.

> **Chapter 15**

Forming Your Corporation

Part One

Part Two

Part Three

Part Four

Part Five

Part Six

Naming Your Corporation

Corporations are governed by state law, and each state has its own way of doing things. Although many states have adopted similar statutes, little differences appear throughout. Naming your corporation is no different. Each state has explicit rules on the books that control the way you name your corporation. Luckily, most of the rules surrounding this issue are pretty much the same. First, the name of your corporation can't be the same as that of another corporation already on file. Second, the name has to end with a particular term or abbreviation that indicates corporate status—such as Corporation, Corp., Incorporated, Inc., Limited, or Ltd. Finally, it can't include any specifically prohibited terms (the common ones here are Bank, Federal, and Reserve). On top of that, the corporate name can't violate another company's trademark.

The biggest impediment to choosing your corporation's name is finding one that no one else is using. A lot of excited entrepreneurs think up a clever name and start using it right away—ordering business cards, letterhead, and signs. But because hundreds (maybe thousands) of companies register names every single day throughout the country, buying anything with the name you want before it gets approved by the state is a big mistake. Most states commonly reject names that are similar to or could easily be confused with the name of another corporation registered in the state. So don't do any shopping until you're holding a certificate of incorporation (or whatever your state sends out as an official acceptance) in your hands.

To make it easier on yourself, do a name search before you fall in love with one. In addition to the numerous online name search providers, most states will let you search their databases online for existing registered corporate names. If you come up with a name that no one else is using, reserve it right away by filing a form (called something like a "corporate name reservation") with the appropriate state office and paying a small holding fee.

> Buying anything with the name you want before it gets approved by the state is a big mistake.

Deciding Where to Incorporate

Once you know that you want to incorporate, you'll need to figure out in which state to do it. You don't have to incorporate in the company's home state, which really means the state in which it will conduct most of its business.

For a small, closely held corporation operating only locally, incorporating in your home state is usually the best way to go. But you may want to consider some other factors before making a final decision.

The big things to think about when you're trying to choose the state of incorporation are costs and legal differences. Cost can be a big factor, especially with a fledgling business that may not have a very positive cash flow to start out with. You should compare the costs of incorporating in your home state with the costs of incorporating somewhere else and operating as a foreign corporation in your home state (see below for a full discussion of foreign corporations). If you register your corporation in one state and do business in another, you'll probably have to pay taxes and annual report filing fees in both states (or however many states you conduct business in).

In addition to the money factor, the differences in state statutes can make a big difference in how easy (or hard) it is to maintain your corporation. In fact, compliance is much easier in some states than in others. And as you learned in the previous chapter, some states even have a special statutory designation for small closely held corporations that helps them to stay in compliance at all times.

Even taking those factors into account, though, most small local companies do best incorporating in their home states. Every corporation transacting business in a state outside the one they've registered in must qualify to do business there—and that usually just means paying fees and taxes. And when a corporation has a significant presence in a foreign state (such as a company that incorporates somewhere other than its home state), the foreign state's laws may apply when problems come up, no matter where you actually formed your corporation.

If you still think you want to incorporate somewhere other than the home state, you'll have to choose the state you want to register in. The two most popular choices for nonresident corporations are Delaware and Nevada—and you'll soon see why.

Delaware

For decades, Delaware has been the clear choice for out-of-state incorporation. More than half of the corporations listed on the New York Stock Exchange were formed in Delaware. The big boys know what you're about to learn. Delaware offers a lot of tangible benefits for corporations that you just won't find anywhere else.

The most important advantage the state has to offer is its Court of Chancery. Delaware has had a completely separate court system for businesses for more than 200 years. Its judges are appointed based on their experience and worth, with no juries at all (a great thing in this day of huge decisions made by emotional jurors). Every decision made is issued in the form of a written opinion, and that gives the judges a very large body of legal precedent to rely on. So for a corporation, Delaware provides perhaps the most stable legal ground on which to stand.

Some of the other advantages of incorporating in Delaware are:

Efficiency—The office of the Secretary of State of Delaware is run more like a business than like a government agency bound in red tape, making it quick and easy to incorporate.

Cost savings—Delaware has traditionally charged relatively low setup costs and annual fees.

Tax breaks—Delaware has a very low corporate franchise tax, plus it levies no income tax on corporations who don't do any business in Delaware.

Nevada

Delaware still rules when it comes to incorporation, but Nevada is quickly gaining popularity for a lot of reasons. The biggest benefit of forming your corporation in Nevada is no state taxes at all: Nevada doesn't levy any corporate income or franchise taxes, or taxes on corporate shares, plus there aren't even any personal income taxes. Nevada also charges extremely low annual fees, and imposes very minimal reporting requirements.

Another area where Nevada excels is privacy protection. Shareholder information isn't considered to be a matter of public record, and that means owners of Nevada corporations remain completely anonymous. Nevada also doesn't require notification of such things as stock issuance, stock transfers, or out-of-state places of business. And on top of all that, Nevada doesn't share information with the IRS.

Understanding Foreign Corporations

When a corporation conducts business anywhere outside the state where it was formed, the outside state counts the company as a *foreign corporation*. Most states require foreign corporations to "qualify" (a.k.a., pay some fees) before they can begin to transact business.

If you operate your corporation in an outside state without registering as a foreign corporation, your company could be subject to tax fines and penalties. If you're not sure whether you're actually conducting business in another state, you're not alone. The definition of transacting business varies quite a bit from state to state, and may even vary based on your particular situation. Your corporation could even technically be conducting business in an outside state without knowing it. (You should definitely consult a lawyer to figure out which laws apply and what they mean to your company.)

Many states look at a group of factors when deciding if a corporation is really transacting business within the state. Some of the more common factors include:

- An office or shop (or other place of business) in the state
- An active checking account (or other bank account) within the state
- Employees performing work in the state
- Accepting orders in the state

Normally, ordering and receiving goods from suppliers in the outside state doesn't count toward transacting business there. Those transactions are considered to be the suppliers' transactions.

To qualify your corporation in another state, you have to register it for a Certificate of Authority. You have to make sure that the name of your corporation isn't the same as one already registered in the state. You also have to obtain and present a Certificate of Good Standing (or some similarly named form) from the home state to prove you have an existing corporation there. Then all of the proper filing fees have to be paid. As you might guess, these fees are often higher than the same fees charged to domestic corporations.

> To qualify your corporation in another state, you have to register it for a Certificate of Authority.

Once your certificate is accepted, your company can begin trading in the outside state. You'll usually receive your acceptance within about six to eight weeks after the filing. If you're in a rush, you may be able to get expedited acceptance service—for an additional fee, of course. Once your company is an official foreign corporation, it will be subject to taxes and annual reporting fees. And you will need to set up a registered office with a registered agent within the state.

Your Registered Agent and Office

Most states require that corporations doing business within their boundaries name a registered agent who will maintain a registered office within the state. Both the registered agent and the registered office are a matter of public record. The registered office has to be an actual place—it can't just be a mailing address like a post office box.

The registered agent is really just a local contact person for the corporation. All he really does is accept service of process and other official notices, such as tax notices, on behalf of the corporation. If your company is incorporated in a state other than the one where it will carry out all or most of its business, you can simply hire a registered agent.

Articles of Incorporation

To create your corporation, you'll need to fill out a lot of paperwork. The first document you'll create—and the one that's the key to organizing—is your articles of incorporation (also known by some other names, like *corporate charter* or *certificate of formation*). Once this document is filed and accepted, your corporation exists. Although you'll have to do a lot of other paperwork to keep the corporation going, the articles of incorporation is the only document necessary to create the business entity.

> The articles of incorporation is the only document necessary to create the business entity.

What gets included in the articles of incorporation varies somewhat from state to state, but they typically contain basic entity information. Regardless of the state of formation, your articles will certainly include at least the corporation's name and address and its registered agent and office. Many states will also require the names (and maybe addresses) of the members of the board of directors; the corporation's capital structure (which just means how much and what type or types of stock you'll be issuing); and the purpose of your corporation. Many states also allow optional items to be appended to their standard forms, and they'll provide you with a list of other things you may want to include (typically this would cover things like a very complex stock structure).

Almost every state provides fill-in-the-blank forms for preparing articles of incorporation, making it fairly easy to create the document on your own. You can even fill in the form online at many states' Web sites; others provide downloadable forms that you can fill out manually, then fax in. The Web sites also provide instruction sheets and fee lists, so you'll have all the information you need to comply. If you need help filling out the form, you can contact the appropriate state office (their phone number will be on the Web site) or ask your attorney for assistance. Along with the articles of incorporation, you'll need to pay some state fees, usually in the $100 to $150 range. When you file electronically or by fax, you can pay by credit card to keep things moving right along.

Once you've submitted your paperwork and payment, it will take any-where from twenty-four hours to two weeks for your articles of incorporation to be returned, stamped as filed, by the state. If you can't wait to get started, most states provide rush services for an additional fee. Your corporation's existence will begin officially when a certificate of incorporation (or a similar document) is issued by the state.

Some Other Start-up Costs

Corporations are the most expensive business structures to establish, and those state incorporation fees are just the start. Additional costs you may encounter include:

- Legal fees (when you use an attorney—which is highly recommended)
- Incorporation service fees (if you use an online incorporation service)
- Notary fees (to verify documents and signatures)
- Foreign registration fees (if you'll be operating outside the state of incorporation)
- Corporate seals (optional in most states, used for official corporate documents)

Be Careful If You Use an Incorporation Service

If you're looking for someone to take care of the bulk of the incorporation details for you, you can hop on the Internet, launch any search engine, and type in the word "incorporate." You'll get a huge response—hundreds of Web sites will appear, and they're all willing to incorporate your business for you. Of course, there are fees involved, but to attract your business some sites post extremely low fees (some even as low as $25.00). When you start to click on these bargain basement service providers, remember the saying "Let the buyer beware." These displayed fees can be very deceptive, and the service providers touting them may not be reputable or current.

Before you sign on with an online incorporation service, look at all of your options. The surest and safest way to form your corporation correctly is to use the services of a qualified attorney, but this is typically also the most expensive option. If you decide to use an incorporation service, make sure the firm is both reputable and experienced by checking them out with the Better Business Bureau and your state incorporation office. Then compare the total actual costs, not just the price they advertise to get you in the door. Many times that advertised price doesn't include everything required for a complete legal corporate filing.

Corporate Bylaws

Now that your corporation is officially formed, you'll need to draft your corporate bylaws. Corporate bylaws act like operating agreements for your corporation, as they include all the rules that it will run by.

Corporate bylaws are internal documents, not filed with the state. They serve as a rulebook for all parties to the corporation to follow. Bylaws typically address such issues as how often directors and shareholders have to hold meetings, how they have to be notified that a meeting is coming up, and the rules for running the meetings. They also specify the rights and duties of the directors, and how the corporation will indemnify directors and officers in the case of a lawsuit.

Some states give corporations the option of including these operating procedures in their articles of incorporation instead of in corporate bylaws. Although it sounds easier (creating one document instead of two), it's not a

> Corporate bylaws act like operating agreements for your corporation.

good idea. If you want to make some procedural changes through corporate bylaws, you just amend them at either a directors' or shareholders' meeting (depending on who has this responsibility). But if you've put these provisions in your articles, you actually have to file a formal amendment to the articles with the state corporate filing office (and probably pay some fees) to make any changes approved by the board or shareholders.

Following Corporate Formalities

Now you're officially incorporated—and the paperwork has just begun. Before your corporation can actually start doing business, you've got to choose a board of directors and then they have to hold a meeting, making sure to keep the minutes (remember, that's like a meeting diary). This initial board meeting records some of the necessary start-up formalities on paper.

The board of directors has to set all of the major corporate policies and make all of the major financial decisions. Their other responsibilities include appointing the corporate officers, authorizing the stocks to be issued, and establishing operating guidelines for the corporation. Finally, actual stock shares have to be issued to the initial shareholders.

Stock Certificates

All new corporations have to issue stock to their initial investors, and they do that by giving stock certificates to the shareholders. Although a lot of states don't actually require formal paper stock certificates be issued, a lot of shareholders still like to have visible proof of their ownership rights—even if they just frame it and hang it on a wall.

When actual certificates are issued, the state requirements are really pretty basic. You need to include the corporation's name, the state of incorporation, the type and number of shares issued to that shareholder, and the signatures of two corporate officers. You can find out your state's printed certificate requirements at the Web site, or by calling the office where you incorporated.

Blank stock certificates can usually be found at stationery stores, and you just fill in the blanks. If you want them to look fancier, you can have them printed by a legal printer, but that will cost more.

The Consequences of Not Following Corporate Formalities

You incorporated your business for a reason, and you went through a lot of effort and expense to do so. If you want to preserve the important benefits of incorporating, all state legal formalities have to be strictly observed. When you neglect to follow any of the necessary steps, your corporation can be dissolved, even retroactively. So if you are the sole shareholder, director, and officer of your corporation, these formalities must be followed to the letter.

What happens when your corporation gets dissolved? First, you lose the personal liability shield, meaning you're now personally responsible for all corporate debts. Second, there could be serious tax consequences, such as having to include all the corporate income on your personal income tax return. Finally, you could be barred (either permanently or temporarily) from forming a new corporation in that state.

Special Rules for S Corporations

All S corporations start out as C corporations. So to create an S corporation, you first have to create a regular corporation under state statute. The second step is to get the formal (and that means written) consent of every one of the corporation's shareholders, and record this agreement in the minutes. If even one of the shareholders doesn't want to switch to S status, you can't do it.

Once the shareholders unanimously agree to make the change, you (or your accountant or lawyer) have to complete IRS Form 2553—Election by a Small Business Corporation. The one-page form is pretty straightforward, and you can download it along with complete instructions from the IRS Web site (*www.irs.gov*). New corporations have to file the form within two months and fifteen days from the beginning of their tax year. To be on the safe side, file Form 2553 right away, and certainly within two months and fifteen days of your official incorporation date.

Although this one-page form is relatively easy to fill out, a lot of people fill it out wrong and their request for S status gets rejected. (If the IRS finds the mistake even years after the filing date, for example, S corporation status will be disallowed from the beginning.) When the IRS does notice the mistake, they'll send the form back and reject the election. You can always refile the application, but that will change the timing of final IRS acceptance of the form. The most common errors people make when filing are neglecting to have every shareholder sign the form and waiting too long to file.

To avoid that first common error, make sure that every shareholder signs his consent on Form 2553 or on a separate written consent statement that you'll attach to the form. These separate written consents are typically used when a shareholder is out of town or otherwise unavailable to sign the form. If you use these written consents, make sure they include the shareholder's name, address, and social security number; the number of shares he owns; the date he acquired the shares; and the day and month of the end of his tax year (usually December 31); and his signature. And, of course, they need to say that the shareholder agrees to operate as an S corporation.

Creating a Shareholders' Agreement

If your corporation will have more than one shareholder, a shareholder's agreement can help avoid future conflict, much like a partnership agreement. When you map out an agreement on paper, you'll have to look ahead and consider the possible issues that could arise—and that can only help you plan and run your business in a way that makes you all happy.

What issues you'll include in your agreement should be based on your unique combination of shareholders and your specific business circumstances. Some of the issues most commonly included are who can be a shareholder

Why You Need Buy-Sell Provisions

Buy-sell provisions don't just protect you from having to work with your co-owner's obnoxious Uncle Bob; they can also protect the existence and status of your corporation. Sound overdramatic? Think about this: Transferring shares to a prohibited party can terminate an S corporation.

If that's not reason enough, here are some more. If you want to maintain control over your business, you want a co-owner who agrees with that. If he owns more shares, he can outvote you and even fire you. In fact, a shareholder who owns the majority of the company can even liquidate it, leaving you with no corporation at all.

A Quick Look at Securities Law

Securities laws were written to protect investors. To ensure that, corporations have to comply with a lot of legalities before they can offer shares to the public. Corporations have to register the sale of shares with the Securities and Exchange Commission (SEC) and the appropriate state office before selling even their initial shares. This registration process is very complicated, and you'd need both attorneys and accountants to do it right.

Luckily, most small corporations are exempt from this registration process under both federal and state law. The main exemption comes under the SEC rules for private offerings to either no more than thirty-five people or to only people who can be reasonably expected to understand the investment process. Since small corporations are usually formed with less than thirty-five owners, they get out of following all the strict guidelines involved in offering securities.

(very important with a small closely held corporation), who can be a director or officer, and buy-sell provisions.

Buy-sell provisions control how and to whom the shares of your corporation can be transferred, and should be included in every shareholder agreement. There are a lot of events that can cause a stock transfer, from a divorce settlement that gives stock to a shareholder's spouse to an offer from an outsider that's too good to refuse. Whatever the cause of the transfer, how it's done is critical to the continued existence and success of your corporation.

In a small closely held corporation, ownership and management typically overlap. So if one of your co-owners wants to sell, the buyer can have a huge impact on your business. To make sure no shares are transferred to someone you don't want involved in your company, include detailed buy-sell provisions in your shareholders' agreement as soon as your corporation is formed.

Accounting Basics for Corporations

Like all other business structures, corporations have to make all of their accounting decisions when the first tax return is filed. If you want to make changes after that, you'll need permission from the IRS.

C corporations are prohibited from using cash basis accounting—most of the time. And that means it can't really use delayed receipts or accelerated expense payments as a tax-planning strategy.

But most of the time doesn't mean all of the time, and as with most IRS rules there are exceptions. Qualified PSCs mostly owned by employee-shareholders can use cash basis accounting. Plus, small corporations can also use the cash method; the IRS currently defines small corporations as those having gross receipts of $5 million or less for any prior three-year period, when they don't hold inventory for sale to customers.

Other than that, basic bookkeeping is pretty much the same for corporations as for any other structures. The big difference comes in the capital section of the balance sheet, which is somewhat more complex than that of other entities. Here the owner's equity has several components:

1. The capital stock accounts (of which there may be more than one)
2. The additional paid-in capital account (for capital contributions above the stated par value of the stock)
3. The retained earnings account (which could have subcategories)
4. Declared dividends (income payments to shareholders)
5. Current net income (or loss)

Maintaining Your Corporation

Corporations have a lot of formalities to follow. And now that your corporation is formed, up, and running, you'll have ongoing formalities to deal with. These tasks are crucial to your corporate status, and failing to maintain each and every formality can cost you that status.

Like everything else, specific corporate requirements vary from state to state, and even within some states depending on the type of corporation. Some of the most common required official procedures are holding regular board meetings (even if there is only one director), conducting regular shareholder meetings (even if you're the only shareholder), writing up an agenda for every meeting, keeping minutes for every meeting, and recording corporate resolutions. In addition, your directors should meet at least once a year with the company's accountant and any other business advisors.

The Minutes

No one likes taking notes—this goes as far back as grade school. But keeping corporate notes, called minutes, makes the difference between maintaining your corporation and losing it. When you religiously keep the minutes, you'll be complying with state and federal laws that require thorough documentation of all corporate issues and decisions. You'll also be compiling a history of all those decisions, and your reasons for making them—which can go a long way toward satisfying the IRS or the courts, should the need arise for you to justify any actions taken by the corporation (or by you on behalf of the company).

It's especially easy to blow off this tedious task when you're the only shareholder, director, and officer. But with single-person corporations, it's even more important to keep minutes. When you don't, it will be very easy for corporate creditors to get a judge to pierce the veil of liability protection, and make you liable for everything.

What kinds of things should you include in the minutes? All significant events or decisions made by the corporation. This would cover things like amending your bylaws, declaring dividends, increasing officers' salaries, getting a bank loan, and launching a new product. Basically, any decision you make that has or could have an impact on the company should be recorded in the minutes. If you're not sure, write it down. Better to record too much than too little.

Corporate Resolutions

When you make any really big decisions during meetings of either the shareholders or the directors, you'll formally record them as corporate resolutions. You don't legally have to record big decisions this way, but doing so can serve as proof to outside parties that the decisions were made by and on behalf of the corporation.

Corporate resolutions (which also get recorded in the minutes) usually cover major issues like making changes to the articles of incorporation, deciding to dissolve your corporation, and declaring corporate bankruptcy. But they can also include some more typical business decisions, like starting an employee retirement plan, purchasing large and expensive assets, and applying for S status.

Chapter 16

Corporate Taxation

Part One

Part Two

Part Three

Part Four

Part Five

Part Six

The Type of Corporation Determines the Taxation

Taxation is an issue you should absolutely consider when you're deciding which type of corporation you want to form. Both C and S corporations offer advantages and disadvantages to their owners. When making this decision, you need to take your personal tax situation into account. But you also need to look at the current tax climate.

Historically speaking, the graduated federal corporate tax rates for C corporations have usually been lower than individual tax rates, especially for high-income individuals. That made C corporations the entity of choice for successful corporations with successful owners. But right now, personal rates are lower than they've been in a very long time, and may be lower than corporate rates (depending on your personal situation). That makes S corporations more attractive, since the income will be taxed at the lower individual rates instead of the currently higher corporate ones. However, because tax rules and rates change as frequently as you change the battery in your smoke detector, don't let this be your only deciding factor.

The regulations regarding corporate taxation are less likely to change than the rates. So you should focus at least part of your decision on those issues. First, the C corporation. On the plus side, fringe benefits are tax-free to owners, and income-splitting capability lets you really minimize your tax bill. On the downside, double taxation on corporate dividends is a definite drawback. When it comes to S corporations, their claim to fame is pass-through taxation—especially beneficial to start-up businesses with initial losses. The drawbacks include taxable fringe benefits (to the owners) and less tax planning capabilities.

This chapter will help you understand some of the more complex issues surrounding the taxation of both types of corporations. As with any tax matters, talk to a CPA if there's anything you don't understand—taxes are complicated, and business taxes even more so. Don't be afraid to ask for help; it's better to do a preemptive check with a professional than end up trying to explain your position to the IRS later.

> Tax rules and rates change as frequently as you change the battery in your smoke detector.

How C Corporations Are Taxed

Unlike the other available small business structures, C corporations are responsible for paying taxes on their own income. In fact, the name "C" actually refers to the tax status of the company. Corporations basically figure out their income in the same way as other companies. But instead of the owners reporting the income somewhere on their personal tax returns, the C corporation files its own annual return on IRS Form 1120 and pays the balance due. And just like individuals, if the corporation expects to owe taxes at year-end, it has to make estimated tax payments.

Federal Income Tax on C Corporations

Historically, federal corporate income tax rates have been lower than the federal personal rates (at least on the first $75,000 of corporate income). That's not the whole story in 2004, but the personal tax rates schedule could revert to the norm (read "high") at any time. Right now, the federal corporate tax rates are the same as they've been for years—but personal rates are relatively low. Whether C corporation taxes would be more or less than individual taxes for the same income depends on your personal financial situation and filing status. The 2004 corporate rates are shown in the table below.

2004 FEDERAL CORPORATE INCOME TAX RATES

Taxable Income Above	But Not Over	Corporate Tax Rate
$0	$50,000	15%
$50,000	$75,000	25%
$75,000	$100,000	34%
$100,000	$335,000	39%
$335,000	$10,000,000	34%
$10,000,000	$15,000,000	35%
$15,000,000	$18,333,333	38%
$18,333,333		35%

The exception to the corporate rates above is for PSCs, which are taxed at a 35 percent flat rate on all profits.

Corporate Estimated Taxes

When your corporation is having a successful year, it will have to pay estimated taxes on the expected income throughout the tax year. Like people, C corporations are subject to additional taxes when they underpay their estimated taxes. Your corporation can avoid this tax penalty by making payments that come to 100 percent of the current year's tax liability—or meet the special allowance for small corporations. Small corporations can sidestep the extra assessment by making four on-time payments of at least 25 percent of the tax due for the year before (unless there was no tax due for the last year).

Lots of Tax Advantages for C Corporations

In addition to excellent liability protection, C corporations offer a lot of flexibility when it comes to income tax planning. And the benefits to you, as the owner, are pretty substantial, too—fringe benefits that is. With a C corporation, 100 percent of most of your fringe benefits will be tax-deductible to the company and tax-free to you. This includes even life insurance, which is typically not allowed the same treatment with other business structures.

As you might expect, there are IRS rules and restrictions that control how much income you can shift, and limitations on the amount of tax-free fringe benefits. The IRS also pays close attention to dividend payments (or nonpayments) to make sure that people aren't disguising dividends as tax-deductible salary. To avoid potential tax traps that can make your corporation less advantageous, talk to a tax professional about the best ways to lower your overall business and personal tax bills.

> C corporations offer a lot of flexibility when it comes to income tax planning.

C Corporations Allow Income Splitting

To make sure you pay the least possible taxes when your corporation is profitable, you can "split" income with your company. By paying yourself salary, bonuses, and other items that are tax-deductible to the business, you can actually control how much taxable income the corporation has, and how much will show up on your individual tax return.

Salary is the expense that most business owners fiddle around with. For every salary dollar you pay yourself, the corporation gets to deduct a dollar from its income. When you increase your salary and bonus payments, corporate income decreases while your personal income goes up—a good strategy when personal income tax rates are relatively low. When the opposite situation exists, you can reduce your paycheck and lower your personal income and increase the company's profits.

When your salary hits a high point, the IRS may step in to make sure that your paycheck still falls into the "reasonable" category. On your side, you want to get as much tax-deductible cash as you can out of the corporation. On their side, they want to collect as much tax revenue as they can. To keep the peace, make sure your salary is reasonable—meaning a fair paycheck for the job you do (when compared to others with similar job responsibilities). It absolutely can be on the very high side of fair, but should not border on the ridiculous.

Of course, there's no set limit on how much you can pay yourself. But if the IRS deems your salary "unreasonable," they'll recharacterize some of it as dividends, and you'll end up paying more taxes (and possibly penalties as well). To avoid this potential tax hit, you can mix up the ways you take money out of the corporation, and still keep most of it tax-deductible to the company. Once you've taken as much as you can in reasonable salary, the next step is to consider which fringe benefits you want.

Fully Deductible (and Tax-Free) Fringe Benefits

Employees can receive fringe benefits on top of their regular salaries and bonuses. And when you work for your corporation, you're an employee, too. C corporations can offer any number of tax-advantaged benefits to their employees—including you as an employee-owner—providing a definite advantage over pass-through entities. Although due to changes in the personal income tax regulations health insurance premiums are tax-deductible for everyone, there are other fringe benefits that are only tax-deductible/tax-free under the C corporation structure.

The first of these is group term life insurance, which is exactly what it sounds like: employer-paid term life insurance coverage for a group of employees. In fact, your corporation can pay for up to $50,000 worth of life insurance coverage for its employees completely tax-free to them (and to you as one of them). The plan does have to adhere to all the IRS guidelines and limitations (mainly that it doesn't discriminate in favor of only certain employees), but they're pretty easy to deal with in this case.

Another benefit involves college costs. C corporations can deduct qualified educational assistance provided for employees, including you (as an employee-owner). That means your company can pay for things like tuition and books—and get a tax deduction for it. Employer-provided educational assistance (up to the $5,250 limit) is totally tax-free for employees. But, there is a catch here. Many small, closely held corporations won't meet the guidelines for this benefit. The biggest problem is that the company's education program can't provide more than 5 percent of its benefits for the year to shareholder-employees who own more than 5 percent of the corporation. But if one of your children is an employee (not an owner) of the corporation and you don't take her as a dependent on your personal tax return, she can qualify for the full tuition payment exclusion. Meaning you can send your child to college on the company dime, and the company gets a tax deduction for it.

Expense Reimbursement and Travel Allowances

Many small business owners frequently pay company expenses with the cash in their wallets. As a corporate owner, you can benefit from an expense reimbursement plan, and so can your corporation. Employees don't get a 100 percent income tax deduction when they pay for business expenses; but the corporation can deduct 100 percent of all the legitimate business expenses it incurs (except for those subject to limits), including expenses originally paid by employees then reimbursed by the company. For proper documentation, adopt a written plan that covers all shareholders and employees and specifically states that all reasonable business expenses will be reimbursed when receipts are presented within a set time period.

You know that your corporation can reimburse you for travel expenses. But did you know that you have the option of reimbursing yourself at the IRS standard daily per diem rates? You can choose whichever method gives you the bigger deduction—actual or per diem. The choice gets made for each reimbursement, so you can always figure out which is higher and use that one for your reimbursement and deduction.

Rent Property to Your Corporation Tax-Free to You

One of the lovely loopholes in the tax code lets you rent out property for fourteen days or fewer every year completely tax-free. So you can rent your house, your vacation home, or your cabin in the woods to the corporation for a few days every year—you'll get tax-free income and the corporation will score a deductible expense. To keep it all above board, you need to put some things in writing like the business purpose of the rental (like an employee meeting) and an authorization from a corporate officer (which can be you).

Make sure the corporation pays fair market rental. For example, if you rent the company your ski lodge for a week in January, charge whatever the going rate for ski lodges is at the time.

Downsides to C Corporation Taxation

The most commonly talked about drawback of C corporations is double taxation. This comes into play when the company transfers its earnings to its owners. Here's what happens: When the corporation has profits, it pays tax on them; when it pays you dividends out of those earnings, you pay tax on them. That's how the same income gets hit with a double tax burden—one for the company, one for the owner(s). Under current tax law, dividends are eligible for a special low tax rate, making this problem slightly less burdensome, but that could change at any time.

In addition to that tax drawback, corporations are sometimes also subject to more than just the regular income tax. First comes the alternative minimum tax (AMT), similar to that paid by high-income individuals. Next is the accumulated earnings tax, levied on corporations that don't distribute their earnings. Finally comes the personal holding company tax.

> Under current tax law, dividends are eligible for a special low tax rate.

All about the AMT

The AMT is really a sort of tax prepayment, because your corporation will get a tax credit for the added-on tax in future years. That doesn't make it any better when you have to shell out the cash, but at least it isn't gone forever. Even worse than paying the AMT is calculating it (you definitely need an accountant for this) and then storing the records required to ensure full compliance.

Luckily, there's an exemption from the AMT for small corporations. The tax code lets small corporations that meet some gross revenues tests avoid dealing with the AMT at all. Right now, your corporation will qualify for the AMT exemption if its average gross receipts for the past three-year period aren't more than $7.5 million (if you've not been in business that long, it looks at the shorter time frame). So if it's your first year in business, the AMT probably won't apply. You may never have to deal with the AMT, but leave all the tax calculations to your CPA just in case.

The Accumulated Earnings Tax

When a corporation holds on to too much of its earnings (according to the IRS), it can be hit with the accumulated earnings tax (AET). The AET is assessed by auditors when they think shareholders are trying to skate around double taxation. But it takes a lot of retained earnings to get the IRS involved: Corporations can keep up to $250,000 of their earnings, no questions asked; PSCs are allowed to amass $150,000.

Even corporations that hold on to more than the limit can avoid paying the extra tax if they can show a reasonable business purpose for not distributing the earnings. The AET will not apply to earnings that a company keeps because it needs to. For example, if your corporation wants to buy a warehouse that's selling for $1,000,000, it would be reasonable to save up earnings for a substantial down payment.

The Personal Holding Company Tax

The rule affecting small, closely held corporations with income from personal service and/or investment activities is called the personal holding company (PHC) tax. The PHC tax works similarly to the AET, but is self-assessed by shareholders.

Your corporation counts as a personal holding company if it meets two conditions. First, more than half of the stock is owned by no more than five shareholders during the last half of the tax year. Second, 60 percent or more of your company's income comes from things like dividends and rents. The

PHC tax will come into play any time the corporation's income doesn't get distributed to the shareholders. If you want to avoid the PHC tax, pay out some dividends.

IRS Audit Risk

Unlike pass-through entities, C corporations are taxpayers—and that makes them potential IRS targets. In fact, since the corporate tax law is so complicated, it's pretty easy for the IRS to make a case that a company owes more taxes. Plus, for corporations they have extra ways to levy taxes, like the AMT, the AET, and the PHC tax. Because the IRS can potentially levy a lot of extra taxes here, C corporations get audited pretty frequently, second only to sole proprietorships.

S Corporations Offer Pass-Through Taxation

C corporations get audited frequently, second only to sole proprietor-ships.

When you have a small start-up company, using the S corporation business structure can be more beneficial for federal income tax purposes than a regular corporation. Statistics show that new companies usually sustain losses in the first couple of years after they're formed. S corporations offer pass-through taxation (unlike C corporations), so those losses can be used to offset your other taxable income and reduce your personal federal income tax burden.

Although they typically don't have to pay taxes, S corporations still have to report their profits or losses to the IRS on Form 1120S. Like partnerships, the corporation also reports the year's activity to its owners on Schedules K-1. Then the shareholders each report their portion of the corporate income or loss on their personal tax returns. Just like partners, S corporation shareholders have to pay taxes on their shares of the company's income whether or not they actually get any money. On the plus side: Profit distributions are never subject to self-employment tax, even when you're active in the business.

Because the rules of S corporation accounting are confusing, use a professional for tax preparation. The tax situation gets even trickier when the company has out-of-state shareholders or does business in more than one state. All out-of-state shareholders have to file tax returns in both their own home states and in the corporation's state of formation. When the S corporation does business in multiple states, all of the shareholders will likely have to file tax returns in each of those states—and that's a lot of tax returns.

Then comes the question of state income taxes. Most states follow the federal example for taxing S corporations, where the shareholders are taxed on the profits instead of the company. But in some states, S corporations are treated just like regular corporations and have to pay their own taxes. Other states do recognize the S status, but still require the S corporations to pay some taxes just like C corporations. The states where your corporation could be subject to state income taxes include:

- Arizona
- Connecticut
- District of Columbia
- Michigan
- New Hampshire
- New Jersey
- New York
- Rhode Island
- Tennessee
- Vermont

Tax Issues for S Corporation Shareholders

The first issue for S corporation shareholders is how to put the information from their Forms K-1 on their own tax returns. (Again, due to the complexity of the tax law in this area, using a professional is the best way to go.) As with a partnership, the company is invisible for federal tax purposes, so each item that affects taxes is looked at as if the shareholder had earned it himself. For example, corporate interest income turns into shareholder interest income. It sounds simple, but it's really not. Some items may not transfer to your personal return exactly as is because other factors, like your other income, has to be taken into account. Bottom line: You can't just copy the items from the K-1 onto your tax return without knowing all the rules.

The Rules about Tax Losses

The main advantage you'll get from your S corporation's pass-through taxation is being able to claim the business losses directly on your personal tax return. So if your brand new S corporation loses $8,000 in its first year and you're a 50 percent owner, you get a full $4,000 deduction from your other income on your tax return—in most cases.

No Special Allocations Allowed

Another contrast between S corporations and partnerships is how profits and losses are split among shareholders. With an S corporation, all pass-through items must be allocated among the owners in direct proportion to the percentage of stock they own; with a partnership, you can divvy up profits, losses, and any other items in almost any way you like. So if you own 50 percent of an S corporation, you have to get 50 percent of profits, 50 percent of losses, and 50 percent of everything else. Any other allocation can cause the termination of your S status.

First, you can only take losses up to your basis in the stock (more details below). On day one, your basis equals the money you put into the corporation in exchange for your stock plus any money you personally loaned to the corporation. So right off the bat, that total is your deductible loss limit. For example, if you paid $10,000 for your shares and then loaned the corporation $2,500, your initial basis would be $12,500. You could deduct any first-year losses up to that amount, but anything more would have to carry over to a later year.

Second, your deductible losses can be limited by at-risk rules (a fancy tax code way of saying the total amount you could lose if the corporation went bust). As a shareholder, you're considered to be at risk for all the money and property you contributed to the business plus any business loans for which you are personally liable to repay (like if you had to cosign for a business loan from the bank).

Finally, shareholders who aren't active in the business (people who just put up money but have nothing to do with running or working for the company) could be subject to passive activity loss (PAL) rules. Those PAL rules basically say that these loss deductions can only be used to offset income from other passive activities.

Luckily, most small business owners are affected only by basis issues. That means you have some control over when you'll be able to deduct corporate losses by adjusting your basis up or down. For example, if your share of losses for 2004 came to $10,000 but you had only $8,000 of basis, you could loan $2,000 to the company and take the full loss. If you didn't have other income to offset the loss, you could just leave things as is and carry the $2,000 forward to use against next year's income.

Paying Estimated Taxes

As a shareholder-employee earning a salary, you'll have regular income taxes withheld from your paycheck just like everyone else. But you won't have any withholding taxes deducted from your share of corporate profits, so you may have to pay estimated taxes on that income. If you're expecting to owe taxes at year-end, pay some estimated taxes so you won't get hit with interest and penalties.

First you have to figure out approximately how much income the corporation will earn for the year. Then that gets combined with all of your other income. Finally, you calculate the total income taxes that would be due, subtracting what's being withheld from your paycheck. If the balance is positive, you should make estimated tax payments. Divide that balance by four, and write a check to the U.S. Treasury. Write your social security number on the check along with "2004 Form 1040-ES" (or whatever year you're paying for). Mail that in with an IRS Form 1040-ES payment coupon. The remittance address varies by where you live, so check out the IRS Web site (*www.irs.gov*) to find the right mailing address. And if all this seems like too much of a hassle, you could always just increase the withholding tax on your paycheck instead.

Shareholder-Employee Salaries

In C corporations, you have to make sure that your salary doesn't seem too high. But with the S corporations, the opposite is true: You have to make sure that your salary doesn't seem too low. Again, the key word here to avoid IRS interest is "reasonable."

Again, you and the IRS are at odds here. While it benefits both you and your corporation to keep your salary to the bare minimum, the IRS gets more when your paycheck is higher. Although federal income taxes are due on all corporate income no matter how it's paid out, only salaries are subject to Social Security and Medicare (called FICA both together) taxes. So where a C corporation doesn't want its owners' salaries reclassified as dividends,

S corporation shareholders don't want their dividends reclassified as salaries. If that happens, the corporation will have to pay retroactive FICA taxes plus penalties and interest.

There are some times when low—or even no—salaries make sense, even to the IRS. In fact, this rule only applies when the corporation is making money. If your company is losing money (as many do in the beginning), you don't have to pay yourself (or the other owners) any salary at all. If you did, the corporation would end up with an even bigger loss. So until your corporation starts making money, don't worry about paying yourself a "reasonable" salary.

> If your company is losing money, you don't have to pay yourself (or the other owners) any salary at all.

Back to Basis

Tracking your basis is one of the most mind-numbing tasks associated with S corporations. Initially, your total basis equals the value of your stock plus all the money you loan the company. After that, it goes up and down based on corporate income or losses, additional loans, and a few other things.

Your basis will increase by your share of corporate profits, any additional investments you make in the company, or any more loans you make to the business. It will decrease (but never below zero) every time you get a distribution, when your loan is repaid, and also by your share of losses. This is the simplified version of calculating basis, but other factors may come into play (yes, this is another reminder to use a professional).

Once your basis hits zero, you won't be able to deduct any further losses. But these disallowed losses aren't gone forever, they're just in limbo until your basis goes back up. To increase your basis right now so you can use current losses on this year's tax return, you can either loan money to the company or make additional capital contributions.

Tax Benefits of S Corporations

Now that you know a lot more about S corporation taxation (probably more than you ever wanted to know), take a look at some of the highlights:

- No double taxation on corporate income
- Pass-through tax treatment that lets you deduct losses
- No self-employment tax on your share of corporate income

- Interest paid on a personal loan used to put money into the company can be 100 percent deductible
- S corporations can use cash basis accounting
- S corporations aren't subject to the AMT, PHC tax, or AET
- The IRS almost never looks at shareholder-employee salaries
- S corporations are hardly ever audited by the IRS

Some Tax Drawbacks for S Corporations

There are two main tax drawbacks for operating as an S corporation. One will probably affect you, the other probably won't. First is the treatment of fringe benefits:

While S corporations can provide tax-deductible benefits to their employees, shareholder-employees who own at least 2 percent of the company have to report some of those benefits as additional taxable income. The added-back amount isn't subject to self-employment taxes, but it is subject to regular federal income tax.

Under the current tax law, benefits that count as compensation include things like accident, health, disability, and life insurance premiums; cafeteria plan benefits; and qualified transportation fringe benefits. The big one, health insurance, isn't really a problem—although it counts as income, it also counts as a 100 percent deduction from income, netting out to a zero effect. The other benefits, though, will add to your total taxable income. And in this case, giving the benefits to your spouse won't make them tax-free; under the rules, your spouse counts as if he were a shareholder, too.

The other S corporation negative tax issue applies to those companies that previously operated as C corporations (another good reason to apply for S status as soon as possible). For a converted corporation, the company itself could end up bearing its own tax burden. Although these taxes only come into play under very specific circumstances, consult a tax practitioner if you did operate as a C corporation before filing for S status.

Loans Between Corporations and Shareholders

It's the life of a small business owner: You put money into the company, you take money out. If you decide that some (or all) of the money going back and forth is a loan, you need proper documentation to avoid any possible IRS complications.

When You Loan Money to the Corporation

There are a lot of good reasons for you to lend money to your corporation. First of all, it's much cheaper than getting a bank loan, with no application fees or audited financial statements. Second, there's minimal paperwork involved, just some basic documentation to prove it's a loan. Best of all, you can get tax benefits when the loan is treated correctly. For example, interest payments (unlike dividend distributions) are deductible to the corporation.

It's pretty easy to make your loan an ironclad transaction. Simply create a note complete with the loan terms. The note should specify things like a specific repayment date or schedule, the total loan amount, a fixed interest rate, and the signature of a corporate officer (which can be you). Then make sure to record the loan in the corporate minutes, just like you would with an outside loan.

The reason for the paperwork is to have proof that your loan is really a loan. Because if the IRS doesn't believe it's really a loan and reclassifies it as a capital contribution, all the interest and principal payments will be treated like dividends and you'll have to deal with double taxation.

Loans from the Corporation to You

The flip side of putting money in is getting money out, and the best way to get tax-free money out of your corporation is to have it loan money to you. Salary and dividends paid are always fully taxable, but loan proceeds are not. And just like a loan the other way, it's pretty easy to protect the loan status and avoid potential taxes.

The first thing you have to do is to make sure the loan carries a reasonable interest rate. Loans to you that carry either a very low interest rate—or no interest at all—may be subject to special "below-market" loan rules (if total loans to you are more than $10,000). The IRS considers a loan to be below-market if the interest rate is lower than the published applicable federal rate (AFR) for the period. If your loan is below-market, your corporation has to report interest income at the AFR—regardless of the amount you actually pay.

The best way to get tax-free money out of your corporation is to have it loan money to you.

Plus, the difference between what you really pay and what the IRS thinks you should pay has to be reported as dividends on your tax return.

The second step is to complete the same paperwork you would if the loan went the other way. You'll create a written note detailing the loan terms, and this one should contain both your signature and that of a corporate officer (this time it shouldn't be you, unless there is no other officer). A note should be written up for each shareholder loan, even ones that are less than $10,000. After the note is all set, record the loan in the minutes. And remember, any loan that's not fully documented could be recharacterized as a taxable dividend by the IRS—and that could be a lot of dividends to pay tax on.

Special Considerations for S Corporations

If you do use loans as a way to move money into and out of your S corporations, use extreme caution when you set up the loans. This is definitely not the time to skimp on paperwork, or just do it later. Because here the worst-case scenario is losing your S status—and that could cause an awful lot of tax problems. Along with the procedures discussed above, there are a few more things you need to do to keep your loan from being recategorized.

To keep your loan a loan, it must be crystal clear that the debt can never be converted into stock ownership. In addition, the loan holder has to be eligible to hold S corporation stock. So, for example, if you get a loan from your corporation, then transfer the debt to someone else (a pretty common business practice), the person the loan was transferred to must also be eligible to hold shares—even if he doesn't actually.

An option that can benefit S corporation shareholders is a back-to-back loan. These arrangements work well when the corporation needs borrowed money to get by but can't get a loan on its own. So you'll take out a personal loan in your name, deposit the proceeds into your personal bank account, then loan the same money to the corporation. When the company pays you back, you pay the bank back, and everybody wins. Plus, you get the side benefit of increased basis, which allows you to deduct more pass-through losses.

> Chapter 17

Corporations Provide the Best Protection for Personal Assets

Part One

Part Two

Part Three

Part Four

Part Five

Part Six

Learning about Limited Liability

When entrepreneurs hear the word "corporation," limited liability protection automatically springs to mind. For good reason, too—corporations provide all of their owners with limited liability. And that means the owners' personal responsibility for *business* debts can't be more than what they've invested in the company. But it does not mean that the company itself also has limited liability. In fact, the corporation has unlimited liability for its debts, and can potentially lose everything it owns.

Here's how it works in a nutshell: Legally speaking, a corporation is its own entity, totally separate from its owners. So corporate creditors can't go after the personal assets of the shareholders. And the opposite is also true: The corporation won't ever be responsible for the personal debts of its owners. The only thing that a shareholder can lose is his investment in the company, but he can lose 100 percent of it if the corporation loses everything.

Do you need all of this protection? The only answer to this question is, "That depends." Incorporating is not cheap and it's not easy. Corporations are the most expensive businesses to form and maintain, and they require the most paperwork and formalities to meet all legal requirements. And there are some circumstances that do not merit using this entity—for example, you don't have any personal assets, you're running a seriously low-risk business, or any real liability concerns can easily be addressed by insurance. In other cases, though, you may really need the bulletproof liability protection offered by this time-proven business structure.

You Need Corporate Liability Protection If . . .

The first thing you need to look at when deciding if you need considerable personal liability protection is how much you have to lose. If you have very little money in the bank, rent (instead of own) your home, and don't currently own significant assets, the corporate business structure could be overkill. You could always start your business in one of the easier, cheaper forms, then incorporate when your business takes off and you do have some assets to protect. On the other hand, if you do have a lot to lose, you should absolutely form your business in one of the protective entities, of which the corporation is the oldest and most solid.

Regardless of your current personal financial situation, if your business is inherently susceptible to potentially large-award lawsuits or significant debt, you should consider incorporation. These days, when it's possible for creditors to attach even your future earnings and assets, it makes sense to shield yourself when you're engaging in risky business.

Business Factors to Consider

Certain businesses are naturally prone to debt, much more than others. To start with, if you need to incur a lot of debt to start or run your business, that's a risk. Retail and manufacturing companies take a lot more cash outlay to get going than service-oriented businesses, for example. Retailers usually must maintain inventory levels and inventory requires storage space—these factors make borrowing almost a given for this type of company. Manufacturers also need inventory to make their products, plus machinery, equipment, operating facilities, and much more. That typically requires substantial debt to suppliers and other creditors. If your business structure doesn't limit personal liability and the company can't pay up, these creditors can come after you.

In addition to requiring an awful lot of money to start up and stay in business, manufacturing concerns also have a lot of potential liability exposure. From environmental issues (like waste disposal, chemicals leaking into water supplies, and emissions) to possible product defects, any company making products could get hit with huge fines, penalties, and lawsuits. Even products that don't seem to be dangerous or that don't require hazardous chemicals to produce could end up costing the company a lot of money in claims settlements. In times when people can bring lawsuits against fast food companies because they gained weight when they ate there, is any product really safe from the court system?

Finally, having employees always increases your company's liability potential. With a risky business (like one that uses flammable liquids, poisonous chemicals, or hands-on

A Picture of Protection

Suppose you own a business. You've invested a total of $5,000 in the company, and now the company has $50,000 in assets. You have personal net worth outside the company of $40,000. The company has some financial troubles, and ends up with total debt of $100,000.

First, the company would lose everything, and satisfy whatever portion of the debt it could handle. The rest depends on your business structure. If you're a sole proprietor or a general partner, you could stand to lose your whole $40,000 personal assets plus the $5,000 you had invested in the company. If you're a shareholder in a corporation, on the other hand, you could only ever lose your $5,000 investment and you'd get to keep all of your personal assets.

machinery), having employees perform potentially hazardous activities boosts your lawsuit likelihood to near 100 percent. Even activities like lifting or carrying heavy boxes could be considered potentially hazardous to the people who work for you. One on-the-job injury could set your company back pretty far financially. And when your employees do things that could endanger the public (like make deliveries or demonstrate exercise equipment), your liability potential doubles. These situations could injure your employee and an innocent bystander to boot.

Common Personal Liability Issues for Shareholders

Now you know that your maximum liability for corporate debts equals your investment in the company. And you also know that your personal debts can't become problems for the corporation. Most people think that's the end of the story, but it's not. There's still one more category of debts and obligations that overlaps both personal and business concerns and opens up both you and your corporation to liability.

Your limited liability shield as far as business debts are concerned will not protect you from any claims brought on by your own professional malpractice, negligence or other tortious acts (meaning anything for which a lawsuit could be brought against you). On top of that, you could also be held personally responsible for such acts committed by an employee under your control. You are fully protected, though, against financial responsibility for the tortious acts of a fellow shareholder. The corporation has no protection in any of these cases—since the tortious actions were directly connected to corporate business, the corporation can be sued as well.

So basically, forming your business as a corporation will protect your personal assets (as the "innocent" shareholder) from liabilities brought about by your co-owners in the ways discussed above. However, the corporation itself can (and probably will) be sued. In fact, all of your corporate assets could be wiped out by any one shareholder's professional malpractice or other tortious act. You won't be held personally financially responsible, but you could end up losing your investment in the corporation, and losing your company to boot.

Aside from lawsuits, there is still another circumstance in which you (as a corporate shareholder) could be held personally responsible for a company debt. If you personally guarantee a loan to the company, and the company can't make the payments (meaning the corporation defaults on the loan), you will have to make the payments out of your own money. This is not an uncommon scenario, particularly among new small companies. Shareholders are frequently required to guarantee any bank loans to their fledgling corporations. While other corporate debt is not your personal problem, for these loans your personal assets will be at risk if the corporation defaults.

Protecting Corporate Assets

No business is ever completely safe. In fact, all businesses have some inherent liability risks. In order to protect your corporation's assets from out-of-the-ordinary business liabilities, you should take some proactive steps to control any potential loss. As with any small business, you should purchase some general business insurance. If you have a professional practice, you should also buy adequate malpractice insurance and require that your co-owners do the same. If you have an obviously dangerous business (like a skydiving service for the general public), you should maintain more than the bare minimum in liability policies. And all businesses, no matter how small and how safe, should acquire umbrella coverage.

A Real-Life Example

You and two friends (John and Rob) open up a takeout and delivery pizza restaurant. You've each put $15,000 into the business, and you all work there full-time as corporate employees.

One day, business is suddenly much greater than usual. So John decides to make deliveries in his personal truck to help out the regular delivery guy. Three deliveries go off without a hitch, but on his way to the last one, John swerves to avoid a raccoon and hits a parked car, causing severe damage to both vehicles. John leaves a note on the parked car telling the owner how to get in touch with him.

The owner of the parked car can sue John for damages. If John doesn't have enough money to cover the claim, the owner of the parked car can sue the corporation. The only ones protected from direct liability are you and Rob.

In addition to insurance protection, there are a few other ways to keep the corporation's assets protected. One commonly used strategy involves systematically transferring cash out of the company—after all, cash it doesn't have is cash it can't lose to a judgment. Another method used frequently involves setting up two entities, but that arrangement requires a lot more planning and paperwork. If your company is a high-risk business, one (or both) of these strategies should be used in conjunction with ample insurance policies. But when your company's liability potential is on the minimal side, these approaches (especially the multiple-entity setup) probably won't be necessary.

The Minimum Cash Strategy

One asset protection strategy aims to keep your company's liquid assets (like cash) at a bare minimum. The reason for this is that any assets held by your corporation are vulnerable to corporate debts and obligations. But assets held by the shareholders can't be touched if the corporation can't meet its financial commitments.

> Any assets held by your corporation are vulnerable to corporate debts and obligations.

The best way to reduce the amount of cash held by the corporation is to systematically withdraw it. You can arrange to do this in a few different ways:

1. Through your (and other owners') regular salary and bonus payments.
2. By paying out dividends three or four times a year.
3. With monthly lease or loan payments to yourself (and the other owners).

This strategy usually works as long as the business continues to meet its regular obligations. This means that payments to you (and the other owners) are not being made in place of payments to outside parties (like suppliers), but are being paid in addition to the normal bills and invoices. If regular obligations are kept up, creditor challenges to the payments probably won't hold up in court. But if you pay yourself so much that your everyday creditors aren't being paid, you may face some problems—and they could include losing your liability protection.

What should you do if your company needs money for expansion or large purchases but you still want to keep corporate cash balances pretty low? Simply use one (or a combination of) the withdrawal strategies, then either lend or contribute the cash back to the business when it's ready to act.

Transferring Cash Out of Your Corporation

The whole point of your business is for you to make some money. And when you're making money—and paying the bills—no one will complain. If you're struggling to make ends meet, though, and your suppliers are the ones not getting paid, you can expect to hear some grumbling. If the corporation's debts aren't being satisfied, or your company is suddenly hit with an obligation too big for it to swallow, the corporation could be sued for payment. Should that worst-case scenario occur, the courts will go over the corporate finances with a fine-toothed comb, especially when it comes to transactions between the company and you (and the other owners).

When cash is paid out to corporation owners in return for value, such as with salary or lease payments, the courts usually accept these as customary, reasonable, and necessary business expenses. This payment classification is particularly beneficial if your corporation is stuck in the middle of a financial downturn, when salary and lease payments will still be looked at as ordinary and essential expenditures to keep the company in business. On the other hand, earnings distributions like dividends could be challenged when your corporation is having a lot of difficulty meeting its outside financial obligations.

Under most circumstances, loan and lease payments are the best ways to get cash out of your business, for many legal and tax-related reasons. First, loan and lease payments are the most advantageous disbursements for tax purposes. Lease payments and the interest portion of loan payments are fully deductible to the corporation (and also taxed as regular income to you). Shareholder-employee salaries are also deductible, but they are also subject to employment taxes, which causes an extra cash expense for the company. And if your company is set up as a C corporation, you will probably want to limit the amount of money you distribute as dividends anyway so that you can avoid the whole double taxation issue. As you can see, loan and lease payments are your best choices for tax purposes.

Using loans and leases for your financial strategy can also provide you and your corporation a lot of legal benefits, especially with a small closely held corporation. When physical property, like warehouse space or computer equipment, is owned by the shareholder and leased to the corporation, it will not be available to the company's outside creditors. That means no one can force you to sell off the assets in order to satisfy the corporation's debts. And in the case of a secured loan from you to your corporation, you will have first rights to the assets used as loan collateral if the corporation starts having financial troubles. On top of that protection, the courts have consistently found that loan and lease payments are typical, legitimate business expenses—regardless of to whom the payment is made.

Using Multiple Entities Adds Extra Protection

For businesses that are innately dangerous or prone to lawsuits, an extra layer of insulation for the owners may be warranted—especially if those owners have substantial personal assets that they don't want to risk losing. Under these circumstances, a third level of asset protection should be employed. This ironclad strategy uses multiple business entities as a way to thoroughly limit both personal and corporate liability.

Using multiple business entities just means setting up two or more corporations. The underlying goal is seriously solid liability protection, and the best way to accomplish that is to set up both an operating entity and a holding entity. Both of these business entities would be set up as formal corporations.

Here's how it works: The holding company will own all of the business assets, from desks and chairs to production machinery and delivery vehicles. The operating entity will handle the regular day-to-day business transactions, from ordering supplies to making sales. The operating company will bear all of the potential liability risk, but has absolutely no assets to lose. The holding company has all of the assets, but no potential liability risk. Plus, since the holding company doesn't conduct any business, it won't incur any business debt.

The operating company is the real business. That corporation is the one that enters into transactions and contracts, and makes all the money. The holding company is also a corporation on its own, plus it is a shareholder of the operating company. And as a shareholder, the holding company is legally protected from liability exposure from the operating company. You will be a shareholder of the holding company, leaving you with virtually no liability exposure at all.

Since it costs money and time to set up and maintain two corporations, this strategy really only makes sense when there's both a lot of risk and a lot to be lost. If you do choose to go this route, you will have to make sure to meet all the formality requirements for both corporations, or risk losing their protective status. This setup will protect you and your corporate assets from business liabilities, but there is still one potential loophole that creditors can slide through. If you are having personal financial difficulties, it's possible that your creditors can attach your stock in the holding company corporation—and if you're the only or the major shareholder, that creditor could vote to liquidate the company.

S Corporations Have Additional Liability Concerns

If you've set your company up as an S corporation, you have extra concerns as far as liability goes. Although you are absolutely protected from liability for corporate debts, your corporation is not protected from your creditors. That's true of any corporation, but it's especially a problem when you've elected S status.

When you have personal liability issues, creditors can attach your assets—and that includes all of your shares of your S corporation stock. Any creditor with a valid charging order can try to have your company liquidated, whether you've formed it as an S or a C corporation. But if the creditor who ends up getting your stock shares is not eligible to be a shareholder of an S corporation, the S status will be automatically and immediately terminated. That in itself can have big (and serious) tax implications for you, your fellow shareholders, and for the corporation itself. Plus, once a corporation loses its S status, it has to wait five years before it can be eligible to apply again.

There are two different limits on S corporation shareholders: the maximum number allowed and also restrictions on ownership eligibility. First, you can't have more than 75 shareholders. If you have more than the maximum allowed at any time, the S status will be revoked. Second, some entities are prohibited from owning S corporation shares. Only individuals (the legal way of saying "people") who are legal U.S. citizens or residents, their estates, certain kinds of trusts, and other S corporations (as long as they are the sole owners of the corporation) can own shares. Partnerships, other types of corporations, pension funds, individual retirement accounts, and nonresident aliens are not allowed to be shareholders.

There are two different limits on S corporation shareholders: the maximum number allowed and also restrictions on ownership eligibility.

Having even one prohibited shareholder for even one day can cause the termination of your S corporation status. So if a personal creditor who's not eligible gets a hold of your shares, your corporation will be automatically reclassified. How common is this? It's much more common than you'd think—because the kinds of creditors who get these judgments are typically companies, and most companies can't own S corporation shares.

Piercing the Veil of Limited Liability

> Corporations provide their owners with the best, most reliable protection from business liabilities.

Business advisors throughout the country will all tell you the same thing: Corporations provide their owners with the best, most reliable protection from business liabilities. This excellent protection from corporate debt comes with a pretty big price tag, though. In addition to actual money (corporations are typically the most costly entities to set up and maintain), forming your business as a corporation will cost you a lot of time doing paperwork. As a shareholder, you must make sure to comply with the many legal formalities required to guarantee that your corporation gets to keep its separate entity status. If you don't preserve the separate existence of your corporation, it could be considered (by the courts) as your "alter ego," and that could lead to the "piercing of the corporate veil."

What does all this legal jargon mean? The alter ego theory says that your company is truly just a legal extension of you, meaning no separate entity, and no separate debt. If the court finds that your company is really not separate, your corporate veil will be pierced—and that means that you and your fellow shareholders could become personally liable for all debts of the corporation.

In order for a court to actually order the corporate veil pierced, it must find that your entity is a fake. Not that your business isn't a real business, just that your business structure isn't proper. If you don't take your corporation seriously, this type of judgment could be the result. A court decision to pierce your corporate veil could happen if:

- You don't follow each and every corporate formality.
- You or your fellow shareholders have mixed personal assets with corporate assets.
- The corporation wasn't formed with enough assets for it to reasonably succeed.

It's pretty simple to make sure that your corporate veil doesn't get pierced. All you really have to do is act fairly, honestly, and legally with third parties. Make sure that your corporation is adequately funded by putting enough money into it to at least meet all of its short-term obligations. Follow all of the required corporate formalities, which can help prove to the courts that you truly intend your business to be a separate entity. And definitely keep your personal finances totally separate from those of the corporation.

Even If You Hate Paperwork, Do It Anyway

The first line of attack on small corporations by almost every creditor will be the following of formalities. Failing to follow even a single requirement can result in loss of your corporate entity. Could that really happen to you, just because you forgot to hold one lousy shareholders' meeting? Absolutely, so make sure that you do everything your state demands to keep your corporate charter intact.

Here are some of the things that small business owners may overlook:

- Having an initial organizational meeting
- Actually issuing the corporate stock
- Adopting and complying with corporate by-laws
- Holding regular board of directors' and shareholders' meetings—especially when you're the only one of each
- Keeping current corporate minutes
- Recording major business decisions (especially those related to yourself) in the minutes
- Getting all state and local business licenses in the corporation's name
- Properly filing all state annual report and registration forms on time

Without complete compliance, you won't have a corporation. Yes, all the paperwork is annoying. And it does seem a little silly to have meetings with yourself—and keep a journal of those meetings. But in order to have proof that your company is a true separate entity, you'll just have to do it.

The Most Common Threat

Believe it or not, the biggest threat to your corporate veil is how you move money into and out of the company. Regular payments, like salaries and declared dividends, when officially called for during a directors' meeting and recorded in the minutes, don't pose a problem. But when you use the corporate checkbook to pay your own personal expenses, you could be buying yourself some trouble.

Make sure that you set up a separate corporate checking account in the corporation's name. Have a different checking account for yourself, in your name (and the same goes for all of your co-owners). Don't make corporate deposits into your checking account, and don't make payments for corporate expenses with your personal checks. The reverse also holds: Don't deposit checks you receive from outside sources in the corporate account, or pay your own bills with corporate checks. Doing any of these things is considered a commingling of assets—and it's just a short walk from there to show legally that there's no true separate entity.

Small business owners frequently make liberal use of their corporate checking accounts, making checks out to their personal creditors instead of making the checks out to themselves. Many also use the company credit cards for personal purchases, simply because that's what's in their wallets. But this casual use of corporate funds poses a serious threat to their limited liability status. If this is standard operating procedure for your corporation, the courts may find that your corporation doesn't really exist.

The easy way to get around this potentially sticky issue: don't do it. When you need corporate money to pay your personal bills, give yourself the cash officially. Hold a meeting with yourself (and your co-owners) and declare a dividend. Give yourself a raise or a bonus (complete with all of the appropriate payroll taxes coming out). Make the checks out to yourself, deposit the money into your personal checking account, and pay your bills yourself.

Make Sure Your Corporation Is Fully Funded

A lot of new small business owners are strapped for cash. They put just enough into the business to get it started, and they hope that somehow more money will start flowing in. That's typical, but it can also lead to problems if the company starts going under. If the courts find that you underfunded your corporation, that may be enough to undermine the entity. The solution: Borrow, even beg if you have to, but make sure your company has enough cash to pay at least three months' worth of expenses even if no cash comes in.

Even if you started out with enough cash, you may find that the ongoing expenses are higher than expected—or that incoming cash is lower than expected. That can cause cash crunches. You may go to family or friends to tide your company over, max out your credit cards, or even get a bank loan. Usually, that kind of borrowing won't be a problem. But if you borrow funds when you know that your company is on the verge of bankruptcy, you could end up being responsible for repaying them.

Charging Orders for Corporations

If you or one of your fellow shareholders aren't meeting personal debt obligations, the unpaid creditors could get a charging order from the courts. First the creditor will attach your (or your fellow shareholder's) interest in the corporation to satisfy the debt you owe. Then the charging order allows the creditor to actively participate in the management of the corporation. Theoretically, this court decision is to protect the interests of the creditor. If he can be involved in the company's management, he can get his money back.

The creditor, however, typically doesn't want to manage the corporation—he just wants his money and he wants it now. So instead of playing manager, he may vote his shares in favor of liquidation or take other actions that can make it very difficult for the corporation to stay alive. Small closely held corporations are particularly at risk for this treatment, especially those with only a single shareholder. If the creditor ends up with a controlling interest, what he wants to happen will be what happens.

> If you borrow funds when you know that your company is on the verge of bankruptcy, you could end up being responsible for repaying them.

> **Chapter 18**

Getting Out of the Corporation

Part One

Part Two

Part Three

Part Four

Part Five

Part Six

PART FOUR   CORPORATIONS

■ CHAPTER 14 The ABCs of Corporations ■ CHAPTER 15 Forming Your Corporation ■ CHAPTER 16 Corporate Taxation ■ CHAPTER 17 Corporations Provide the Best Protection for Personal Assets ■ CHAPTER 18 **Getting Out of the Corporation**

Passing It Down to the Next Generation

Corporations have perpetual life, and that means they theoretically live forever. They can remain in existence indefinitely, regardless of the fates of their owners. Whether the shares are sold to outsiders, inherited by the next generation, or gifted to friends and family, the corporation remains in existence.

Ownership of a corporation is easier to transfer than any other type of business structure. No one would think twice if you gave your daughter 500 shares of IBM; giving her 500 shares of your own corporation is just as easy (in most cases). As far as legalities go, shares of stock are completely freely transferable (meaning you can transfer them however, whenever, and to whomever you like) unless you have a shareholders' agreement that specifically outlines restrictions. So while the standard body of business law doesn't put any restrictions on stock transfers (as long as they conform to all of the applicable state and federal securities laws), you and your original co-owners may have limited how and to whom shares may be transferred. If you're the only shareholder, though, you can basically do whatever you want.

> Ownership of a corporation is easier to transfer than any other type of business structure.

Once you've decided you want to give your children shares of your corporation, the question is when to do it. You have three options: to give them a little more every year until they have controlling interest; to hand over the whole corporation at once when you retire; or to leave it to your children as part of your estate. Each method comes with its own set of benefits and drawbacks, some personal, some tax-related. You should carefully consider which strategy works best for your situation. Consult with an estate planning professional (who may also be your attorney or accountant) beforehand in order to make sure there are no long-term adverse consequences to your decision.

Minimizing transfer taxes (which include gift and estate taxes) is a major goal when you're passing down your corporation. Also important is current control of the company. If you want to keep the reins for yourself, make sure you retain enough shares to make your votes the ones that count; if you're easing yourself out of the business, your level of control is much less important.

A Brief Look at Gift and Estate Taxes

Like all other taxes in the United States, gift and estate taxes are subject to change—and under current law, they're guaranteed to do so. The current law affecting these taxes sets a timetable for their reduction and eventual phase-out through 2010. At that point, the law will revert back to how it stood in 2001 unless Congress passes legislation to keep the repeal in place. What will happen in 2010 is anyone's guess, so be sure to keep your plan flexible and you'll be able to deal with whatever legal changes occur.

Here's the basic theory behind the law, at least for how it works right now. As of 2004, you can give anyone up to $11,000 worth of gifts with no tax consequence to either of you. If you have three kids, you can give each of them $11,000 this year and pay no gift taxes. Giving such gifts has two possible tax benefits. First, if you give the children income-producing property (like shares of stock in your corporation, or equipment that your corporation will be leasing), the income produced will be taxed at your child's lower rate (assuming your child makes less money than you do). Second, anything you gift now (up to the total lifetime limit, which is $1,000,000 = even though the estate tax exemption increases to $1,500,000 for 2004–2005) will not be included in your estate, and therefore will not be subject to estate taxes.

Keep in mind, though, that gifts of stock that you make to your children will be based on the current fair market value of the stock at the time you make the gift. So just because you originally put $10,000 into your corporation in return for 1,000 shares of stock doesn't mean that the stock you're giving to your children today is worth $10 per share. Consult with your business advisor to determine the value of your company's stock before you gift it away. That way you can make sure not to exceed this year's gift limit.

Who's in Control?

Giving up control of a corporation you've built from the ground up isn't easy—in fact, it can be downright thorny. This is especially true when you're giving up that control to your children, and even more so if your children won't have equal stakes in the company. So how is a loving parent to resolve these dilemmas?

In the first place, the ages of your children make a big difference. If your kids are too young to really take part in the management of the company, they shouldn't have direct controlling interests. But when they are old enough to participate, and they have the desire to do so, how much control you relinquish to them should depend on their experience and their commitment to

the family business. One option to consider (depending on how your corporation is formed) is creating a second class of stock that doesn't allow its
holders voting rights. That way the children have an ownership stake in the
corporation without a controlling interest. As they begin to take more actual
control of the company, you can "trade" shares with them, allowing you to
retain ownership while allowing them to make all the key decisions for the
future of the business.

When you have more than one child, their actual participation in the
business can also make a difference in how you grant shares. Conventional
wisdom says that only those children who are directly involved in the company should own shares; parental wisdom says that if you have more than
one child, you have to divide things equally. This part of the decision lends
itself to a family conference (assuming the children are old enough to participate). Listen to what they have to say, and try to work out solutions that don't
cause family rifts. If all of your children work for your business in pretty equal
ways, equal shares make sense. If one child is really running the business and
the others are not involved, it makes business sense for the one actually participating to get the most stock. Perhaps you have other assets you could gift
to the remaining children, so everyone gets gifts of equal value; maybe you
could go the two classes of stock route so that everyone has equal shares, just
not equal control. The bottom line here is that you know your family better
than anyone else. A cookie-cutter solution from a book may not work for your
personal situation. Talk to your family, and come to a decision together.

Selling Your Shares

Technically speaking, corporations are the easiest entities to sell. Shares of
stock are bought and sold by the millions every day, with little or no effect
on the underlying companies. Small closely held corporations may be a little
less easy to buy and sell than their *Fortune* 500 counterparts, but the nuts and
bolts of the transfer remain the same. You offer your shares for sale, find a
buyer, make the exchange, pay some taxes, and go on with your life. The difference here is that you may be restricted by your shareholders' agreement as
to who can buy your shares and how much you can sell them for.

Regardless of what it says in your shareholders' agreement, when you
sell your shares of the corporation, there will be a tax effect. The tax effect

largely depends on whether you have a C corporation or an S corporation. With an S corporation, you'll really only have to deal with paying taxes if the corporation held assets that substantially increased in value (like real estate). With a C corporation, you'll probably owe taxes on the sale no matter what.

With pass-through entities, the taxable income earned by the company increases the basis of the owners' interest—and that means their basis is roughly equal to the true market value of the stock. But with a C corporation, the taxable income it has earned has absolutely no effect on the basis of shareholders' stock. When C corporation earnings are retained instead of paid out as dividends, the intrinsic value of the stock shares increases. That's a good thing—it means you can get more money when you sell off your shares. The downside is that you'll have a tax bill to pay. And, yes, it's one of those double taxation issues.

Here's the underlying accounting-tax issue. When the fair market value of your stock increases but your basis doesn't, you end up with unrealized (meaning you didn't actually get any money yet) and unrecognized (meaning you haven't reported it for tax purposes) gain; that is, until you sell your shares. At that time, you'll have a taxable capital gain (if the value of your shares has declined below your basis, you'll have a deductible tax loss). But when your shares are of a C corporation, the same income gets taxed twice. The first time when the corporation originally earned the money, and a second time when you sell your stock and realize a capital gain.

> When your shares are of a C corporation, the same income gets taxed twice.

S Corporation Shareholders May Be Restricted

Most owners of small closely held corporations have to comply with shareholders' agreements, with the big exception being for those with only one owner. These agreements typically lay out restrictions on when stock can be sold, to whom you can sell, and other such items. But S corporation shareholders face additional restrictions that must be followed in order to preserve the S status. And losing that precious tax status can be a big problem, as you'll see in the next section of this chapter.

To start with, S corporations are limited as to the maximum number of shareholders allowed. For now, the magic number is 75, but the small business community is lobbying hard to get that cap raised to 100 shareholders or more. Sounds like a lot of shareholders for a small corporation—and it is probably not something you'll ever have to worry about. But keep in mind, if you exceed the limit by just one person for even one day, your corporation will be reclassified and you'll have to deal with any legal and tax fallout.

The next restriction on S corporation shareholders is the type. Only individuals, their estates, certain types of trusts, and other S corporations (as long as they are the sole owners of the corporation) can own S corporations. On top of that, nonresident aliens are explicitly forbidden to be shareholders. How can that affect you? If, for example, one of the qualified shareholders of your corporation is married to a nonresident alien and they own the stock jointly (even if just because of community property laws), your corporation is ineligible.

The safest way to ensure that no restricted parties ever get a hold of shares of your S corporation is to have your shareholders' agreement include buy-sell provisions that specifically bar stock transfers to ineligible parties.

Losing S Status

If any one of the eligibility requirements for S corporation status isn't met at any point during your corporation's existence, it can (and probably will) lose

Adding Up Shareholders Is Tricky

Your corporation may only have a few shareholders. But if you've used equity financing, or begun to transfer shares to family members, you may get dangerously close to the limit on the number of shareholders for an S corporation.

Typically, a husband and wife will own shares of corporate stock jointly, either as tenants in common, joint tenants, or as community property. The couple will then count as a single shareholder. But if spouses own their shares individually, they will be counted as two separate shareholders. If you gift stock to your married children in one joint gift, they are one shareholder; with separate gifts, they will be considered as two. And, when spouses divorce and both continue to own shares (regardless of how they owned the shares before the split), they will be treated as two shareholders.

When two unmarried individuals own shares jointly, they are still considered to be two separate shareholders. This is largely because they can't file joint tax returns, and the S status is, in fact, a tax status.

its S status. This status change has some nasty tax implications, so make sure that you take some preventive measures to make sure you are always in compliance with all of the requirements. You read about restrictions on shareholders in the previous section. Now you'll learn about the other big issue: different classes of stock. In addition to that, you'll see what you can do if your S status does get terminated.

Different Classes of Stock

Basically, S corporations can have only one class of stock. That means that all of the outstanding shares give their owners identical rights to the profits and assets of the business. In plain English, you'll all get dividends and other distributions in direct proportion to the relative number of shares you own. One minor difference is allowed, though: You can have stocks of the same class with different voting rights, and those will still be considered the same class.

It's easy for your corporation to be in compliance when the stock is originally issued. But in some cases, certain transactions or agreements can be classified as a second class of stock even if you didn't mean for that to be the result. To cut through some of the legal mumbo jumbo, here's what the regulations really mean. If your corporation enters into some kind of transaction where the other party gets rights to distributions and to liquidation proceeds, that could be interpreted by the IRS as allowing shareholder rights—even if you never issue or transfer any actual shares of stock. Your saving grace here is that the IRS typically only makes the reclassification if the true principal purpose of the agreement is to get around the one-class-of-stock rules.

What kinds of transactions could be considered a technical stock issuance? Here are a couple of common examples. First, we'll look at a loan to the corporation from a nonshareholder family member. On the surface, it's just a loan. But if the loan agreement says that the loan holder will get his principal paid back out of corporate income, you've just accidentally created a new shareholder. Here's why: Distributions of income are for shareholders, not loan holders. A person who loaned money should be paid back regardless of the corporate bottom line, and tying repayment to income could reclassify the transaction as equity-related. The simple solution is not to put anything linking loan repayment and corporate income in any of the loan paperwork.

Example two involves shareholders and state taxes. If these shareholders have their state income taxes on corporate pass-through earnings either withheld by or directly paid by the corporation, you've just created a second class of stock. Why? Because the taxes for each shareholder will be different based on his total income, not just corporate income. Plus, shareholders living in different states may be subject to different tax rates. The simple solution is to pay yourselves proportional dividends, making sure they're high enough to cover everyone's state tax bill.

Appealing S Status Termination

As you can see, it's actually pretty easy to accidentally trigger a termination of your S status. If your corporation loses its S status because it inadvertently stopped qualifying, the IRS may decide to waive the termination and just let you continue on as before. The IRS will consider reversing their decision if the cause of the termination truly was accidental, with a couple of caveats. First, the corporation and all of the shareholders have to correct the problem within a reasonable time period. So if the corporation lost its S because you had one too many shareholders, you'll have to get rid of a shareholder. Second, both the corporation and all of the shareholders have to agree to act as if the problem never happened in the first place.

In order to get the IRS to change their mind, your corporation will have to apply for a private letter ruling. Basically, a *private letter ruling* is a solution for a single tax entity—you have a particular tax problem, and the IRS decides how to treat your problem individually without any official change in the tax laws. There are a laundry list of items that must be included in your request, like the names, addresses, and tax ID numbers of all shareholders and of the S corporation; an explanation of what happened that triggered the termination; and what you're all planning to do to fix things. Because the S status is pretty important, have your tax professional draft the letter. They'll put in all the right information in the right language, helping to ensure that the IRS considers your appeal.

A *private letter ruling* is a solution for a single tax entity.

Dissolving Your Corporation

A corporation cannot simply cease to exist. Its shareholders have to hold a vote to dissolve it, even if there is only one shareholder. Once the decision is made, a complete set of dissolution forms have to be filed in the corporation's home state (the state in which it was originally formed). If the corporation does business in multiple states, it may have to fill out multiple sets of paperwork. Some states require that even foreign corporations that are ceasing operations have to file dissolution forms there in addition to any home state procedures.

After you've taken all of the appropriate actions to fulfill state legal requirements (in both the corporation's home and any foreign states), the corporation has to wrap up all of its affairs. All creditors with outstanding balances must be paid in full, any existing contracts must be satisfied, and any leftover corporate assets have to be sold with the proceeds distributed to the shareholders in proportion to their ownership interests (unless you've agreed to accept physical assets that you'll keep or sell on your own).

The Final Formalities

If you want to dissolve your corporation, you must first hold a meeting of the board of directors. The board has to officially propose the corporate dissolution, and this proposal has to be formally recorded in the minutes. Then the shareholders must vote on the proposal (yes, even if you're the only shareholder, you have to hold and record an official meeting where the vote is held) and a majority must approve the dissolution. (Some states require a two-thirds majority to dissolve, but if you are the only shareholder this clearly won't apply.)

Once the internal decision has been made to end things, you have to let the state know. State laws vary in regard to corporate dissolution, so contact your attorney to make sure you do everything properly. If everything isn't done exactly right, your corporation could remain in existence, liable for registration fees and report filings. For example, some states require that you file a Statement of Intent to Dissolve before you start winding up the business, then require you to file articles of dissolution once all pending business is resolved. Other states allow you to file the articles of dissolution before the business is wound up and don't require any "intent" statement at all. Still other states require only the articles of dissolution, and those must be filed after all corporate business is wrapped up. In addition, many states demand that you get a tax clearance certificate (meaning your corporation isn't delinquent in paying any state taxes) before they'll process your dissolution.

Once you've gotten all the state paperwork out of the way, you'll have to notify all of your known creditors that you'll be dissolving your corporation. Generally speaking, this notice has to include your intent to dissolve, a mailing address to which the creditor can send a final statement, a specific deadline for any claims (most often 120 days from the date of the notice), and an explicit statement that any claims submitted after the deadline will be forfeited.

Then you'll have to notify all of your unknown claimants of the dissolution. (An unknown claimant is someone the corporation has no current knowledge of, such as a customer who will sue the company three months from now because he bought a defective product.) Because you obviously don't know how to contact these unknown claimants, this notification is typically published in the newspaper. The information to include is pretty much the same as you'd include for your known creditors, but the deadline date is based on statute—usually five years. (Check with an attorney here; you could face legal difficulties if you do this wrong.)

Wrapping Up the Business

In addition to formally dissolving your corporation with the appropriate state offices, there are some basic steps you should follow to wind up the actual business of your company. Although these loose ends should be tied up for any business entity, it's especially important to make sure they're done when your company is incorporated. If any items remain outstanding, you may not be able to officially end the business. For example, if you have outstanding accounts receivable, you can't close your corporate bank account or you won't be able to deposit the payments when you receive them. If you still have a corporate bank account, you may not be able to dissolve your corporation (depending on the laws of the state in which your corporation was formed). In another example, you may have open contracts outstanding that need to be fulfilled. If that's the case, you may not be able to legally end your business without the express consent of the other party to the contract.

Typical business items that need closure before you can officially finalize your corporation include:

- Canceling any outstanding leases (in accordance with all provisions in the lease)
- Fulfilling or canceling open contracts

- Paying all open invoices
- Canceling any unnecessary insurance coverage
- Maintaining insurance policies that must remain in force
- Canceling any outstanding business licenses or permits
- Closing your corporate bank accounts and credit card accounts
- Fulfilling any federal, state, and local requirements for employees
- Filing all final tax returns (including income, sales, excise, and employment taxes)
- Distributing any remaining assets among the shareholders

Ongoing Insurance Needs

Depending on the types of insurance your corporation used, you may need to keep some policies in force for another year or two—even if your corporation will no longer exist. How long you need to maintain the insurance depends a lot on the terms of your contract. For example, if you'll still be covered for past acts even if you cancel today, you may not need to keep the policy going. On the other hand, if your coverage for everything ends if you end the policy, you may want to keep paying premiums in case your corporation gets sued next year for something that happened last year.

Final Tax Returns

In most cases, filing an official final tax return is as simple as checking a box. In some cases, additional forms may be required. Because a corporate liquidation has to result in a gain or loss, some taxes (or a tax refund) may be due. The best way to make sure you file everything necessary correctly and on time is to have your accountant file for you.

One of the additional filings you may need to prepare to dissolve your corporation (at least for federal tax purposes) is IRS Form 966, Corporate Dissolution or Liquidation. This simple one-page form really just serves as a notification to the IRS that you are planning to dissolve your corporation. The form should be filed within thirty days after you've officially recorded your plan to dissolve the corporation.

As for payroll taxes, you have a bit more to do here. (If you're using a payroll service, they'll handle everything for you.) First, you'll have to file

> The best way to make sure you file everything necessary correctly and on time is to have your accountant file for you.

final quarterly or annual employment tax forms (depending on the tax type). But you'll also have to issue final W-2s to your employees—including yourself if the corporation has paid you salary in its final year. Finally, make sure to pay in full all withholding taxes; if you don't, you could be subject to the trust fund penalty.

Exit Plans for S Corporations

Winding up your business is a life-changing event. Whether your business was wildly or mildly successful, you've been there since the beginning. You've poured a major portion of your life and energy into this "baby," and now it's time to cut the cord. As with any financial event in life, the IRS will be involved here. Luckily for you, however, having operated as an S corporation can have a significant tax benefit when you end your business.

Most of the time, liquidating an S corporation is less expensive than liquidating a C corporation. This savings is really another avoidance of double taxation that you would have been subject to had you not gone the S route. Now, any gain you realize when the assets are finally distributed will be subject to taxes only once. (By the way, different rules may apply if your S corporation previously operated as a C corporation.)

The only real tax bill you might face comes into play if the corporation owns assets that have appreciated in value (such as land or buildings). If that's the case, you'll be liable for federal income taxes on the asset appreciation even if the assets are not sold at the time of the dissolution. For example, suppose the corporation bought a piece of land for $40,000 that's now worth $100,000. When you liquidate the company, you take the land to hold for yourself. At that time, you'll have to pay tax on the $60,000 increase in value even though you didn't get any money. This is one of the rare times that you'll have to recognize (meaning pay tax on) a gain when you haven't yet realized it (meaning gotten money).

> **Chapter 19**

Learning about Limited Liability Companies

Part One

Part Two

Part Three

Part Four

Part Five

Part Six

PART FIVE   LIMITED LIABILITY COMPANIES

■ CHAPTER 19 **Learning about Limited Liability Companies** ■ CHAPTER 20 Starting an LLC ■ CHAPTER 21 LLCs and Taxes ■ CHAPTER 22 LLCs Offer Solid Protection for Personal Assets ■ CHAPTER 23 Leaving the Business

A Cross Between Partnerships and Corporations

In 1977, a brand-new business structure was created (by the Wyoming legislature) to accommodate the changing needs of entrepreneurs. No longer would they have to try to squeeze their budding businesses into one of the existing entities that didn't quite fit. Sole proprietorships and partnerships offered pass-through taxation and freedom from paperwork, but offered their owners no freedom from personal liability for business obligations. Corporations gave them strong liability protection, but stuck them with complex tax, legal, and compliance issues.

With more small businesses being created every day, a new entity had to evolve that fulfilled the needs of the entrepreneurs. After Wyoming, it took about five years for the next state to adopt this flexible entity—Florida enacted its original body of statutes for this innovative structure in about 1982. Back in those days, very few professionals were advising entrepreneurs to use this business form because the IRS was still waffling over how to tax it. When the IRS decided that pass-through taxation was an option for this entity, all of the other states eventually jumped on the bandwagon and enacted new business legislation.

The resulting entity is called the *limited liability company*, or LLC for short. This fairly new business structure fits squarely in the middle of the other entity choices, offering the best elements of partnerships and corporations with few of their negative aspects. LLC owners get limited personal liability and complete management flexibility, in addition to more important advantages. At the same time, they don't require the time-consuming administrative

Fifty-One Different Laws

Although it took a while, fifty states and the District of Columbia now have full LLC statutes in place. And while there is a lot of similarity among the state laws, they are by no means uniform. Formation procedures don't differ much from one state to another, and each set of laws includes explicit limited liability protection for all LLC members (as the owners are called). Wherever you do form your LLC, pay close attention to the laws of that state to make sure you do everything properly.

tasks required for corporations, and there aren't a laundry list of restrictions on ownership as there are for S corporations. And when the IRS granted their seal of approval in 1997 by allowing pass-through taxation with the mere checking of a box, LLCs became the business entity *du jour.*

All of the pluses combined with minimal minuses make LLCs the darling of business advisors throughout the United States, and it's easy to see why. LLCs give you the biggest benefit of incorporation (complete personal limited liability for the members) without the burden of a corporation's biggest nuisances: formalities and paperwork. Unlike their much more formal cousins, LLCs don't have to hold any ownership or management meetings. They aren't required to keep written minutes for any meetings that they do decide to hold. In fact, complying with LLC regulations is very simple, and that significantly reduces the risk that owners will make mistakes that can cost them their liability protection. On the tax front, LLCs offer you a choice between pass-through or corporate taxation on the federal level, plus they allow special allocations for profits and losses.

On the other hand, LLC statutes do require more paperwork than either sole proprietorships or general partnerships. LLCs have to file articles of organization to start up, pay original and annual state filing fees, and follow any formalities required by the states they trade in before they can declare themselves open for business. That's a small price to pay for freedom from personal liability for business debts. But, remember, neglecting to meet any state requirements could result in the dissolution of your LLC, meaning that you and all of your fellow members would lose your liability protection.

What's a Member?

LLC owners are called *members*, regardless of their level of participation in the business. Members are quite similar in nature to partners, with the exception of liability issues. For example, members can be either active or passive, participating in the company's management or merely providing money and collecting distributions. Members can be individuals, corporations, partnerships, trusts—basically any person or any entity can be an LLC member. Also like partners, members are responsible for paying their own taxes on the LLC's income, including computing and remitting estimated quarterly tax payments.

In every state except Massachusetts, one person can form an LLC on his own. Massachusetts requires LLCs to have at least two members. So, if you really want to create a one-person LLC there (practically speaking, that is) and you're married, you can simply make your spouse the other member.

Every state allows you to form multimember LLCs. In fact, no state places a legal limit on the total number of members your LLC can have. And though there is no maximum, it's just sensible to keep the total owners to a manageable size, at least where active members are concerned. Practically speaking, you should probably limit the number of active members to five or six, as more than that can get unwieldy when it comes to making the day-to-day business decisions.

If your LLC will be a professional practice, your home state laws could require that all of the members are properly licensed in the same profession. Check with the secretary of state or your professional licensing board to make sure your profession is eligible to form an LLC before you get started.

Should Your Business Be an LLC?

Although the LLC is currently the most popular choice for small business structure, it doesn't necessarily work for every business. In fact, some types of businesses are not even allowed to choose the LLC for their entity (according to the laws in some states). Banking and insurance, for example, are specifically barred from operating as LLCs in most states.

In addition, some professional practices may also be barred, either by state law or by the state's board of professional standards. Typically, when professionals want to form an LLC, all of the founding members have to be fully (and currently) licensed professionals in the same field. The states that allow professionals (like doctors, lawyers, and accountants) to form LLCs usually require each member to get a letter of good standing from the appropriate state licensing board and include the letters in the entity's formation documents. Some states put these professional LLCs in a separate category with special naming requirements (which you'll learn about in the next chapter) and additional rules (like requiring each member to have a minimum amount of malpractice insurance). Finally, some states (including California) may not allow professionals to form LLCs at all.

Factors to Consider

If you are allowed to form your business as an LLC, here are some things that could swing the vote in favor of this popular entity:

- Your business will have co-owners.
- You expect the business initially to incur losses.
- You want pass-through taxation.
- You'd like profits or losses to be allocated differently than ownership percentages.
- The business has some inherent liability risk.
- The business will have nonowner employees.
- You want to limit your personal liability.
- More than one of the owners wants to actively participate in the company's management.

In addition to the business factors listed above, your personal financial situation should be considered when you're choosing your business entity. As you will learn in greater detail in Chapter 22, LLCs almost always provide the best protection for the business from your personal creditors. So if your personal financial situation is a bit murky right now, or if you've incurred a lot of personal debt to get your business up and running, forming your company as an LLC will go a long way toward protecting it from your creditors.

Finally, if you plan for your company to be a family business, structuring it as an LLC may be the best choice. In fact, the family LLC is quickly overtaking the family limited partnership as the best way to pass the family business down to the next generation without running into a brick wall of gift and estate taxes. That's because with a family limited partnership, someone still has to act as the general partner, subject to full personal financial responsibility for all of the debts of the partnership. But with an LLC, no one will be stuck with unlimited liability regardless of the fate of the company. And because of

Why Family LLCs Make a Lot of Sense

Perhaps the best way to transfer ownership of your company without giving up any control is with a family LLC. Because LLCs can have different types of ownership interests (such as nonvoting, nonmanager interests), children can be members while parents retain complete discretion over the decisions that impact the family business.

And since there are no restrictions on what type of entity can be an LLC member (in contrast to the very strict ownership regulations for S corporations), you can actually hold your children's shares of the company in an irrevocable trust—with you and your spouse as the trustees. (This setup definitely requires the assistance of a competent attorney.)

the liability shield for the company from its owners' personal debts, you won't ever have to worry about your company being hit by claims from one of your children's creditors.

Sometimes an LLC Is Not the Best Choice

In some cases, even when your business is legally permitted to be formed as an LLC, it may not make practical sense. For example, if your business isn't prone to high creditor bills or large liability claims you may not need significant liability protection from your business structure—especially when that protection will cost your new (and possibly struggling) company money and time to maintain. If you will be the only business owner and you need every penny you can keep your hands on, it may be better for you to start out as a simple sole proprietorship; you can always convert to an LLC once business picks up. (Due to the joint liability inherent in general partnerships, it's almost always better to form an LLC regardless of the liability quotient of the business itself.)

When money is a big issue for your fledgling company, taxes and fees can make the LLC form very unattractive, at least in some states. Every state charges some level of fee to get your LLC up and running—but a few states charge very high fees, like California. As for ongoing fees, many states charge about $50 a year to keep your LLC in existence, but others charge upward of $300 annually. Plus, in some states LLCs have to pay their own income taxes on top of any personal taxes you have to pay, making them a less desirable entity choice when money is a big factor (which it is for the vast majority of small businesses).

Untested Statutes Add Risk to the LLC

The LLC is a relatively new business structure. That means it hasn't been tested by the courts as much as the other entities, and there are not a lot of case law precedents for judges to follow. Precedent, meaning prior decision, is one of the most important aspects of case law. Generally speaking, judges don't want to make new law with their own interpretations of state statutes; when they do, they run a greater risk of being overturned on appeal. They prefer instead to follow existing opinions that have already held up under the scrutiny of the appeals courts. The other structures have literally centuries of case law that spell out exactly how they have to conduct business. In contrast, LLCs have been around for less than thirty years, and have very little legal precedents for judges to stand on. That means they'll be forced to make new decisions, and those can be difficult to predict.

What does that mean for you? It means that there is no guarantee that your limited liability protection will hold up if a creditor tries to sue you for business debts. While there is also no such guarantee with corporations either, there is a vast body of case law there that outlines specific and definite situations where the corporate entity will be held invalid. In plain English—with a corporation you know for sure what you're getting into; with an LLC, there are still a lot of questions surrounding the lengths to which your liability protection goes.

That's not to say the protection doesn't really exist—it does. But what legal holes can be poked in it are yet to be seen. State statutes and individual operating agreements do cover an awful lot of legal ground, but in real life actual events may not fit perfectly into the existing legal framework. Without numerous reliable legal precedents, no one is really sure which way judges will rule when issues do come to court. For example, LLC members may be more susceptible to decisions piercing the limited liability veil than corporate shareholders, particularly with single-member LLCs.

Many small business advisors and attorneys think that the state courts are likely to go along with corporate precedents when they make decisions regarding LLCs. Should that be the case, you'll probably be pretty safe from veil piercing as long as you follow any state formalities and operate your business as a truly separate entity (for more information about preserving your limited liability protection, see Chapter 22).

> There is no guarantee that your limited liability protection will hold up if a creditor tries to sue you for business debts.

Many Different Sets of Laws

As you learned previously, LLCs are governed by state law. Though those fifty-one sets of laws have a lot of similarities, it's the little differences that can cause difficulties for small business owners. To make sure you understand the laws for LLCs in your state (and any state in which your company will be operating), read them. That's right, read them. The statutes are some of the easiest—and shortest—to read, and you can easily find them on the Internet or in whichever state office handles LLCs (usually the secretary of state). If the thought of reading legal jargon makes you queasy, pay an experienced small business lawyer a few hundred dollars to tell you what they say.

Now that every state has a body of LLC statutes in place, there are some attempts to homogenize them. The most well-known "model" law is called the Uniform Limited Liability Company Act (ULLCA), but this body of statutes has not been adopted by all of the states. The ULLCA is still in the development stages (albeit the final ones), but conventional wisdom holds that most states won't adopt these laws in full. Rather, they'll cut and paste parts they like into their existing bodies of statutes. That will add at least a little more commonality to the various state regulations.

Differences in States' Laws Can Impact Your LLC

There are three main reasons why differences in state laws can matter to your LLC. First, state fee and tax treatment varies, and that can impact both your business and personal finances. Second, as with a corporation, you can form your LLC in any state you want to minimize fee and tax implications and ongoing maintenance requirements. Finally, if your company will be operating in more than one state, it will have to follow more than one set of rules.

When it comes to fees, all states charge them when you create your LLC. Most states make this pretty painless, in the $150 or less range. A few states, like Illinois and Massachusetts, actually charge pretty high fees to form your company as an LLC ($400 in Illinois, $500 in Massachusetts). And that's just the formation fee—many states also impose an annual filing fee to keep your LLC in business (the name of this fee varies also, from renewal fee to franchise tax).

The variations in state laws may also have a negative tax effect: Some states make LLCs pay income taxes at the entity level regardless of their federal tax treatment. Luckily, this state tax treatment is limited to a very few. But those that do impose an LLC income tax charge that in addition to the tax the owners pay. In California, for example, LLCs that make more than $250,000 a year have to pay a minimum $900 tax bill. And Texas will tax your LLC as if it were a regular corporation even if it's taxed as a pass-through entity for federal tax purposes.

The next factor to look at is multistate operations. This will impact your LLC whether you form it in one and operate in another, or you have business dealings in several states.

When your LLC transacts business in more than one state, it may not always be clear which set of state statutes will take precedence if there's ever a dispute. Depending on the particular issue, your case could be heard in the LLC's state of formation or in the state in which the business was transacted. If your business will be operating in multiple states, you (and your attorney) should look carefully into the applicable laws of all of those states to figure out which will be the controlling statutes.

One thing is certain, though—if your LLC spans more than one state, you will be paying more than one set of fees. In addition to your home state fees (the state in which you've formed your LLC), you will have to register your company as a foreign LLC in all the other states in which you operate. Each of those will have its own list of charges, some of which will be higher than if your LLC was originally formed there. To register as a foreign LLC, you'll have to qualify to conduct business in the state, basically by applying for a Certificate of Authority.

When Securities Law May Apply

Most of the time, LLCs are pretty small enterprises—at least when it comes to membership. The typical LLC has somewhere between one and five members, all of them active in the business. Less common are LLCs with more

Home State Laws Apply . . . Usually

In most cases, the laws of the state of formation will rule (at least according to current states' statutes), but some exceptions do apply. For example, Montana subjects the members of LLCs operating there to Montana's laws pertaining to personal liability, regardless of the state of formation. Remember, however, that even though most states' laws say that when conflicts arise with foreign LLCs, the companies' home state laws will apply, there haven't been many cases testing this.

than five members, many of whom act like limited partners. For companies set up like this, securities law may actually come into play.

Right now, whether LLC interests will be considered securities is addressed on a case-by-case basis. The courts will look at how much members control the LLC versus the extent to which members are only passive investors. If the LLC is judged to have many (and "many" is a matter of judgment, not math) passive investors, membership interests might be treated as securities. If that happens, the LLC will be subject to both state and federal securities laws, which can be cumbersome to understand and follow.

Your LLC will probably not fall into this category (unless you have a lot of "silent" members). Just in case, though, there are some simple provisions you can put in your operating agreement to help make sure your LLC's interests don't get recategorized as securities:

- Require members to carry out all regular management functions.
- Don't allow members to delegate their management duties to anyone else.
- Limit membership to people who are familiar with the business and will work regularly for the LLC.
- Keep voting rights for members of manager-managed LLCs, especially the right to fire managers.

> **Chapter 20**

Starting an LLC

Part One

Part Two

Part Three

Part Four

Part Five

Part Six

Naming Your LLC

You'll want the
name of your
company to
clearly identify it
and what it does.

As with any business, an LLC's name is the first thing people will know about
it. You'll want the name of your company to clearly identify it and what it
does, to be easy to remember and spell. The state, however, requires that one
part of the name be as clear as glass—and that's the part that identifies it as a
liability-limiting entity.

The name of an LLC has to clearly identify it as such, and that holds true
in every state. Either you have to actually use the words "Limited Liability
Company" or "Limited Company" in the name, or one of the state's allowed
abbreviations. The permissible abbreviations are a little different from state to
state, but they generally fall along the lines of "LLC," "LC," and "Ltd." The permitted abbreviations used for professional LLCs are close to their counterparts. For these types of companies, the name must typically include either
"PLLC" or "Professional Limited Liability Company." By using one of these
naming conventions, you'll be explicitly informing creditors that the structure
used for your business limits the liability of the owners. This matters to creditors because it lets them know right up front that if the company can't pay its
bills, its owners won't have to.

In addition to the rules regarding what must be included in the name,
there are also some rules about names and words you can't use. First off, as
with any other type of entity, the name can't be the same as that of another
LLC on file in that state. So before you order engraved letterhead, do a name
search to make sure yours is an original. Second, the name you choose
absolutely cannot include terms that are barred for LLCs by state law, such as
"Corporation" or "Inc."

If your LLC will be doing business in more than one state, the naming
requirements of each must be met. Be aware, though, that if the LLC doesn't
use its exact name in all of its business dealings, it could lose its status. That
unpleasant fate would leave all of the members (even inactive ones) exposed
to the same total personal liability as general partners. So if your home state
requires periods among the initials, use them. Don't lose your precious liability protection over a couple of silly little dots.

Articles of Organization

Although it takes more work than a sole proprietorship, creating an LLC is easy enough that you could do it by yourself. (If you're unsure about any points of law, or if you just want to be 100 percent sure no mistakes are made, talk to an attorney before you create your LLC.) Once you've made the key decisions—what your business will be, its name, and that you want to structure it as an LLC—you'll be ready to form the entity. Each state has a set of steps to follow, but to actually create the LLC you'll have to file articles of organization in your business's home state and pay the listed filing fee (somewhere from $40 to $900). Be aware—some states call the articles of organization by a different name. Some (including Delaware and New Jersey) call them "certificates of formation," and Massachusetts and Pennsylvania call them "certificates of organization."

Every state has its own requirements for the information that must be included in the LLC's articles. These documents are pretty short and easy to fill out. Most states even have fill-in-the-blank forms available on their Web sites to make it even easier to do it yourself. In fact, it shouldn't take you more than about twenty minutes to create your own LLC. To help the do-it-yourself crowd, most states now have LLC formation offices staffed with personnel whose only job is to help entrepreneurs form their companies.

Though the exact wording and content does vary by state, you'll almost certainly have to provide the following information:

- The LLC's name and address
- The type of business (or business purpose)
- The names and addresses of all founding members
- The name of the registered agent and address of the registered office

In addition to the basics, some states require even more, like information about the LLC's management and the expected duration of the LLC (meaning how long you expect it to be in existence).

Once you've filed your articles of organization, sit back and wait for the state to accept them. Depending on the state, this can take anywhere from three business days to three weeks. Almost all states do offer expedited service, meaning twenty-four or forty-eight hour turnaround time, for an extra fee. How will you know when your LLC has been approved? You'll get a copy of your articles of organization in the mail, stamped by the state as accepted. This official stamp will include the effective date of your LLC (that means the date it officially started).

The Operating Agreement

The articles of organization may form your LLC, but the operating agreement truly governs the company's scope, spells out the members' rights and responsibilities, and helps protect your limited liability status. This legal document lets you shape your financial and organizational relationships with both your LLC and your co-owners. An operating agreement is not legally required in every state—in many, you can form and run your LLC without one—but it's a good idea to have one in place anyway, even if you are the sole owner of the company. If you do have co-owners, though, such an agreement is particularly important. Because when tricky issues come up—and they almost certainly will—the solution provided by state law may not be the answer you wanted to hear.

Why a Formal Agreement Is Important

Every state provides some statutory guidance in very basic language about the legal relationships and obligations of LLC members. If you don't have your own operating agreement, the state's rules will apply any time conflicts arise. The statutes deal with things like distributions, management, profit and loss allocation, and dissolutions—but not necessarily in a way that you and your co-owners will like. For example, when it comes to allocation of profits and losses, the default rule may be that they are dished out equally regardless of ownership percentage—hardly fair if you're the member who put up the most cash to get things going.

To make sure that the LLC is run how you want it to be, an operating agreement should be drafted, preferably by a competent business attorney. This way you can custom-tailor the rights, responsibilities, and obligations of all the members, and set up clearly defined procedures to follow when conflicts do arise. Another important point is to make sure that your operating agreement is in line with your articles of organization. If there's any disagreement between the two documents, the articles will rule and that section of your operating agreement will be considered invalid by the courts.

Things to Put in Your LLC's Operating Agreement

The key point of this agreement is protection. Protection for you and your co-owners from each other when tempers flare, protection for all members when an outsider threatens your personal limited liability, and protection for your LLC from members' creditors. You want this protection to be thorough and strong, explicit and clear. While there's no prescription for the perfect document, and there's no limit as to what you can include, there are certain basics that belong in your LLC operating agreement.

At a minimum, an LLC operating agreement should include things like:

- Each member's percentage interest in the business
- Definitions of different types of membership interests
- Responsibilities of the members
- How the company will be managed
- Members' voting rights, plus how and when votes will be taken
- Allocation of profits and losses
- Rules governing members' capital accounts and distributions
- Procedures for withdrawal of members from the LLC
- Transfer of ownership interests by members (a.k.a. buy-sell provisions)
- Events that will cause dissolution

Even with all the things it can do, there's one thing your operating agreement can't do. The agreement will never supersede mandatory provisions dictated by your LLC's home state, like those put in place to protect creditors. Other than that,

The Registered Agent and Office

In order to be eligible to conduct business within any state, an LLC must have a legal presence there. Every state in which your LLC has transactions requires a physical address (a post office box won't do) and an actual person that the public can deal with. So your LLC must have a local registered office (not necessarily the company's principal place of business in the state) where its local registered agent can receive service of process and other official documents. If you don't have someone who can act as your company's registered agent, you can hire one—for a fee, of course.

your LLC operating agreement can be customized to meet the needs of you and your co-members.

Capital Contributions and Distributions

You can acquire a membership interest in an LLC with money, property, services, or a legally binding obligation to contribute any of the three at some time in the future. When cash is the contributed capital, it should be deposited into the LLC's bank account right away. If property is contributed, make sure that you retitle the property in the name of the LLC as soon as possible. Once you've contributed capital to the LLC, you can't take it back unless you completely withdraw from the LLC, sell all or part of your membership interest, or the LLC itself is terminated.

The LLC's operating agreement will spell out each member's contribution, including the amount he's putting in, the form of the contribution (such as money or services), and the date by which the contribution must be made. In the case where a member trades services for his part of the LLC, a work schedule or timetable would be included in the document.

In return for their contributions, each member receives a distributive share of the LLC's income. Usually each member's share is based on his percentage interest in the business (for example, if you contributed 25 percent of the capital, you would be entitled to a 25 percent distributive share). But if circumstances call for a different arrangement, you and your fellow members may divide up profits and losses however you want, as long as you follow all

An Operating Agreement for One

A single-member LLC should also have a written operating agreement in place, whether or not it's a legal requirement in the company's home state, even though it may seem like overkill to have an agreement with yourself. But these one-owner companies run the risk of being treated as sole proprietorships by the courts, and that means with absolutely no liability protection for their owners. The formality of a written operating agreement can help make sure that the LLC is treated as a separate entity from its owner.

of the IRS guidelines regarding special allocations. (For more information, see Chapter 21.) Plus, when the ownership interests will be proportionally different than the members' capital contributions, the allocation has to be spelled out in the operating agreement (otherwise the default state rules will apply, and they definitely won't mirror the intent of your special allocation).

Details about Distributions

Now that everyone's contributions have been made, each member is entitled to his distributive share of the LLC's net income. But whether you'll actually get a distribution is entirely another story. Specific steps for exactly how and when funds will be distributed should be clearly written in the LLC's operating agreement. Although you can put in as much about distributions as you want, there are at least four items you should make sure to include.

First, you should decide what portion, if any, of each member's distributive share has to be paid out to the members each year. For example, if there are four equal owners of the LLC and each has a total distributive share of $2,500 for the year, what percentage of that $2,500 absolutely must be paid to each member? Remember, just because you have profits of $10,000 doesn't mean that your LLC will actually have $10,000 in cash. Plus, the company may need to retain a portion of the profits to pay bills, finance an expansion, or cover minimum bank account requirements. On the other hand, no member wants to slave away all year, watch their company profit, and go home with empty pockets. Therefore, you should decide on a reasonable percentage that each member will definitely be paid each year—you can always add to that when circumstances allow.

The second issue comes right on the heels of the first. Here the question is whether the LLC will be required to distribute to each member at least enough to cover his income tax liability on his full distributive share. LLC members must pay tax on their percentage of profits, whether any actual cash is paid out, just like partners and S corporation shareholders. So you may want to include a provision in your operating agreement that gives each member the right to receive enough money in distributions to cover his tax bill, regardless of other cash needs of the LLC.

The third issue is timing. You and your fellow members must decide when distributions of profits will be paid out. During your first few years in business, you may want to take the wait-and-see approach, and make one big distribution at year-end. Or, depending on the cash flow needs of the members and the LLC, you may decide to make periodic distributions throughout the year. Whichever you choose to do, set specific dates for member distributions so you can plan for the momentary cash depletion.

Finally, you'll want to spell out whether members can draw from business profits whenever they choose, sort of like advances on their eventual promised distributions. This may sound like a good idea from a personal standpoint, but it may not be beneficial from a business standpoint. The draw-as-you-go plan has quite a few drawbacks for your company. For example, a member may withdraw cash when the LLC needs that same money to pay its bills. Or if members make out checks to their personal creditors instead of to themselves, that could eventually help the LLC's creditors pierce the veil (see Chapter 22 for more information). Also, if a member takes his draws willy-nilly based on projected profits that don't materialize, the other members would be hard-pressed to get that member to pay back his excess distributions.

Problem Distributions

As with any business, there are some times when distributions shouldn't be made, or when making them triggers a taxable event. So when you and your fellow members decide to make distributions, make sure you don't inadvertently create one of the following problems.

Problem number one: *taxable distributions*. When a member receives a cash distribution in excess of his basis in the LLC, the excess portion is subject to personal income taxes. There are, however, two simple solutions to this problem. First, the member in question could delay receipt of his distribution until he builds up his basis. Second, the member could take a noncash distribution, like a computer or a vehicle (if allowed in the operating agreement or by state law). The member would only incur taxes when he sold the property for a profit.

Problem number two: *wrongful distributions*. Any distributions to members when the LLC is already insolvent or that cause the LLC to become insolvent are considered wrongful by law. If any third parties suffer damages because of these wrongful distributions, the LLC will be held liable for them and can be forced by the creditors to get the distributions back. As a member, you won't be held directly liable to those creditors, but you will be legally liable to the LLC to the extent of your distribution (unless you were unaware that the distribution was wrongful and your state law provides protection in that case). The solution: If you know or suspect that your LLC is having financial trouble, don't take any distributions.

Defining Voting Rights

Typically, the everyday business decisions will be made by the LLC's management team. However, sometimes issues will come up that require a member vote. These are usually pretty big issues that can alter the current path of the company. Such issues, like whether to expand or to begin offering health insurance to employees, are much too important to be decided without hearing from all of the members.

There are two ways in which you and your co-members can allocate votes—one is based on ownership percentage, the other is per capita. Percentage relates to each member's proportional ownership interest in the business (for example, if you own 30 percent of the LLC, you get 30 percent of the vote). Per capita means one vote per member, regardless of relative ownership (for example, if you own 60 percent, Joe owns 30 percent, and Al owns 10 percent, you'd still each get only one vote). Using the percentage method is the norm, since members with more capital invested want a greater say than those with less to lose.

Once you've decided whether to go percentage or per capita, you also have to decide how many votes it takes to decide an issue. Some votes (like the health insurance issue) may require a simple majority to pass, others (like whether to expand) may require the unanimous consent of all members. But no matter which voting methods you choose, spell them out in your operating agreement. If you don't, default state law will apply.

> Members with more capital invested want a greater say than those with less to lose.

Choosing a Management Structure

Small LLCs (with two or three members) are normally managed by all of their members, just like general partnerships. And because the vast majority of LLCs fall into this category, the default presumption in most states is that all members will take part in the management of their company. These LLCs are called "member-managed."

The key issue for member-managed LLCs is the definition of voting rights. Although state statutes do include language about voting, whatever the founding members have specified in the operating agreement usually will take precedence. For that reason, it's very important that your operating agreement spell out which issues require a vote, how many votes are needed to decide an issue and whether votes will be counted by percentage or per capita.

Large LLCs (meaning those with more than three members) on the other hand, usually pick a small management team to run the day-to-day operations. These companies have a lot of flexibility in how they define management authority in their operating agreements—pretty much whatever the founding members want. The management team can be made up of a small group of members, or by nonmember employees. LLCs run in this fashion are awkwardly called "manager-managed," even if some (or all) of the managers are also members.

How Manager-Management Works

Although a manager-managed LLC could have some member managers, this section will focus on those companies managed solely by nonmembers. When an LLC is managed by outsiders, the members don't have much to do in regard to daily operations. For example, the members wouldn't be the ones to hire or fire employees (other than the managers themselves), pick suppliers, or place orders. So what decisions would the members take part in? Typically, the members would decide (by vote) things like hiring and firing the managers and other major issues.

If your LLC will be manager-managed, your operating agreement should spell out the ability of members to hire, fire, and authorize the actions of managers. If there are some decisions that you and your co-members specifically want the authority to make, those should be spelled out in the agreement as well. In addition to a mention in your operating agreement, some states will require your articles of organization to include a statement that the company will be managed by managers instead of by members.

> When an LLC is managed by outsiders, the members don't have much to do in regard to daily operations.

Legally Binding the LLC

There are two types of legal authority that exist in connection with binding contracts and agreements: actual and apparent. Actual authority means powers expressly granted in the LLC's operating agreement. This would explicitly list the things that a manager or a member has the authority to do in the LLC's name, and whether the member or manager can legally bind the LLC. Apparent authority refers to the powers a member or manager appears to have to outsiders who aren't privy to the operating agreement. Regardless of the actual authority, most states' statutes will consider the LLC to be legally bound to an agreement if the member or manager who made it has the apparent authority to act on behalf of the company. What does that mean? No matter what it says in your agreement, if a member acting on his own enters into a contract with someone who reasonably thought the member had authority, the contract will stand.

Under most state laws, apparent authority extends to every member of a member-managed LLC and every manager of a manager-managed LLC. Even if there are restrictions on actual authority included in the operating agreement, those are typically considered irrelevant unless you can show that the third party knew about (or should have known about) the restriction. The exception to the authority assumption extends to nonmanager members of a manager-managed LLC—they aren't considered to have the authority to bind the company to an agreement.

LLC Accounting Mirrors Partnership Accounting

Ninety-nine percent of LLCs will have books and taxes that look just like those of general partnerships. (The other one percent is made up of those LLCs that have chosen to be treated as corporations for tax purposes, as explained in the next chapter.) Therefore, the financial statements of an LLC copy those of partnerships, right down to the equity section of the balance sheet.

Just like in a partnership, a member's equity has three components: his capital, his distributions (or draws), and his share of the current net income (or loss). All of his contributions to the LLC count as capital, and all profits left in the company bank account will increase his capital, too. All distributions decrease his capital, whether they take the form of cash or property.

When a member contributes capital in exchange for an ownership interest in the LLC, he doesn't report any gain or loss on his personal income taxes—even when his contribution includes appreciated assets. All subsequent contributions are also free of tax consequences, and they simply increase his basis in the LLC. And just like putting money in, transferring money out of the business won't usually trigger a taxable event, unless a cash distribution exceeds a member's basis. It's important to keep on top of the balance of each member's capital account, promptly adjusting each for any contributions or distributions, especially since each member's current basis can make a difference at tax time.

Also like partnerships, LLCs may use cash basis accounting. However, two exceptions apply:

1. An LLC with annual gross receipts over $5 million for the past three tax years has a C corporation for a member.
2. A multimember LLC is considered to be a tax shelter under the Internal Revenue Code.

Chances are neither of these exceptions will apply to your LLC. If you're not sure whether your LLC can use cash basis accounting, check with your CPA.

Members and Basis

Each member has an ownership stake in the LLC. For accounting purposes, that stake is called *capital*. For tax purposes, that stake is called *basis*. It's crucial that each member know what his total basis is at all times, especially if the operating agreement allows members to take discretionary distributions whenever they choose. It's most important, though, to know the balance at tax time. That's because the value of a member's basis for tax purposes directly affects how the LLC income will be allocated to him, and the way that income will be taxed.

Figuring out the basis for LLC members is the same as doing that for a partner in a partnership. To start with, a member's original basis is equal to the amount of money plus the adjusted basis of any property he contributed to the company in order to acquire his membership interest. Along with that, his basis gets increased by assuming company liabilities and decreased by

> It's important to keep on top of the balance of each member's capital account, promptly adjusting each for any contributions or distributions.

any liabilities assumed by the LLC on his behalf (such as if he contributed a warehouse that was still subject to a mortgage).

Once the company gets rolling, a member's basis will be increased by his distributive share of LLC income and by any additional contributions he makes (whether they're in the form of cash or property). His basis will be decreased by his distributive share of losses, all of the distributions he takes, and certain tax-related items (these are better left to the CPAs).

How Debt Affects Your Basis

When the debts of an LLC change, so does your basis—just as if you'd contributed more cash to the business. On the other hand, when LLC liabilities decrease, so will your basis, just as if you got a cash distribution. This change in your basis is very important—especially at tax time. Your basis determines the amount of LLC loss you can deduct against your other income at year-end. Since your basis can increase without you actually adding any cash to the business, you can take a bigger loss deduction—which also serves to conserve your precious cash. This tax treasure is most important in the early years of your business, when larger tax losses are normally suffered and when cash flow is typically at its lowest point.

The flip side of this coin shows up when the LLC assumes some of your debt. Any time an LLC takes over an individual member's debt (as often happens when a member contributes property subject to liability, like a vehicle with some payments remaining), his basis gets reduced by the amount of the liability that's taken on by the other members. The other members then receive increases in their basis. And just like when the LLC takes on its own debt, these increases and decreases to basis are treated like contributions and distributions of money.

Debt and Basis: Examples with Numbers

First, let's look at how increasing your company's debt can help you at tax time. Suppose you and your partner Joan each put up $5,000 cash to start Tea Time, a catering service formed as an LLC. To buy your van, coolers, and other equipment, your LLC borrows $10,000 from the bank.

Since you and Joan each own equal interests in the business, you each get $5,000 added to your basis in the LLC. If the business suffers a big loss in that first year (as many new catering companies do), you can each deduct up to $10,000 of that loss on your personal tax returns.

Now we'll see how your basis is affected when the LLC takes on some of your debt. For this example, we'll suppose that you and Joan are still both equal owners of Tea Time. But now, instead of getting a bank loan, the LLC gets a van that you've contributed. The van has an adjusted basis of $16,000 (the tax term meaning how much you paid for it in the first place less any depreciation you took), and you still owe $6,000 on it.

When you contribute the van, your basis will increase by $13,000: the $16,000 minus the $6,000 of debt assumed by the LLC plus your $3,000 share of the increase of LLC debt. Joan's basis will go up by $3,000, which represents her share of the increase in the LLC's debt.

Understanding At-Risk Rules

You know that you can deduct LLC losses up to the amount of your basis, and that your basis increases as the LLC's debt does. But you can't deduct losses that are greater than the amount you have at risk in the LLC—meaning more than you could truly lose. That means you can't deduct losses equal to increases in your basis from debt for which you won't have any personal liability. And that describes the at-risk rules in a nutshell.

Unless you have personally guaranteed an LLC debt, your at-risk basis will increase only if the liability is *qualified nonrecourse financing*. That means any loan from a qualified lender that's taken on to hold real property, and for which no individual is personally liable. Why is this the case? Because the LLC entity form protects its owners from personal liability for company debt, you aren't at risk for any regular business debts. And the IRS says, if you're not at risk, you can't get a bigger deduction.

> Because the LLC entity form protects its owners from personal liability for company debt, you aren't at risk for any regular business debts.

Maintaining Your LLC

You formed your LLC to protect your personal assets from business creditors. So don't lose that protection by failing to follow the simple steps that will ensure its survival. In addition to the normal start-up steps (like retitling contributed assets in the name of the LLC, getting federal and state EINs, and opening separate company bank accounts), there are some additional protective steps you can take, plus a few requirements you need to fulfill every year to preserve your LLC.

Most states require LLCs to have certain records on hand, typically at its main office. These records normally include the articles of organization, the operating agreement (if you have one), the company's tax returns, and a roster of all members and managers. You must also be sure to file complete and timely tax returns, plus any other state filings needed to keep your LLC in existence (these vary by state, so check with the appropriate state office if you're not sure what you need to do).

The biggest threat to your LLC is neglecting to treat it as a stand-alone entity. Following formalities—even those not strictly required—is the best way to stave off that threat. To that end, you can issue formal membership certificates (similar to stock certificates) to each member. You should keep a record book detailing each member's capital account and showing any membership transfers. And, as an extra shield, you can keep minutes for your membership meetings as a permanent and official record of any major decisions made by the members.

> **Chapter 21**

LLCs and Taxes

Part One

Part Two

Part Three

Part Four

Part Five

Part Six

PART FIVE   LIMITED LIABILITY COMPANIES

■ CHAPTER 19 Learning about Limited Liability Companies ■ CHAPTER 20 Starting an LLC ■ CHAPTER 21 **LLCs and Taxes** ■ CHAPTER 22 LLCs Offer Solid Protection for Personal Assets ■ CHAPTER 23 Leaving the Business

LLCs Are Default Pass-Through Entities

LLCs are nothing if not flexible. You can have an operating agreement, or not. You can choose your management scheme, using members or not. And there's even a choice for how your LLC will be taxed. The default option for LLCs is pass-through taxation, the other is being taxed like a corporation. Most LLC members choose to go the pass-through route, but there are circumstances (as you'll see below) that make corporate taxation a better choice.

Unless you explicitly state otherwise, you and your co-members will enjoy favorable pass-through tax treatment where the LLC itself is not subject to taxation on its own income. Your single-member LLC looks just like a sole proprietorship to the IRS, with all of the business profits or losses reported on Schedule C of your personal tax return. If your LLC has more than one owner, it will be automatically treated as a partnership by the IRS. Because the overwhelming majority of LLCs choose pass-through taxation, the rest of this chapter will focus on LLCs taxed as a partnership, unless otherwise noted.

When Corporate Taxation Makes More Sense

Most of the time, new business owners will benefit from pass-through taxation, especially in the early years when losses are to be expected. However, for highly profitable businesses—especially those that will need to hold on to all or most of their profits—choosing to have your LLC taxed as a corporation may provide better tax situations for you and your fellow members.

Thanks to IRS "check-the-box" regulations that were put in place in 1997, the choice is yours. Should you opt for corporate taxation, your LLC will pay taxes on its own income. You and your company will get all the benefits and drawbacks of corporate taxation. The pluses include things like tax-free fringe benefits, the minuses include double taxation. (For more detailed information about corporate taxation, see Chapter 16.)

There is, however, one pretty big drawback to this decision: When an LLC opts for corporate taxation, it can't switch back to pass-through taxation for at least five years. On top of that, if it does make the switch back, there could be tax consequences for both the LLC and its members. Because of the potentially big cost to change your mind after the fact, seek professional advice before you make this election.

State Taxes and Your LLC

Most of the time, the states follow the federal tax treatment of LLCs. So unless you've made the election to have your LLC treated as a corporation, your business will file an informational return and each individual member will pay tax on his personal return (for single-member LLCs, the entity is completely disregarded). The two exceptions are Texas, which treats every LLC as a corporation, and Arkansas, which treats every multimember LLC as a partnership.

Some states make LLCs pay income and other taxes on top of those its owners pay even when the company is treated like a partnership for tax purposes. These states include California and Delaware. Plus, some states charge annual taxes for LLCs in the form of a franchise tax or renewal fee. These fees run the gamut from $10 (the LLC renewal fee in Rhode Island) to $500 (Massachusetts' LLC renewal fee) per year; and the annual franchise tax charged on LLCs by California starts at $800.

If your LLC does not make every single required tax payment, some of the states you do business in (which could include your home state) will bar it from filing any governmental forms. If you can't file any state forms, that could lead to an administrative dissolution of your LLC. When that happens, your business will be treated as a general partnership (or sole proprietorship, if you're the only member). So file your forms, pay your taxes and fees, and do it all on time.

Tax Treatment Has Nothing to Do with Liability

Choosing to have your LLC taxed as a corporation won't provide you with additional liability protection when the chips are down. Neither will opting for pass-through taxation weaken your personal liability shield. The truth is that tax treatment has absolutely nothing to do with liability—they are completely separate issues. You and your LLC both get the full benefits of the limited liability protection inherent in the business structure. And for that, taxation is completely irrelevant. The only possible link comes when your LLC neglects to file tax returns or to pay any taxes due—that can result in loss of LLC status and the liability shield that comes along with it.

Tax Issues for Members

As with any type of pass-through entity, LLC members have to pay income taxes on the company income. How they report and pay that tax depends on a couple of things. First, the number of members is a factor. A one-member company acts like a sole proprietorship, a multimember LLC acts like a partnership. The second factor is member participation level, and that affects both where on his tax return the income gets reported and what type of tax it's subject to.

With a multimember LLC, all company income is taxable to the members in their respective proportions regardless of whether that income gets distributed. That means members have to pay taxes on their distributive shares of business income even if they don't actually get any money. This unpleasant phenomenon, referred to as *phantom income*, is a big disadvantage of pass-through taxation. To deal with this unhappy situation, many LLCs have provisions in their operating agreements that provide a mandatory cash distribution to members so they can pay the income taxes on their allocated profits.

Members and Self-Employment Taxes

LLC members are never considered to be company employees by the IRS; they are treated as self-employed. But not all members are created equal. All members who are actively involved in the business get stuck paying self-employment taxes. But members who aren't at all active in the business may be able to avoid paying self-employment taxes on their shares of the LLC's income.

Since with most small LLCs every member takes an active role in running the company, most LLC members do have to deal with self-employment taxes. How much self-employment income they have to declare depends on their distributive shares of the LLC's net income from business activities.

Self-employment taxes are combined Social Security and Medicare (called FICA when referring to both at once), which are often paid through payroll taxes. When you're an employee, both you and your employer each pay half of the tax. As an LLC member, you'll count as both employer and employee, making you responsible for both parts of the tax. That adds up to 15.3 percent on the first $87,900 of your share of income (for 2004), and an additional 2.9 percent on everything greater than that. You'll report your self-employment taxes on IRS Schedule SE each year along with your income tax return.

Members Must Pay Estimated Taxes

LLC members don't have taxes withheld on their share of business profits. To make sure they pay their fair share of taxes throughout the year, they instead have to make quarterly payments into the system on their own behalf. So you'll have to set aside money to fulfill your tax obligation, and make payments based on the amount of income you expect your LLC to have for the year. If you expect the LLC to suffer a loss for the year, no estimated tax payments are necessary.

Determining your estimated tax payments is pretty easy, once you've accurately projected the LLC's bottom line for the year. Once you come up with a reasonable net income, you'll have to figure out your share of the profits. Then you'll calculate the self-employment taxes that would be due (that's the easy part) by multiplying by 15.3 percent. (If your portion of the profits is really big, multiply the amount over $87,900 by 2.9 percent.) The more tricky part is figuring out your income tax bill. That requires you to look at all of your income for the year (and your spouse's, if you have one), your filing status, and deductions. Then you'll look at the tax tables (included in the IRS instruction booklet for Form 1040-ES), figure out your total tax bill, subtract any other income tax payments you've already made, and come up with the balance due. Now divide that estimated total tax figure by four, and send in equal quarterly installments to the government. Along with your payment you'll send in the Form 1040-ES payment coupon to make sure the IRS gives you credit for the payment. Also be sure to write your social security number (and your spouse's, if applicable) and the words "2004 1040-ES" (or whatever year it is) on your check.

Member Classification for Tax Purposes

One of the factors for determining your personal income tax liability for the year is your activity level. As an LLC member,

Corporate Taxation Changes Member Responsibilities

Should you have one of the few LLCs that's opted for corporate taxation, you won't have to pay any self-employment tax. As a corporate shareholder working for the corporation, you'd be considered an employee. Any payments made to you as salary would go through all the normal payroll procedures, which would include withholding taxes. But you personally wouldn't have to pay the employer side of FICA, as the corporation would foot that income-tax-deductible bill. Along the same lines, you probably wouldn't have to pay any estimated taxes, as you would have had income taxes taken out of your paycheck throughout the year. The only exception—if you expect to pay yourself a particularly large dividend, you want to make an estimated tax payment (or increase your withholding) to avoid a big tax bill at year-end.

you can be either active or passive—and both classifications come with a good side and a bad side. For active members, the positive comes with the ability to deduct losses against any of your other income; it's the opposite for passive members, whose loss deductions will be severely limited. The downside for active members is the steep self-employment tax bill on their full shares of LLC income; passive members are faced with no such tax burden.

In small LLCs, there usually aren't any passive members. In fact, if your LLC is member-managed, by definition it can't have any passive members. Members of larger LLCs can go either way—and this is where you may need to be careful, or at least talk to a competent business attorney. If your LLC has a lot of passive members, state law (depending on which state you're in) or federal law could reclassify membership interests as securities, meaning your company will now be subject to securities laws. The threat potential is even greater when those passive members are allocated a disproportionate share of business losses. How likely is that to happen to you? Here's a common scenario. You and a couple of friends start an LLC, then decide you need to take on some silent partners to infuse cash into the company. To keep those new members quiet, you promise them more than their fair share of tax losses, and everyone's happy. Except the government, that is. So if this (or a similar situation) describes the membership of your LLC, consult an attorney.

Passive Members Are Subject to Passive Activity Loss Rules

IRS language is overly complicated, often using five words where one will do. The language defining passive activities is no exception. According to the tax code, a passive activity is one in which the taxpayer did not materially participate. Translation: to be active in the business for tax purposes, you have to be active in the business. If you or a co-member has provided cash to the company but don't meet the IRS's material participation rules, you will likely be treated as passive for tax purposes. This comes up most often with manager-managed LLCs.

If the IRS classifies you as passive, you will only be able to use your share of the LLC's losses against other passive income (for example, if you're a passive member of another LLC and that one has profits). You can't, however, use those losses as a deduction against any other kind of income. So what if you don't have any passive income to offset your passive losses? The losses carry forward forever until you can use them. Although it sounds like nonpassive income comes from obvious sources, some of what the IRS considers nonpassive may surprise you. Nonpassive income includes things like:

- Salary or wages
- Self-employment income
- Interest
- Dividends
- Capital gains
- Unemployment payments
- Gambling winnings (including lottery)

There is only one circumstance in which your passive activity losses can be used against nonpassive income: when you dispose of your entire interest in the passive activity in a fully taxable transaction. This holds true even if you end up with a tax loss. So basically, you can use up all of your accumulated passive activity losses when you get rid of your LLC membership.

If you do have passive activity losses, you have an additional form to fill out when you do your taxes at year-end, IRS Form 8582 (Passive Activity Loss Limitations). This form adds up all of your passive income and subtracts out all of your passive losses. When the result is positive, it is fully taxable this year. When the result is negative, you can't deduct your losses this year; instead you have to wait until they can be used to offset income.

Active Members Must Have Material Participation

Only active members can use their share of LLC losses to offset all of their personal income, no matter what kind. Most people mistakenly assume that working for the business in any way for any amount of time gives them the green light to take the losses every year. But the IRS has different ideas, and has some very strict rules about what counts as material participation. In order to meet the material participation requirements, you have to either:

1. Participate in the business for at least 500 hours during the tax year, which translates to about ten hours each week.
2. Work for the LLC for at least 100 hours during the tax year, as long as no one else (including nonmember employees) worked more than 100 hours during the year.

3. Be the only person who works for the LLC (including nonowners).
4. Meet any of the first three conditions in a personal service activity for three years, after which you'll be considered a material participant for life.
5. Participate in the business regularly, continuously, and on a substantial basis during the year.

Rule number five is just vague enough to allow most members who do participate in the business to qualify, even if they don't quite fit into one of the other guidelines. If you'd like to make sure that all of your LLC's active members meet the material participation requirements, your operating agreement can set out minimum work schedules and spell out specific functions and tasks for each member. For married members, both spouses' participation counts toward meeting the tests.

Which Tax Forms Should Be Filed

An LLC has to file an informational return on Form 1065 just like a partnership, and along with that comes a Schedule K-1 for each member. A Schedule K-1 shows the details for one member's share of all LLC income and loss items. If your LLC has more than ten members, it also will have to file a Schedule K along with the rest of its return.

Each member of the LLC has to report his distributive share of the LLC's income or loss on his personal Form 1040, Schedule E, each year. If you're an active member, you'll probably also have to file Schedule SE to calculate and report your self-employment tax bill. If you're a passive member, you'll have to file Form 8582 to keep track of any nondeductible losses for future use.

When you have a single-member LLC, your entity doesn't really exist for tax purposes. The IRS sees you as a sole proprietor. So instead of the company filing a return and a bunch of K-1s, you just need to file a Schedule C with your annual 1040. A Schedule C is really just a formalized income statement for your company, listing out all of the company's income and expenses until the bottom line is reached. Whatever that bottom-line result turns out to be gets carried over to the first page of your Form 1040. (See Chapter 6 for complete details about preparing your Schedule C.)

When you have a single-member LLC, your entity doesn't really exist for tax purposes.

If you've decided that you and your fellow members will be better off having your company taxed as a corporation, it will have a completely different set of forms to fill out—and you'll have none. First, the LLC must make the election to be treated as a corporation for tax purposes by checking that box on IRS Form 8832. Then the LLC will have to follow all the rules for corporate taxation, including quarterly estimated payments by the company and an annual Form 1120. Now all LLC profits will be taxed at corporate rates and paid directly by the company. No income will be passed through to the members. Instead, you'll just have to list your salary on your Form 1040 (just like you would if you worked for any other company) and your dividends on Schedule B (just as if you got them from any other corporation).

LLCs Have the Same Tax Advantages as Partnerships

When your multimember LLC goes the pass-through taxation route, you'll get all of the tax advantages as a partnership without any of the nasty liability concerns. These advantages include the ability to personally deduct business losses for tax purposes, making profit and loss allocations in a way other than just by ownership proportions, easier estate tax planning, and basis adjustments when membership changes hands. To make sure you and your fellow members can take full advantage of all the potential benefits, work with an experienced CPA or attorney when setting up your LLC.

Deducting Tax Losses

It's quite common for an enterprise to sustain losses for at least the first year (and maybe the first few) it's in business. These losses and a sagging cash flow typically go hand in hand—and that will affect your personal cash flow, too. Luckily, with the pass-through entity you can deduct the company's losses on your personal tax return, reducing your personal tax burden. Owing less taxes to the government means keeping more precious cash in your own pockets and can help your fledgling business survive the lean years.

Here's how it works: When your LLC racks up a loss for the year, you get a deductible loss. If your current basis is less than your share of the loss, your deduction (or at least some of it) will be disallowed for the current tax year. That lost (or reduced) deduction can be carried forward to later tax years when your basis gets back above zero.

Making Special Allocations

If you do nothing, your distributive share of LLC income and loss will be based on your percentage of ownership in the business (for example, if you put up 50 percent of the capital, you'll get 50 percent of the profits or losses). In the real world, though, things don't always work out quite that neatly. Maybe you put up half the cash to get started, but do 90 percent of the work to keep the company in business. If that's the case, don't you think you're entitled to more than half the profits?

If your company is an LLC, you can change that default allocation into something that makes more sense for your actual circumstances. In fact, LLC members can divvy up profits and losses however they see fit, as long as they pay heed to IRS guidelines. Those guidelines basically say that there has to be some obvious and direct link between what you give to the company and what you're getting from it. So if you're doing most of the work, it would make sense that you're getting more of the profits.

Simplify Estate Tax Planning with Your LLC

In the past, family businesses have been formed as either S corporations or limited partnerships to make the transfer of ownership interests as smooth as possible. But now, with the advent of family LLCs, consolidating family assets in your business entity as a method of estate planning is even easier to accomplish. Here are a few of the reasons that using the LLC structure can be the best choice for a family business:

- There are no restrictions on who can be a member.
- There's no limit on the total number of members your LLC can have.
- No LLC member will have personal liability for the company's debt obligations.

To preserve ownership of beloved family assets, they can be transferred to your LLC, then easily spread among family members by transferring LLC ownership interests. It's much easier to gift a full interest in an LLC than to gift an interest in a portion of a family asset. Plus, your operating agreement can keep the LLC's management in the hands of particular members, allowing them to maintain control over the assets and the LLC. That allows you to make gifts to family members of any age, without worrying about which way your five-year-old nephew will vote on crucial business decisions.

> It's much easier to gift a full interest in an LLC than to gift an interest in a portion of a family asset.

A Special Election When Membership Interests Change Hands

You can benefit from some special tax rules that allow a basis adjustment when an interest in the LLC is transferred. Although this is a technical and complex section of tax code (don't try this at home; use a trained professional), the benefits are pretty easy to understand. This very big advantage comes into play when ownership interests change hands and an IRS section 754 election is made.

Without getting bogged down in too much tax detail, take a look at what happens once this election is made. The new member gets a tax basis of the amount he paid to buy the interest. That means his basis is based on fair market value and not the book value of the LLC's existing assets. Plus, his share of deductions relating to those "stepped-up" assets is based on his higher tax basis, not the LLC's lower historical basis—that means he gets bigger depreciation deductions. Finally, if the LLC sells the underlying asset, the gain allocated to that new member will be less because of his higher basis in the property. Take a look at the following example so you can see in real dollars the true benefit of making this election.

Suppose that four guys each own a 25 percent interest in an LLC. For simplicity's sake, the LLC's only asset is equipment that is being depreciated over five years. The original cost basis of the equipment is $40,000 and its accumulated depreciation so far comes to $16,000, making its current adjusted tax basis to the LLC $24,000. The equipment currently has a fair market value of $60,000. One of the original owners wants out, so he sells his 25 percent interest to you for $15,000.

The LLC makes a section 754 election. That means your basis in the LLC asset is $15,000 as opposed to $6,000 (25 percent of $24,000) without the election. The other members' bases stay the same ($6,000 each), but the LLC's total tax basis rises to $33,000. Then you all decide to sell off that asset for $60,000. You have no taxable gain to report—your share of the sale is $15,000 and your basis in the asset is $15,000. The other members, though, will each have taxable gains of $9,000.

Although this seems like a can't-lose situation for the new member, it may have some unforeseen tax consequences down the line. Therefore, you should look into all of the long-term implications with a qualified CPA before the election is made. Because once your LLC makes a section 754 election, it can't be revoked without IRS consent.

Tax Disadvantages for Members

Although business advisors swear up and down that LLCs are practically perfect entities, there are some possible tax disadvantages (albeit fairly minor ones) that should be considered before you make a final entity choice. First, some states impose income taxes on LLCs regardless of their federal tax treatment. Second, you will have to pay income taxes on your share of the LLC's profits even if you never see a dime of them. Third, taking a cash distribution that's greater than your basis will trigger a tax bill. And, finally, you can't deduct losses in excess of your tax basis on your personal tax return.

The states' tax regulations can be the biggest drawback, especially since there's a lot of disparity among the individual statutes. And not only will the company be affected, but your personal tax situation can be affected as well. If your LLC conducts business in multiple states, you'll probably be taxed in every state where the company does business. Many states now require non-resident LLC members to file a written agreement stating that they'll pay any applicable individual state income taxes. If the member doesn't file the agreement, the LLC may have to pay his state tax obligation. (Although the LLC does have the right to recover the total taxes paid on the member's behalf plus interest and penalties.)

> ## Chapter 22

LLCs Offer Solid Protection for Personal Assets

<table>
<tr><td></td><td>Part One</td></tr>
</table>

Part One

Part Two

Part Three

Part Four

Part Five

Part Six

PART FIVE   LIMITED LIABILITY COMPANIES

■ CHAPTER 19 Learning about Limited Liability Companies ■ CHAPTER 20 Starting an LLC ■ CHAPTER 21 LLCs and Taxes ■ CHAPTER 22 LLCs Offer Solid Protection for Personal Assets ■ CHAPTER 23 Leaving the Business

Limited Liability for Members

As an LLC member, you will receive the same strong limited liability protection previously only available to corporate shareholders. This limited liability applies to you as an owner of the LLC, not to the LLC itself. To you, this protection means that your personal assets are safe from the creditors of the company. However, your investment in the business is fully at risk—you could lose all of it—and so are all of the assets of the business.

For example, suppose you are a member of an LLC. Your total investment in the company is $15,000. Aside from that interest in the LLC, you have a personal net worth of $150,000 (including your home, your retirement account, and your vehicles). The company is struggling, and then a severe financial crisis hits. The company racks up debts of $125,000. Although the company can lose all of its assets, essentially putting it out of business, you can't lose more than your $15,000 investment. The remainder of your personal assets are out of the reach of the LLC's creditors.

Members Still Have Some Personal Liability

Regardless of the business entity you choose, there are some situations where you will always be held personally liable. Limited liability for business debts will not protect you should obligations develop from your own professional malpractice or other tortious acts (things you could be sued for in civil court). And it won't keep your personal assets out of the mix on debts (like bank loans) that you have personally guaranteed.

How Protected Are You Really?

The LLC is a relatively new form of business, so there is not a lot of case law out there. Although the various states' statutes and individual operating agreements cover quite a bit of legal ground, the actual events that transpire may not fit neatly into the existing legal framework. Without firm legal precedents, no one really knows for sure which way judges will decide when liability issues do eventually come to court. For example, LLC members could be more susceptible to "piercing the veil" than corporate shareholders are, particularly with single-member LLCs.

In addition to the usual malpractice lawsuits, you could be held personally financially responsible for anything you do that causes damages—to either people or property. The most common tortious act here involves car accidents that occur when you're driving the company vehicle or driving your own vehicle for business purposes. The other party to the accident could sue both the LLC and you personally for his damages.

Although an LLC member will usually be found liable for such things, he will not be held financially responsible for the same acts committed by another member. So if one of your fellow members causes a car accident using a company vehicle or on company time, you're in the clear. The most you could possibly lose would be the amount you invested in the LLC.

When it comes to loan guarantees, you know what you're getting into at the outset. It's the same as co-signing a loan for your sister. You know from the start that if she doesn't pay, you're going to have to. And in the beginning, your LLC probably won't have sufficient credit history or assets to qualify for a loan on its own. Banks may (and likely will) ask that you and your co-members guarantee loans with your personal assets. Even suppliers may ask that you guarantee their debts when your LLC's relationship with them has yet to be established. And anything that you personally guarantee may end up being actually paid by you.

When You're Liable for Something You Didn't Do

You just learned that you won't be held liable for tortious acts committed by a fellow LLC member. But you may end up facing personal financial responsibility if an agent or employee of the LLC commits a tort, and you're found negligent in either your hiring or supervision practices. To protect yourself from this level of liability, you can take steps to prove that you use reasonable care both when you hire employees and when they are under your supervision.

Here are some basic steps you can take to insulate yourself from negligence claims arising from the torts of an employee:

Check references—Making a few phone calls to verify prior work experience shows that you tried to hire an appropriate employee.

Check backgrounds—Verify academic transcripts, professional licenses, credit history, even arrest history, as appropriate to the type of job you're filling.

Conduct drug tests—Most states permit mandatory drug testing for all job candidates when the position involves potential safety risks (like delivery truck drivers).

Once you've hired someone, make sure they receive proper training to do their jobs safely and correctly. Have periodic performance reviews, and document these in writing. If you're not sure your employee is performing up to snuff, stick close by him for a day or two—and let him know right away if he does something incorrectly (or course, document any suggestions you make in this capacity). This is definitely one of those times when an ounce of prevention is worth a pound of cure.

Your Spouse May Have Personal Liability

In an effort to conserve cash, entrepreneurs just starting out often enlist their husbands or wives to help out with the business. The spouses' tasks run the gamut, from bookkeeping to minding the store. This arrangement typically won't pose any legal problems—as long as your spouse lends a hand once in a while, and for no pay. But if your spouse's role is a steady one, a public one (meaning he or she deals with the general public for you), or a paid one, that may change everything.

If your husband or wife is very involved with your LLC, he or she could end up bearing personal financial liability for judgments entered against the company. For example, the courts could consider your spouse to be an independent contractor of the LLC (if he or she is not an official employee but gets paid by the company). In that case, your spouse could be held liable for just about anything related to his or her work for the company. And, since you're married, all marital property could be at stake.

The solution to this potentially sticky problem? Make your spouse a member of the LLC. Do it formally, and according to all applicable guidelines—whether they be from the state or from your operating agreement. To make your spouse a full (and bulletproof) member of your LLC:

- Keep a written record of the decision to admit your spouse as a new member.
- Make any applicable changes to your operating agreement, spelling out your spouse's capital contribution, voting rights, and profit and loss allocations.
- Make sure that your spouse pays necessary income and self-employment taxes on his or her share of LLC profits.

Your spouse's capital contribution need not be cash or property—it can be a pact to provide services to the LLC. If labor will be your spouse's contribution, make sure to explicitly set minimum time and duty requirements, and include those in the operating agreement.

Protection Strategies for Company Assets

No business exists without at least some built-in liability risks. And with the growing creativity of attorneys, the things that turn into lawsuits these days are mind-boggling. Since defending yourself against a lawsuit (frivolous or not) can cost hundreds of thousands of dollars, your small business may feel pressured to settle in the plaintiff's favor—even when you're truly not at fault—just to avoid paying huge legal bills. Even worse: you go to court to defend yourself and the jury sides with the plaintiff, returning a large settlement. Either way you go from there, paying the settlement or appealing it, this can put a serious dent in your assets or wipe out your business completely.

Think that your company won't get sued? Think again. The odds are not in your favor. But there are a lot of ways you can protect your company and its assets, should a lawsuit be filed against your LLC. By implementing some of the strategies discussed before you have any problems, you both protect your company's assets and reduce the risk of lawsuit. No lawyer wants to file a lawsuit when there are no (or very few) assets at stake.

A Real-Life Example

Pete and Edwin started a flooring company, and formed their business as an LLC. They set up shop on a typical Main Street, devoting over half the space to showroom and samples. For their grand opening, Pete decided to hang some banners and signs. As he was putting up one of the banners, he lost his grip and the banner fell to the street. It landed on a very startled woman, causing her to fall down.

The woman sustained some injuries, including a sprained ankle—especially unfortunate as her job was as a dog-walker. The woman sued for damages (including her lost wages) and won. Although insurance picked up the lion's share of the tab, there were still deductibles and co-payments to meet. Since the LLC couldn't cover the full claim, Pete himself was liable for the balance.

Steps You Can Take to Protect Your LLC

There are several things you can do to protect the assets of your LLC from unexpected liabilities. The most important thing to remember when taking preventive measures is that you need to take them *before* something goes wrong. Implementing these strategies after a lawsuit is in place does nothing to shield your company's assets—in fact, some of them, when started after the fact, can be considered fraudulent transactions punishable by law. Putting them in place from the beginning, on the other hand, can do an awful lot to keep your company going in the face of adversity.

Once you've been tagged for a lawsuit, your first line of defense should be business insurance. If yours is a professional practice, make sure that you and all of your fellow members have adequate malpractice insurance in place. Insure your company vehicles for more than the bare minimum liability permitted by law. Innately hazardous businesses should absolutely maintain liability policies. And all businesses should acquire supplemental umbrella coverage.

Next in line is keeping your LLC's liquid assets at a minimum. Any assets held by the LLC—especially cash—are always vulnerable to business debts. To reduce your LLC's net worth, you can regularly withdraw the assets generated by the business.

The third strategy involves separating business assets by creating more than one entity. In the case of a very small business, that separate entity could be you—although that could open up a personal liability can of worms. For more substantial or asset-intensive businesses, creating multiple LLCs can insulate assets effectively.

Keeping the LLC's Liquid Assets Low

It's pretty simple to limit your LLC's liquid assets—give yourself some money. But how you do it can make all the difference. You can systematically withdraw funds in a few different ways:

1. Make guaranteed payments to members.
2. Distribute LLC income on a regular basis.
3. Make lease or loan payments to members.

A word of caution, though, if you choose to use this strategy. Creditors can attack any of these withdrawals as fraudulent conveyances under the Uniform Fraudulent Transfers Act. When you remove the assets from the LLC properly, and the business continues to meet all of its regular obligations, these creditor challenges probably won't hold up in court. That's why it's very important to set up the withdrawals from day one; if you start after you're sued, you could be hit with a fraud charge.

The strongest way to make withdrawals (for an asset protection strategy) is in return for value. Asset distributions to LLC members for these types of withdrawals, such as for lease payments, are typically considered to be exempt from constructive fraud provisions. This is particularly important if your company is in the middle of a financial slowdown—lease payments usually will be looked at as ordinary and necessary business expenditures. Conversely, earnings distributions may be called into question if they're made while your business is suffering from financial troubles.

Here are a couple of things you can do to implement this strategy. First, you can lend money to the company, then have the company pay you back on a regular loan schedule. Or, you can lease your assets to the business for its use; for example, you can buy a computer, then lease it to the company. The company pays you, you pay your credit card bill, everyone's happy. Best of all, the courts have consistently found that loan and lease payments are legitimate business expenses. It does not matter at all to the court to whom the payment is made. So in this way, you can simply and safely remove funds that would otherwise stay in the business bank account like a sitting duck.

If your company has plans that will call for fairly large sums of cash, you may not want to make these types of withdrawals. Of course, a big bank account can make your LLC a much more attractive target for lawsuits. If you want to keep the money in the business, make sure you have more than adequate insurance coverage. As an alternative, you can make the withdrawals, then lend the money back to the company when it's ready to spend the cash.

> Earnings distributions may be called into question if they're made while your business is suffering from financial troubles.

Separate Entities, Separate Assets

If your LLC needs some serious liability protection, using the multiple entities strategy may be your best bet. Why would your company need so much protection? It could be in a hazardous industry (manufacturing poisonous

Lending Money to Your LLC? Get a Note.

Every time you lend money to your company, put it in writing in a signed and dated promissory note. You can also document the "meeting" where the loan was discussed, much like corporate minutes.

You can find preprinted blank note forms at stationery stores, or just type one up yourself. At the very least, it should include the original amount and date of the loan, the interest rate, when payments will start, and how frequently payments will be made.

The note should be signed by an LLC member, preferably not you. Once the paperwork is finalized, make sure that the LLC commences repayment on schedule. The LLC will get a tax deduction for the interest paid on the loan, and you'll have to declare interest income on your tax return for all the interest you receive. By making sure all the legal and tax requirements are followed just as if you were unrelated parties, you'll make your business loan—and the payments—invulnerable to creditor claims of fraud.

chemicals, like bug sprays, for example), or have employees who will be called upon to perform hazardous duties (such as a roofing business). Maybe the type of interaction you'll have with the general public could generate some seriously big liability claims—like food and alcohol service, or petting zoos.

If your LLC is prone to large liability claims, using multiple business entities can truly limit both personal and company liability. The best way to implement this strategy is to set up both an operating company and a holding company, each formed as an LLC. The holding company will own all of the business assets. The operating company will be the one that conducts all the day-to-day business transactions. The result is that the operating company bears all the risk of loss, but owns no assets to lose.

Because the holding company doesn't conduct any business, it can't incur any business debt. And since it won't deal with any entities other than your operating company, there will be no one to initiate a lawsuit against it. Plus, when you set up the holding company as a member of the operating company, the holding company legally cannot be exposed to the liabilities of the operating company. And you will have essentially no liability exposure at all under this structure.

As you can imagine, this strategy can get pretty expensive. So talk to a trusted business advisor to make sure it's warranted before you begin making arrangements. Your attorney should be a key player in this set-up—if you're going through this much trouble to protect your company's assets, make sure you do it 100 percent correctly. If your company has that much at stake, and a lot of potential for losing it all, paying a lawyer and some extra fees will be well worth it in the long run.

When the Limited Liability Veil Gets Pierced

One key benefit of using the LLC entity for your company is the limited liability protection it extends to your personal assets. That means you can't be personally sued for debts incurred by the business. If the business can't pay up on its own, the creditors can't come after your assets—even if they're substantial. The most you could conceivably lose would be your full investment in the business. That could be quite a lot—but at least it's not everything.

This shield that stands between you and your LLC's creditors is called the veil. But should that veil get pierced, your limited liability protection would be lost, and your company's creditors would have total access to your personal assets. Courts typically pierce the veil of limited liability in fairly limited circumstances, since it's a pretty extreme measure. Unfortunately, a lot of small business owners unknowingly put themselves in jeopardy every day. This section will help you make sure you're not among those uninformed entrepreneurs who do end up risking personal assets by doing things that are very easy to avoid.

Courts will only apply a ruling to pierce your LLC's veil if its creditors can prove either one of the following two legal theories:

1. *Undercapitalization Theory:* the owner(s) of the company intentionally underfunded the business when it was formed in order to defraud creditors.
2. *Alter Ego Theory:* the owner(s) did not keep personal financial dealings completely separate from those of the business or did not follow all required legal formalities (these vary widely among states).

In addition to the two theories that can be trotted out in court, LLC members can trigger the veil piercing simply by not filing the form or paying the fees necessary to renew their LLC status. It's crucial that you submit all state paperwork, filled out completely and on time, and pay all necessary fees. Neglecting to do either will result in the automatic dissolution of your LLC, and an automatic end to your limited liability protection.

The Undercapitalization Theory

It's the same old story: New businesses need more cash than they have. And new business owners typically dump all the money they can into their start-ups. While almost all companies have cash struggles for the first few months or years, fraudulent undercapitalization requires an additional ingredient: intent.

How can you prove you didn't intend for your company to be undercapitalized? By starting up intelligently. This does not mean you have to put a lot of money into your LLC, and put your family in the poorhouse as a result. It does mean that you have to put in *enough* money to meet the company's typical, expected expenses. Just as the rule of thumb for personal savings is three months expenses in cash, that's a safe maxim to follow for your LLC.

If you start your business with very little investment on your part, then run up a lot of bills with outside creditors, you're putting your company and your personal assets at risk. The courts will take a look at what you've put in compared to the amount of debt you've run up—and if they don't like what they see, they may disregard your limited liability protection.

The Alter Ego Theory

One quick way to get your LLC disregarded is to run your personal affairs through the company, instead of treating it as a separate entity. Common culprits here are things like paying your home phone bill with an LLC check, or paying for your groceries with the company credit card.

This casual use of company funds is actually the most common threat to limited liability for small business owners. Almost everyone does it—uses the LLC's bank account to directly pay personal expenses. Many small business owners use draw accounts, but making checks out to your personal creditors rather than to yourself is a big mistake. It may not matter when your LLC is in the black and no one's checking; but when your company hits lean financial times, the courts will look through the company checkbook, and they won't like what they see.

If this practice is standard operating procedure for your LLC, the courts may find that the LLC doesn't really exist. And if your LLC doesn't exist, neither does your limited liability protection. So if you haven't yet started doing this, don't; if you've already used company checks to pay your personal bills, stop. The only thing you have to change is the name on the check. Make it out to yourself. Deposit the check in your personal account. Then write out your own check to pay your bills.

This theory goes both ways. You should not write personal checks out to the LLC's creditors, or use your personal credit card to make company purchases. Instead, put more money into the LLC's bank account, and let it pay its own bills.

The bottom line here is that your LLC is an entity separate from you, so treat it that way. Get an EIN. Open a company checking account. Get a credit card in the company name. Let the LLC establish its own credit history. And keep all assets completely separate, titling them in the name of the appropriate entity. If you respect your company as a separate entity, so will the courts.

Charging Orders for LLCs

For protecting your company's assets against claims from your personal creditors, the LLC may offer the best protection around. Many states have drawn from the Revised Uniform Limited Partnership Act (RULPA) when drafting their LLC statutes. The RULPA position actually prevents personal creditors with charging orders against the LLC from forcing a liquidation of the business. That means the creditor cannot step into your shoes and become a member of the LLC, and if he's not a member, he can't force a liquidation.

Statutory Fraud Limits for LLCs Revisited

As you read earlier, state law concerning LLC withdrawal restrictions typically are modeled on the Uniform Fraudulent Transfers Act. If withdrawals that you and your co-members made are found to be fraudulent under the statutes, the veil will be pierced.

What constitutes a fraudulent transfer in the eyes of the courts? Two things: A payment is made by the LLC for which the LLC gets nothing (or something of clearly lower value) in return, and that payment is made when the LLC is insolvent (or becomes insolvent because of it).

All income distributions and ownership redemptions (i.e., the LLC buys you out of your interest) meet the first test, as they are never considered to be in return for value. As for the insolvency test, that's based on court-applied formulas relating to either your company's cash flows or balance sheet.

When a Member Files for Bankruptcy

So far, the U.S. bankruptcy laws don't specifically address LLCs, and that means more state-by-state variance. What bankruptcy code does include is language about contracts—in this case, the operating agreement. Without getting into too much legal mumbo jumbo, a trustee appointed by bankruptcy court gets the power over the debtor's interest in the LLC operating agreement. So depending on the home state laws, the bankruptcy trustee could end up liquidating the LLC to pay off the bankrupt member's debts. (States that follow RULPA would leave that trustee basically in the same place as a creditor with a charging order.)

To protect your LLC, you can include a provision in the operating agreement that lets the other members expel a member who's filing for bankruptcy. This effectively kicks out that member, and lets the company continue as before without having to worry about any bankruptcy court decisions.

On the other hand, some states take the general partnership view, and that does allow for liquidation of the LLC. In fact, the Uniform Limited Liability Company Act takes the general partnership view, and so will all states that adopt it. To provide your LLC with the stronger protection as afforded in RULPA, you can form your LLC in a state that uses that rule even if it's not where you'll be operating. Some of the states that follow the RULPA guidelines include Connecticut, Delaware, Maryland, and Nevada. To find out which method your state follows, you can go to the appropriate secretary of state's Web site and look into the LLC statutes regarding charging orders.

> ► **Chapter 23**

Leaving the Business

Part One

Part Two

Part Three

Part Four

Part Five

Part Six

PART FIVE   LIMITED LIABILITY COMPANIES

■ CHAPTER 19 Learning about Limited Liability Companies ■ CHAPTER 20 Starting an LLC ■ CHAPTER 21 LLCs and Taxes ■ CHAPTER 22 LLCs Offer Solid Protection for Personal Assets ■ **CHAPTER 23 Leaving the Business**

Follow the Operating Agreement

You've devoted a lot of time, heart, and energy to making your business a successful one—and that makes the thought of closing up shop, well, unthinkable. But there comes a time when every entrepreneur must step aside and walk away from the company he so lovingly helped build.

At the dawn of a new company, no one likes to think about how things will eventually end. But preplanning can go a long way toward making the final transition easier for you, or at least less difficult. Whether you are your LLC's sole member or just one of a few, leaving the business will have a serious impact on it. By following the separation steps outlined in your operating agreement, you can help ensure that any transition will be a smooth one.

A properly prepared operating agreement (as talked about in detail in Chapter 20) will include provisions—called buy-sell provisions—that spell out what should happen in the event a member leaves the LLC. Thorough buy-sell provisions give members explicit instructions about what to do in any of the events that can cause a member to withdraw from the LLC. These events include:

> Thorough buy-sell provisions give members explicit instructions about what to do in any of the events that can cause a member to withdraw from the LLC.

- Death
- Disability
- Divorce
- Personal bankruptcy
- Retirement

You Need Buy-Sell Provisions to Protect Your LLC

Things change: people, circumstances, the global economy. Somewhere down the line, your LLC will be affected. If you don't plan ahead, you could lose your LLC. If you think you don't need buy-sell provisions, think again.

Some very common scenarios that can change the shape of your business include one member moving away; one or more members leaving to start another business; a change in the mental, physical, or financial capacity of a member; and one member selling his interest to someone you don't know or don't particularly like. All of these situations can—and do—happen, possibly without any advance warning. And, as you can imagine, the impact on your LLC can be huge.

Just imagine trying to work every day with a business associate whom you literally can't stand. Or think about what would happen if someone with a completely different business philosophy came in and started changing everything—and you couldn't stop him. Worse, envision the LLC you've worked so hard to create simply disappearing. You can stop these worst-case scenarios from becoming the reality, with a simple addition to your operating agreement.

What Buy-Sell Provisions Cover

The buy-sell portion of your operating agreement is almost like a prenuptial agreement, in that it anticipates the "breakup" and explains (unemotionally) how to deal with it from a legal standpoint. The provisions can range from a few brief sentences to several pages, depending on the degree of control the original owners want to have. In fact, some buy-sell provisions are so long that they become a separate agreement, parallel to the operating agreement.

So what kind of things do these provisions cover? First, and probably most important, you can forestall the automatic dissolution of your company. With no "keep going" plans in place, an LLC can cease to exist when even one of its members takes off.

Second, buy-sell provisions define exactly who can buy the withdrawing member's interest in the LLC. Particularly in small closely held companies, the potential buyers may be limited to other members—or at least give them the first rights of refusal. In other cases, transfers to outsiders are permitted, as long as the other LLC members agree to admit the new member. If your agreement does not allow sales to outsiders, it should state that either another member or group of members, or the LLC itself, will have to purchase the departing member's share of the company. Don't box yourself into a corner by saying that no member can sell to outsiders without making some kind of stipulation that the other members would have to buy him out. If that were the case, no member could ever leave—at least not with a settlement for his fair share of the business.

Next, buy-sell provisions can limit the withdrawing member's future activities. For example, you may want to include some kind of noncompete clause in the agreement. That will ensure that one member can't open up a competing business within a certain time period and a specified distance from the existing company.

Fourth, this section of your operating agreement should include some sort of formula for figuring out the value of each membership interest. The agreement should also cover how and when the member who's leaving will be paid. If left blank, he or she could insist on full payment in cash on the date of separation. This could seriously hurt your company—as most small businesses don't keep that kind of cash on hand.

As you can see, buy-sell provisions can be fairly complex. It's often uncomfortable for an LLC's founding members to hash out the details of a split, especially when everyone's wearing rose-colored glasses and the excitement level is running high. But it's better to do it at the outset, when everyone's intentions are good and attitudes are positive, than to have to deal with the details during a bitter breakup.

Details of a Buyout

When your agreement states that only other members or the LLC itself can (and, therefore, must) take over your ownership interest when you leave the company, the agreement must also include a way to set the price for your share of the business.

Specific dollar prices should be avoided—you have no idea now what your LLC might be worth in the future. Instead, come up with a way to calculate the fair market value of the departing member's interest. For example, your agreement could say that an independent appraisal was required to determine the value. To make sure no one gets cheated here, it's best to have experienced professionals involved with the determination.

> Make sure your buy-sell provisions provide for a payment plan, over a reasonable period of time.

To avoid this unpleasant scenario, make sure your buy-sell provisions provide for a payment plan, over a reasonable period of time. Although a substantial down payment is commonplace (usually from 15 percent to 50 percent of the interest, depending on its relative size), so are mortgage-like payments for the balance. Structuring the buyout in this fashion can help make sure that you don't have to sell off crucial business assets to pay off a departing member.

Legal Termination of the LLC

An LLC technically can exist forever, based on the provisions included in the federal check-the-box regulations. (Remember, that's the box to check when deciding how you want your LLC to be taxed.) When those rules took effect, almost all of the states modified their existing LLC statutes to allow the companies to carry on indefinitely. If any member decides to withdraw from the LLC (except in the case of a single-member LLC), the remaining members may choose to continue the business as is. The states that didn't make the change still hold that dissociation by a member automatically terminates the LLC entity—unless the LLC's operating agreement explicitly states that the remaining members can continue it if they want to.

In addition to members leaving (whatever their reasons), there are other circumstances that can cause your LLC to terminate. Under most states' laws, an LLC will dissolve when particular events take place. And once that dissolution occurs, the members have no choice but to wind up the business of the LLC and formally terminate the entity. Some of these events are actions purposely taken by the members; others occur as the result of oversights or errors. In most cases, an LLC will be dissolved when:

- Any termination event that is identified in the operating agreement or articles of organization happens.
- A set number (or percentage) of members, as spelled out in the operating agreement, provide written consent to dissolve the entity.
- A formal judicial decree of dissolution is entered (this typically only occurs when the LLC is deemed unable to carry on its business in accord with its articles of organization and operating agreement).
- The state initiates an administrative termination because your LLC failed to adhere to all of the required procedures (like filing documents or paying fees).

Should your LLC be dissolved by any of the trigger events listed above, the remaining members have to follow all the necessary steps to wind up the LLC. These steps (listed in more detail later in this chapter) include fulfilling all contractual obligations and dividing up all of the remaining assets among the members.

Carrying On When a Member Has Left

If your LLC is terminated under state law because a member has withdrawn from the company, you and your remaining fellow members (or just you, if it was a two-member LLC) will have to form a new LLC if you want to continue in business in that entity form. But this kind of disruption can be easily avoided if you simply include comprehensive buy-sell provisions in your firm's operating agreement. These provisions will allow for a smooth transition without causing an abrupt end to the existing LLC simply due to a change in membership.

Articles of Dissolution

When your LLC is going to be dissolved—whether by choice or by legal termination—there is some paperwork that needs to be filed. This applies even to single-member LLCs; though they're treated as sole proprietorships by the IRS, they still count as official entities at the state level.

Many states require formal legal articles of dissolution to be filed; most of those that don't require the extra paperwork still allow it to be entered. Why should you file articles of dissolution if your state doesn't specifically call for it? Because this filing has a dual purpose. In addition to notifying the state that your LLC will be terminating, the filing also serves as legal notice to creditors that the LLC is being dissolved. You should also send notices to all of the known creditors of the LLC, and alert any unknown creditors via a public notice in the newspaper.

Like articles of organization, articles of dissolution are pretty easy to prepare. And also like their entity-creating counterparts, dissolution paperwork typically must be filed with a check attached. Most states charge a fee to accept your articles of dissolution, and won't recognize the filing without it. Check your home state's Web site to see if a fee must be paid (and how much you have to pay). Typical official articles of dissolution include the following information:

1. The name of the LLC
2. The entity's state identification number

3. Names and addresses for all current members
4. Final date of existence

Those states requiring filing of these documents may call for additional information.

Transferring Your Membership Interest

Your ownership interest in an LLC generally cannot be transferred freely. The first restrictions on the transfer of your share of the business are typically included in the buy-sell provisions section of the LLC's operating agreement. If your company either doesn't have an operating agreement (not recommended) or if your operating agreement doesn't include buy-sell provisions (also not recommended), state law will kick in. The default rules in most states typically allow new members to be admitted to an LLC only with the unanimous consent of existing members. That means that if your fellow members don't like the person you plan to sell your share of the business to, they can simply vote "no" and you'll have to find someone else.

This sounds pretty unfair, but it really serves to protect you and all of the members from having to be in partnership with someone unsuitable. If you can't find anyone that everyone agrees on, the remaining members will have to buy you out. However, should you actually find a buyer that your co-members take a shine to (or someone directly named in your original operating agreement), you can complete your sale.

As you've probably figured out by now, there will be tax consequences from the transfer. You'll have to pay capital gains tax on your profits (assuming there are profits). How much you'll have to recognize as gain depends on your current basis in the LLC. (For more detailed information about your basis, see Chapter 20.)

Multistate LLCs May Need to File Multiple Forms

If your LLC operates in more than one state, you may have to file more than one set of articles of dissolution. Because the requirements due vary among the states (like all other aspects of LLC paperwork), make sure to check the regulations for every state in which your company conducts business. The rules may be different for foreign LLCs than they are for home-state companies.

If you fail to file the paperwork in a state in which it's required, your LLC will continue to exist, at least for the record. That means the company will still have to pay taxes and fees, and follow all the state formalities. If these filings aren't filed and these fees aren't paid, interest and penalties will likely accrue. And that may turn what should have been a $30 dissolution fee into hundreds of dollars due from your company to the state.

Retirement Planning for Children

When most people think about saving money for their kids, college funds immediately come to mind. And while these can be great savings vehicles, they can also cause problems when you're seeking financial aid. Since the money in the college fund technically belongs to the child for the purpose of paying his tuition, he may not qualify for many asset-based aid programs.

The solution is to start a retirement plan for your kid instead. Retirement plans are often not included in the asset calculations used to determine financial aid status. Plus, the extra savings time can turn modest contributions into huge retirement accounts, thanks to the compounding effect.

When your children actually work for your business—and receive regular on-the-books paychecks for their work—you can make retirement plan contributions for them. And, as anyone with a retirement plan knows, the earlier you start, the more your money multiplies.

The Section 754 Election Revisited

The quirky law—known as the Section 754 election—that allows incoming LLC members a one-time basis increase can make it easier to sell your ownership interest to outsiders. (This tax election was discussed in detail in Chapter 21.) This basis adjustment can be made when an exiting LLC member transfers his ownership interest to someone else. Essentially, it allows the new member to receive basis equal to the amount he actually paid for his interest—the fair market value—instead of the book value of the underlying assets.

Although the election typically is beneficial to the new member, there may be some circumstances where the long-term implications may be unfavorable from a tax perspective. Since the election is irrevocable once made, make sure to consult with a competent tax advisor before you submit any paperwork to the IRS.

Tax Implications of Transfers to Family

The words "family business" evoke images of mom-and-pop soda shops, father-and-son carpenters, and restaurants full of uncles and aunts and cousins. And most small businesses do fall into the stereotype: Mom or Dad starts a business, then brings the kids in, then hands the business over so he or she can retire—but never far enough away so that one hand can't stay on the cash register. And while the family dynamic can add complexity to the family business, so can the tax system.

Once a family business is up and running successfully, transfers to the younger generation usually begin. Often this strategy is used to shift income from the adults (in higher tax brackets) to the children (in lower brackets). This division of income lowers the income taxes for the family as a whole.

The other tax to consider when handing over shares of the business to your children is the gift and estate tax. Although under current law the estate tax is set to disappear in

2010, it's also set to reappear in 2011 unless Congress does something to keep the repeal in place. No one really knows what will happen, so it's best to talk with an experienced estate planning specialist when you draw up your plans to hand over the family business, even if you do it in a piecemeal fashion. Depending on the value of your LLC and the size of the shares you hand over, gift tax returns may need to be filed.

Wrapping Things Up

When you've decided to close the doors of your LLC, there are some basic things you need to do to wind up your business. Once you've taken care of all the federal and state requirements (like filing articles of dissolution and final tax returns), you'll have to wrap up all of your outstanding business obligations as well.

Some of the steps you'll need to take are:

- Notify existing customers and vendors to let them know you'll no longer be in business.
- Fulfill or renegotiate all contract obligations (such as outstanding sales or purchase orders).
- Sell, transfer, or junk the company's physical assets.
- Cancel or reduce insurance coverage.
- Pay off all known business debts (and possibly set up a reserve in your own name for any unforeseen debts).
- Close out the company bank account.
- Distribute all of the remaining assets among the members in proportion to their ownership interests (or in accordance with the operating agreement).

Your business advisor (such as your accountant) can run you through everything that needs to be done to close your books.

Although your business will be officially closed, you still have to maintain your business records in case of lawsuits or tax issues. To be on the safe side, you should hang on to all of your files for at least seven years.

Chapter 24

> Chapter 24

The Normal Business Progression

Part One

Part Two

Part Three

Part Four

Part Five

Part Six

Almost Everyone Starts as a Sole Proprietor

More and more people are starting their own businesses these days. With an uncertain economy, and the constant threat of corporate downsizing, thousands of people decide to take their fates into their own hands every day. The entrepreneurial spirit has always run high in the United States—but never higher than it does now.

Technology constantly improves, getting more sophisticated and faster all the time. Almost everyone has a computer—and a fax, a scanner, a copier, and a printer with it. Homes are equipped with high-speed Internet connections as often as they are with regular old telephone lines. All of this easily accessible technology—at much lower prices than ever before—makes starting a business as easy as printing out your own business cards.

The other side of the equation is people. People are tired of corporate scandals and schemes, tired of calling a "help line" only to get connected with an endless stream of machines. People like to use technology, but they don't like to deal with it. More and more, people want to deal with people—they want to call a company and talk to a person. They want individual attention, and genuinely friendly and polite service.

And that's where small businesses come in. They can't usually offer the lowest prices, but they can come in with the promise of the best service. They can tailor products and services to customers' needs and wants, instead of trying to fit everyone into the same mold and selling everyone the same thing.

When you have finally had that epiphany—that you can really do it better yourself—you'll want to jump out of bed and just get started. And that's how the sole proprietorship is born. Because that's all it takes to start a sole proprietorship: an idea and the drive to see it through. And as you learned in Part Two, IRS statistics show that more Schedule Cs (the tax form for sole proprietors) are filed than any other type of business tax return.

Going It Alone in Business

If you're working for yourself, you're a sole proprietor. Since you don't actually have to do anything to form a sole proprietorship, it's truly a default business entity. That means the minute you incur business expenses or earn revenue, you're a sole proprietor. And that's why practically everyone starts

A Small Beginning for a Big Business

In 1946, a young woman with some skin cream and big dreams started her own company. While she still lived over her father's shop in Queens, New York, she began selling special skin creams that had been created by her uncle. No one expected this "potion peddler" to be very successful—but she was. Her drive and ambition won her some coveted counter space at Saks Fifth Avenue just two years after she'd launched her company. Today, you can't turn on the TV without seeing her commercials, or go into any major department store without seeing her name—Estée Lauder.

out as a sole proprietor—they start working for themselves before they ever even think about forming a formal business entity.

If you're self-employed, you're a sole proprietor. If you earn 1099-MISC income by performing services (even if those services are for a big company), you're a sole proprietor. When you really get down to it, if you babysit for your neighbors or cut their lawn, you're technically a sole proprietor. Bottom line: If you work for yourself by yourself, you're a sole proprietor—whether you knew it or not. (By yourself meaning with no partners, not with no employees; you can still be a sole proprietor if you have employees.)

The Testing Ground

It costs money to create a formal business entity. Even a general partnership—another very simple entity to form—costs more, in tax return preparation alone. Most entrepreneurs starting up new businesses don't have buckets of unneeded cash lying around. So most of them try out their business ideas before they do anything more sophisticated. And that's why almost everyone starting a new business begins as a sole proprietor.

Sole proprietorships may not be the most beneficial entities when it comes to taxes and liability protection, but they do take the cake when it comes to formation and maintenance costs and simplicity. And that makes them the ideal testing ground for new businesses without a lot of start-up capital, and for new entrepreneurs who aren't quite ready to give up sovereignty.

From the Basement to the Boardroom

More than two decades ago, Martin Edelston started his own business with just $5,000, and an office in his basement. Although you may not know his name, you'll probably be familiar with his company, now Boardroom, Inc.—the publisher of Bottom Line Publications. His largest newsletter, *Bottom Line/Personal*, has over two million readers.

The company also publishes newsletters—full of small business advice, retirement planning tips, and money management—presented in a clear and easy-to-read format. Martin Edelston knows how hard it is to both start a business and live your life—he did it himself. And that's how he knows that you don't have time to wade through ten or twelve page articles to find the information you need right now; he skips the fluff and gets right to the point. The Boardroom Inc. publications are great sources of information for new small business owners; for more information, go to the Web site at ✎*www. bottomlinesecrets.com*.

Taking on a Partner Means Changing Your Form of Business

The minute you add a business partner, you can't be a sole proprietor any more. Many sole proprietors have to turn to outside investors—meaning bringing on partners—to find extra cash for their ventures. The easiest way to do this (although it may not be the best way) is to take on a general partner, forming a general partnership. Like the sole proprietorship, no legal formalities are required to either create or maintain this business entity. So, by default, when most companies add another owner to their rosters, they become general partnerships.

Of course, as you've learned throughout this book, there are several other options available to multiowner companies:

1. Limited partnerships
2. Limited liability partnerships (LLPs)
3. Limited liability limited partnerships (LLLPs)
4. Limited liability companies (LLCs)
5. C corporations
6. S corporations

Each of these alternatives is more expensive to start and to run than a general partnership. But they all offer at least some level of liability protection for their owners (limited partnerships only offer this feature to their limited partners).

When you take on a business partner, regardless of the entity you choose to house your business, you may have to give up some of your independence. Unless you take on strictly silent partners (like limited partners or small-percentage shareholders), you won't be able to make decisions on your own anymore. If you're looking for a fresh voice and new opinions, that's a good thing. If you really only want to raise money, but remain in (almost) complete control, your entity choices are more limited.

When Growth Dictates a Structure Change

The good news: Your small business is thriving, and on its way to becoming big. You considered taking on a partner, but didn't want to lose any autonomy. You've got plenty of funding, enough to sponsor your next wave of growth, and the profits are literally pouring in. You're working for yourself, it's paying off, and you love it. But you probably shouldn't be a sole proprietor anymore.

Don't worry—you can change your entity without taking on any partners. You can keep your autonomy, and protect your personal financial status, with a simple change in your business structure. How do you know when your business has gotten big enough to merit a change? Here are some benchmarks that can help you decide:

- You need to take on employees.
- You have enough profits to take some home.
- Your business owns substantial assets.
- Your business has a lot of debt.
- You've added new products or product lines.
- You need more space (whether warehouse, office, or retail).

Business growth is a good thing. But with increasing business, you'll also be taking on increased personal liability risk—and that's not a good

Lynch Joins Merrill

Way back in 1907, Charles Merrill (then just twenty-two years old) met Edmund Lynch (also twenty-two) at a YMCA in New York City. The two men took an instant liking to each other, and became lifelong friends.

In January of 1914, Charles Merrill formed his first company: Charles E. Merrill & Co. His daring attitude and personal style, combined with his focus on investment advice based on the customer's personal circumstances, quickly drew in many clients. By May of that year, he had persuaded Edmund Lynch to come work with him; and together they opened their first office on Wall Street. In 1915, the company transformed into Merrill, Lynch & Co.

thing. The fees you'll pay to create a more formal business entity are well worth the added protection you'll receive. Because, unfortunately, in a highly litigious society, success can lead to lawsuits. And you want to make sure that those lawsuits stop at the office door, and don't extend to your private affairs (and vice versa).

Tax Concerns Can Influence Your Choices

The other (minor) downside to business success is bigger tax bills. To start with, sole proprietors, general partners, and active LLC members usually have to pay self-employment tax on their share of business profits. That comes to 15.3 percent of all profits up to $87,900 plus 2.9 percent of all profits over the $87,900 mark. And self-employment tax is in addition to regular federal and state income taxes. The combination could easily put the tax bite on significantly more than half of your profits!

If you're making enough money to be griping about taxes, it may be time to incorporate. Yes, it costs a lot to form and maintain a corporation. And, yes, there are plenty of corporate formalities to follow. But at least all of the costs and fees and some of the taxes are actually income tax deductible at the corporate level. For example, the employer portion of FICA would be both paid for by and deductible to the corporation.

If You Want to Be Alone, Consider a Loan

Many small business owners take on partners because they think it's the only way to raise money. They don't really want to share the decision-making function (or profits), but feel they have no other choice. But there is another option—debt financing.

Granted, loans may be hard to get, especially for a new business in a less than robust economy. But if your company needs more money because it's growing too fast for you to keep up with, the bank may look upon your application favorably. In other words, if your business is attractive enough to appeal to a new business partner, it will probably also interest your banker. The bank will charge you interest, and require periodic financial statements (prepared by a CPA)—but all of the daily business decisions will be yours alone to make.

In addition to self-employment taxes, federal income tax rates can make one entity choice seem more attractive than another. For 2004, personal federal income tax rates are relatively low, making pass-through entities very attractive to small business owners. But the scales may tip back in the favor of corporations (the ones that pay their own taxes on their own income), which may prompt a whole new generation of entrepreneurs to form C corporations.

Finally, most small business owners avoid C corporations (even when their tax rates are lower) because of the double taxation phenomenon. But with today's special tax rate for dividends, this argument becomes less persuasive. Add to that the tax-free fringe benefits typically not available for owners of pass-through entities, and you've got some serious thinking to do.

When should tax issues precipitate a change in your business form? Only your accountant knows for sure. Your situation is a unique blend of personal and business factors. What will work well for someone in a seemingly similar situation could end up costing you more money in the long run. Before you make a change solely for tax purposes, consult a tax professional.

When Your Personal Holdings Change, Re-evaluate the Business

Business factors aren't the only ones that change. When you experience any kind of major alteration in your personal financial situation, you should rethink the business structure of your company. Regardless of the direction of the change in your own net worth, it can have a direct impact on your business and on the two-way street of liability implications.

Your personal financial picture could change for many reasons that have absolutely nothing to do with your business. You could get married or have children. You could inherit a fortune or win the lottery. You could amass a lot of personal

Remember, Liability Is a Two-Way Street

Taking your sole proprietorship to the next level, in entity terms, will help shield your personal assets from business debts and obligations. But it can also protect your thriving company from attacks by your personal creditors. You might think you don't have any personal creditors, but are you really sure? Do you have any student loans still outstanding? Have all of your prior year's tax bills been paid in full? Did your spouse come to the party with questionable credit? Any of these types of unpaid debts can provoke an attack on your business assets.

On top of existing obligations, there's always the threat of new ones. If the paperboy slips on your icy front steps and his parents decide to sue, the assets of your sole proprietorship are considered to be your personal assets. But you can protect your company by changing entities, and protect yourself along the way.

If You've Got Money, Avoid General Partnerships

If you have personal wealth that you want to keep, avoid the general partnership entity like the plague. As a general partner you are personally liable for pretty much any debt incurred by the business, and you may end up being held liable for the personal debts of your partner(s).

Suppose you form a general partnership with a friend who has great business ideas but isn't so swift in the personal financial department. Your buddy has a lot of debt, while you have a healthy nest egg and are fairly debt-free. If your partner gets into debt over his head, his creditors will probably go after the partnership. Plus, if he's trying to pay his bills using company credit cards, you're on the hook for that, too. He may also be taking his share of cash distributions as he needs them, depleting the business of the cash it could use to pay its bills.

Protect yourself, your finances, and your future. Do not form a general partnership, and if you already have—change it to one of the liability-limiting structures available out there.

credit card debt or need to file for bankruptcy. And believe it or not, any of these events can and will affect your business.

When your personal net worth increases, you personally become a bigger target to creditors (and potential creditors) of your business. When your personal net worth hits zero and keeps going, your personal creditors will start looking at your business assets.

The best way to protect your personal assets from business debt will also protect your business from your personal debt. If you structure your business using one of the liability-shield entities (LLC or corporation), facing financial downfall in one area of your life won't have to affect all others. Truthfully, the best time to protect yourself is before you have something to lose. But in this case, better late than never really holds true. If your business is successful or you have personal assets you don't want to lose, make sure your business entity has a solid firewall between the two aspects of your life.

New Laws May Make Restructuring Beneficial

Tax laws aren't the only ones that change—although they do change rather frequently. With the multitude of lawsuits being brought in the United States today, new precedents are being set all the time. Between new interpretations of old laws and the need for new statutes to govern new business issues, the "best" entity for your business could change at any time. That's not to say you should restructure your company every time a law changes. But a significant change that could impact your company or industry specifically may merit the reconsideration of your current entity choice.

Here's a quick glance at some general law categories that could end up being the impetus for a change in your business structure:

- Tax law, including rates (you knew this would be first)
- New entity created by either state or federal statute
- Change in how charging orders are applied
- Personal or business bankruptcy limits or requirements

Of course, there are many more possible statute changes, but these groupings sum up those most likely to affect your choice of business structure.

> **Chapter 25**

Comparing Entities

Part One

Part Two

Part Three

Part Four

Part Five

Part Six

PART SIX   EVALUATING YOUR OPTIONS

■ CHAPTER 24 The Normal Business Progression ■ CHAPTER 25 **Comparing Entities** ■ CHAPTER 26 Switching from One Structure to Another

Sole Proprietorship vs. Single-Member LLC

As you learned in the previous chapter, almost every small business starts out as a sole proprietorship by default. As the business grows, many people simply forget about the structure aspect of their companies, and just keep on as before. That may work out fine for some companies, but others may fare better using a more formal business entity.

The single-member LLC is a very popular choice for businesses with only one owner (except in Massachusetts, where the minimum number of members required to create an LLC is two). Although when it comes to federal taxation, there is literally no distinction between sole proprietorships and single-member LLCs, there are some differences between the two business structures.

Personal Liability Goes from Complete to Almost Nonexistent

With a sole proprietorship, there is no liability protection for either you or your business. You are not separate legal entities. If one of you owes money, you both do. So if your business is in trouble, you could lose your children's college fund. If you're having some personal financial difficulties,

Single-Member LLCs Are More Vulnerable to Veil Piercing

It's not fair, but it's true. You go through all the trouble of forming an LLC, and the courts still look at you as suspiciously as if your business was a sole proprietorship. When your company starts falling behind in meeting its obligations or gets sued and loses a large settlement, creditors will run to the courthouse and ask the judge to pierce the limited liability veil—and they may just win.

Strengthen your veil by officially separating all business and personal assets. Have a lawyer prepare a formal LLC operating agreement. Make sure your LLC is adequately funded for regular business transactions. And run your company as if it's completely distinct from you, at least financially. Then if you do get hauled into court, you'll have plenty of proof that your LLC is truly a separate entity, and you'll be able to protect your personal assets.

your business could be liquidated by the courts. There is literally no distinction—in the eyes of the law—between your personal assets and your business assets, regardless of the practical steps you've taken to separate the two.

The LLC, in contrast, offers liability protection technically as strong as that offered by incorporating. Although somewhat untested in the courts, on paper LLCs provide complete limited liability protection to their members. That means you will not be held personally responsible for unpaid debts and obligations of the company, and that the company's creditors won't prevail if they name you personally in a lawsuit. All you really stand to lose is your investment in the company; the remainder of your personal assets won't be at stake.

LLCs Are More Expensive to Create and Maintain

When it comes to the costs of business structures, sole proprietorships are hands down the least expensive. Other than required licenses and permits that would be needed by any business, sole proprietorships are pretty much fee-free.

LLCs, on the other hand, cost money. You have to pay to form them, pay annual filing fees, pay registration fees, and (sometimes) pay lawyers to properly form the entity and prepare legal documents. In some states, LLCs have to pay unincorporated business taxes; in others, they are taxed as if they were corporations. Some states actually charge LLCs higher fees than corporations!

Whether the added expense is worth it is up to you. But think of it as insurance. When you have a lot to lose, isn't the $300 (or $500 or $800) annual "premium" worth it? If you or your business has accumulated a nice pot of gold, the answer is probably "yes."

Sole Proprietorship vs. Corporation

The decision to incorporate your sole proprietorship boils down to two key issues: liability protection and tax savings. When your business becomes profitable, thereby increasing your personal net worth, these considerations become much more important.

To start with, corporations offer virtually ironclad limited liability protection to their shareholders—even when there's only one. Only you can threaten your liability shield, by treating your corporation as your personal checkbook or by failing to follow corporate formalities. Yes, there's a lot of paperwork that goes along with forming and running a corporation, compared to virtually none for sole proprietorships. If you know that you won't keep up with it, hire someone to handle it for you—or reconsider the corporation as your entity of choice.

As to tax savings, these can tip the scales in favor of corporations. When you operate your company as a sole proprietorship, every penny of profits—even if you leave them in the business—is subject to self-employment taxes. That means at the very least, you'll have to pay 15.3 percent in FICA taxes on all business income. With a corporation (whether you choose the S form or the C), you can allocate a portion of your income to salary subject to FICA, and consider the rest dividends not subject to payroll taxes.

Corporations do cost more than sole proprietorships; in fact, they are typically the most expensive business entities to form and maintain. But tax savings can offset some of that. And the seriously strong limited liability protection is well worth the cost.

Should You Change Your Partnership Type?

If you're operating your small business as a general partnership, the answer is an unqualified "yes." In fact, with all of the other entity choices out there today, many small business experts predict that the general partnership will go the way of the dinosaur. The liability risks simply outweigh any possible benefit that exists within the general partnership business structure.

Should you really want to maintain a partnership as your underlying entity, at least consider one of the more protective forms. Of course, the appropriateness of either of the other partnership forms has to be looked at. But should they suit your circumstances, both are preferable to straight general partnerships.

To Bring in Family Members, Use a Limited Partnership

As you now know, general partnerships are particularly vulnerable to liabilities created by partners. But many small businesses are family businesses, of which the purpose is to gradually bring in the next generation of entrepreneurs. The next generation, though, may not be the most financially responsible—especially when they are college age or younger. Today's kids seem very sophisticated, and they seem to know an awful lot about business; but they are still kids, and they still make the same mistakes all the kids for generations before them have made.

One very strong piece of advice: *Do not make your children general partners in your business.* That applies to younger children in particular, but also to those with insecure personal financial footing. In fact, this caveat also applies to any family member who doesn't have control of his or her own finances. You can still have these family members involved in the business in an ownership capacity (usually this is so they don't feel left out) without making them general partners. Simply alter the entity to limited partnership, and give them limited partnership interests.

Bringing in the younger generation as limited partners can help develop their sense of responsibility and interest in the business without subjecting your company to their personal creditors. In addition, as limited partners, they will have absolutely no power to bind the partnership. Best, under the business-friendly rules of the RULPA, creditors with charging orders against limited partners generally walk away close to empty-handed.

The rules governing limited partnerships are quite a bit more complex than those relating to general partnerships. Therefore, you should definitely talk to a qualified estate and tax planning attorney to help you both form and maintain this entity. He'll also be able to advise you on how shares should be apportioned among family members for the most beneficial tax treatment.

If You Can, Form an LLLP

Very few states offer this beneficial partnership form—the limited liability limited partnership—but if yours does, jump on it. The extra L's add limited liability to the general partner of a limited partnership. And those extra L's mean that no one has complete and total personal liability for partnership debts. So if you have a limited partnership in a state that allows LLLPs (like Maryland, Colorado, and Delaware), pay the fee and free your general partner from unlimited liability.

LLPs Offer Varying Levels of Protection

The state laws governing LLPs are among the most varied business statutes in the nation. But they all do one thing. They add at least some personal liability protection to general partners without removing any of the benefits of the structure. LLPs are identical to general partnerships in every way except for unlimited liability and state fees. But how much those fees are and how much protection the entity affords its owners depends on the home state of your business.

At the very least, an LLP will offer you protection against liabilities generated by the tortious acts of other partners. This level of liability protection is called a limited shield—and while it may not sound like much on paper, it could turn out to save you a lot of money if one of your partners is sued for malpractice.

In some states, LLPs offer their partners personal liability protection similar to that enjoyed by LLC members. Plus, as LLPs gain in popularity, those states originally offering only limited shields are adapting their laws to offer more comprehensive protection.

Partnership vs. LLC

In almost every aspect, you couldn't tell the difference between a partnership and an LLC. But there are several features that are different: one very much so, the others fairly minor. The big difference can be found in the formal

Is the LLP Form an Option for Your Business?

A few states allow only professional firms to form LLPs. In fact, in California that is even further restricted to attorneys, public accountants, and architects. New York also limits LLPs to professional practices, but their list of allowed professions is much broader. In both cases, only properly licensed professionals in the home state can be partners in these LLPs. If your company doesn't meet with these guidelines, forming an LLP in such states is not an option.

name of the LLC: limited liability. The minor differences exist mainly at the state level, in the form of added paperwork, fees, and taxes.

If there's nothing legally impeding you from creating your small business as an LLC instead of as a partnership (whether general or limited), form the LLC. Some states do, however, restrict the use of LLCs to certain professions and industries. To find out if your company is eligible to form an LLC, check out your home state's business creation Web site.

Limited Liability Is a Significant Advantage

In case it has not yet sunk in, repeat the following phrase: "General partners are 100 percent personally liable for all debts of the partnership." Even with limited partnerships, you must have at least one general partner, and he will be fully and personally liable for all of the debts of the business. LLC members, on the other hand, bear no personal responsibility for debts or obligations of the partnership.

In addition to the all-purpose limited liability afforded by state law, LLC members can bolster their protection through their operating agreement. For example, you can specifically limit some members to nonmanagement roles, essentially making their ownership interests similar to those of limited partners. In this way, you can restrict them from having the actual authority to legally bind the company. On the other hand, should all members want to actively participate in the business, they can do so without jeopardizing their limited liability protection (as opposed to true limited partners).

Fees, Paperwork, and Taxes

LLCs cost more in both time and money than general partnerships (limited partnerships have only slightly less paperwork and fees than LLCs). Although the list of formalities can be counted on one hand, that's still more than are required for general partnerships.

As to taxes and fees, they vary by state. However, regardless of the amount due, it's almost guaranteed to be more than would be due for a general partnership. In some states, LLC fees are even higher than corporate fees. There are fees for formation, and annual upkeep fees. Some states charge taxes at the entity level, similar to those they would charge regular corporations.

Partnership vs. Corporation

When comparing partnerships with corporations, variety matters—at least where taxes and eligible owners are concerned. But when it comes to liability protection, any form of corporation wins hands down over partnerships.

Corporations have undisputed dominion when it comes to protecting their owners from liability claims related to the business. With decades of precedent to back it up, the shield of limited liability for corporate shareholders is almost impossible to pierce. In fact, the biggest threat to having the veil pierced comes from you. But as long as you care for your corporation properly, you can rest assured that no corporate creditors will be coming after you at home.

In a partnership entity, though, your personal assets can be on the block for any claims against the partnership. Even an LLP may offer only a scaled-down version of liability protection, and limited partnerships protect only limited partners. Plus, LLPs don't have a long courtroom history, having only been around for a relatively short time. When you want to shield your personal wealth, partnerships are definitely not the best way to go.

> When you want to shield your personal wealth, partnerships are definitely not the best way to go.

Although general partnerships come out the big loser in the liability competition, they sweep the simplicity contest hands down. There is literally no paperwork required to form a general partnership, you don't even need a partnership agreement (though you absolutely should have one). General partnerships don't have to keep minutes, take votes, or come up with bylaws. There are no formation documents, no maintenance documents—the only paperwork you really have to deal with has to do with taxes. For corporations, on the other hand, the paperwork comes in piles. It's almost as though you earn your exceptional liability protection by doing paperwork penance. And if you even skip one piece of paper, even one little requirement, you risk having your corporation dissolved.

Sometimes C Is Better, Sometimes Not

From a tax perspective, the answer to the "Which is better?" question is mixed. In some aspects, regular corporations hold the advantage; in others, partnerships have the upper hand. C corporations are individual tax entities—they pay their own taxes on their own income. And that makes the IRS look somewhat more favorably on their owners, especially those who work for the company. But the IRS rules, as always, pose a double-edged sword—and that's where partnerships have their edge.

The advantages of C corporations over partnerships related to taxation include:

- Being able to split income
- Tax-free fringe benefits
- More flexibility in choosing the tax year

The biggest tax-related advantages of partnerships over regular corporations include pass-through taxation and no double taxation. These advantages can be pretty big, especially in the early years of a business, when it typically suffers "growing pain" losses that can be used to offset the owners' outside income. When profits finally begin to show up, owners often need to replenish their own battered bank accounts with distributions from the business. These distributions are tax-free for partners, but taxable to C corporation shareholders—even though the corporation has already paid taxes on its income.

S Corporations Are Taxed Like Partnerships, But . . .

The tax rules for S corporations mirror those for partnerships. The entity itself pays no income taxes, and all items of income and loss flow through to the business owners. However, there is one major area in which the tax regulations part ways: special allocations.

As long as they have a good reason for it (interpret: as long as the IRS buys the reason), partnerships can distribute profits or losses to their owners however they like. That means fifty-fifty partners could split up profits sixty-forty if they want to. S corporations have no such flexibility, forcing shareholders to split the proceeds strictly in proportion to their respective ownership percentages.

The other drawback to S corporations when compared to partnerships is the ownership restrictions. The number of total shareholders is limited, and who may be a shareholder is also limited. Partnerships are not subject to any of these ownership limitations. Should an S corporation admit an extra or an ineligible shareholder, its S status disappears, reverting the corporation to its original C format.

S Corporation vs. C Corporation

All corporations start out as C (or regular) corporations. Some of those go on to elect S status by filling out an IRS form. S status is mainly a tax distinction, but there are some additional factors to consider. Many corporations initially choose to operate as S corporations, then switch to C corporations as they grow. You can switch the other way, but it's much more complicated and much less common.

Some corporate features remain the same regardless of which letter (C or S) you choose. Limited liability for shareholders is unaffected. Raising additional funds is as easy as selling shares of stock. It's pretty simple to transfer ownership interests. And the entity enjoys the privilege of eternal life (at least theoretically).

The primary difference between the two types of corporations is federal tax treatment. C corporations pay their own income taxes on their profits, and their shareholders must pay additional taxes on any distributions of corporate income (typically in the form of dividends) or capital gains earned when shares are sold off. S corporations pay no income taxes, instead passing their income through to their shareholders, thus avoiding the double taxation issue.

The other differences may seem minor, but can become big issues for some business owners. First comes the number and type of owners: C corporations can be owned by anyone—any type of entity, any number of investors; S corporations must adhere to very strict guidelines when admitting new shareholders. In addition to restrictions on the types of allowed owners, there is also a limit on the total number of owners permitted for S corporations. Second is treatment of fringe benefits: Even though you technically can be an employee of your S corporation, you're treated as an owner when it comes to fringe benefits. C corporation owner-employees, on the other hand, are entitled to tax-free fringe benefits that are also tax-deductible to the corporation. Finally, C corporations have a lot more flexibility when it comes to choosing their tax years.

The choice between corporate types depends on the unique circumstances for your company. The general rule of thumb involves what you plan to do with your profits. If you plan to take profits out of the corporation, using the S form can be more beneficial when it comes to tax treatment. But if you plan to leave most of the profits inside the company (to fund growth, for example), you'll save tax dollars by using the basic C format.

LLC vs. Corporation

If you are an active participant in the business you own, you have two basic entity options to limit your personal liability. You can either incorporate or form an LLC. Each has advantages over the other—but the LLC is quickly emerging as the most popular liability-limiting entity of choice for small business owners.

The biggest advantage of LLCs over corporations is reduced paperwork. But these relatively new business structures also have some financial advantages. For example, unlike any type of corporation, the LLC entity allows its owners to share profits in proportions other than that directly related to their ownership percentages (this is called *special allocations*). Second, most states (though certainly not all) charge lower formation and ongoing fees for LLCs than they do for corporations. Third, LLC membership interests typically are not subject to securities laws (unless they have a disproportionate number of passive members); corporations (except in certain circumstances) may have to comply with both federal and state securities laws.

With all the good press LLCs receive, it's easy to overlook the fact that corporations do offer some advantages. Corporations have unlimited life spans, while LLCs may not (some states don't allow this, for example). Stock shares are typically easier to transfer than LLC membership interests by law (although small corporations often have shareholder agreements limiting ownership transfers). Finally, and probably most important, corporations have a proven track record when it comes to liability protection. Decades of legal precedents

Consider a Close Corporation If Paperwork Is the Issue

You want serious liability protection for your company. You think a corporation will provide the strongest shield. But you hate (and I mean HATE) paperwork, and corporations typically come with much more of that than LLCs do.

If forming an LLC instead really doesn't fill the bill for you, you may want to consider creating a *close corporation* (if your state allows it). Close corporations offer all of the features of other corporations, with much less paperwork. These spin-off entities were developed to help small business corporations stay in business without the overwhelming burden of typical corporate formalities. Easier compliance means less threat of having the corporate veil pierced. And isn't that why you wanted to incorporate in the first place?

Remember, Double Taxation Doesn't Only Apply to Dividends

One of my clients had a vintage car business. On the advice of his next-door neighbor (a plumber, not a professional business advisor), this client—who we'll call Ted—formed a C corporation for his business. For his first few years in business, he successfully avoided excessive double taxation by making his annual salary and bonus roughly equal to his annual profits.

When Ted decided to retire, he had three vintage cars remaining in inventory. He found a buyer for the company, including the cars—selling it at a substantial profit. The way the tax law works, Ted's corporation had to pay taxes on the profits from the sale of the inventory. Then, Ted had to pay tax on the whopping capital gain he realized on the liquidation of the corporation.

The moral of this story is that with a C corporation, you can't avoid double taxation forever.

have shown the corporate liability shield (in most cases) to be virtually bulletproof.

The rest of the differences are specific to the type of corporation you form. The remainder of this section will focus on comparing LLCs to each specific corporate structure.

Comparing the LLC to the C Corporation

In general, an LLC will be a better choice for a small company than a C corporation. In addition to the smaller paperwork burden, forming an LLC will help you avoid the problem of double taxation. So if your company will own assets that will probably increase in value substantially, an LLC can save you some taxes.

But in some circumstances, structuring your company as an LLC instead of a regular corporation may not be the best choice. First, if you're in Massachusetts and want to be the sole owner of your company, you can't form an LLC. That leaves incorporation as your only choice if you want or need to limit your personal liability. The second scenario is almost the polar opposite. If you need to obtain financing from multiple investors (or sell pieces of your business to the general public), a corporation makes more sense. LLCs work great when you have up to five members—especially when members will want to be active in the business. But when the number of owners increases above that, an LLC is no longer practical.

Two other factors may make the C corporation a more attractive choice than the LLC: fringe benefits and stock bonus incentives. When you work for your corporation, you count as an employee—not so with an LLC. As an employee, you are entitled to more tax-free benefits than you would be as an owner. An added benefit: These extras are tax-deductible to the corporation. So if you want to provide yourself with benefits (like group term life insurance), forming a C corporation may be the most tax-effective way to do that. The other factor applies to nonowner employees: stock incentives. First, the obvious fact: LLCs don't have any stock. So if you want to reward employees with stock incentives, you have to have a corporation.

If none of the circumstances that tip the scales in favor of incorporating exist for your company, using the LLC structure may be a better choice for you. LLCs are typically easier to deal with, more flexible, and less expensive.

LLC vs. S Corporation?

Both LLCs and S corporations offer their owners favorable pass-through taxation, completely sidestepping the double taxation issue. The main difference in these entity choices from a tax perspective is self-employment taxes, which typically affect only active business owners. Here's the scoop: With an S corporation, you have the option of classifying a portion of the business income as your salary, and only that portion of profits is subject to FICA (the corporation pays its half, you pay yours through withholding, but it all still comes out to the 15.3 percent). The rest of the company earnings flow through to you as dividends, subject only to income taxes. On the other hand, as an active LLC member, your entire share of profits is subject to self-employment taxes. When it comes to the issue of self-employment taxes, S corporations hold the advantage over LLCs.

In other areas, though, LLCs can make your business life easier. For example, there are no restrictions on the number (except for Massachusetts LLCs) or types of owners for LLCs. S corporations, on the other hand, are subject to a heap of restrictive ownership regulations. Also, S corporations can have only one level of ownership; LLCs can have many different classes of ownership interests. Plus, the special allocations (referred to above) available to LLCs allow profits and losses to be divvied up in any manner you see fit. If you share profits in any manner other than in direct proportion to ownership interests in your S corporation, it will be deemed a second class of stock and you'll lose your S status.

> **Chapter 26**

Switching from One Structure to Another

Part One

Part Two

Part Three

Part Four

Part Five

Part Six

PART SIX   EVALUATING YOUR OPTIONS

■ CHAPTER 24 The Normal Business Progression ■ CHAPTER 25 Comparing Entities ■ CHAPTER 26 Switching from One Structure to Another

From Sole Proprietorship to Single-Member LLC

When it's time to think about integrating liability protection into your sole proprietorship, forming a single-member LLC is the easiest way to go. In addition to allowing you to be the only owner of your company (except in Massachusetts), there are no tax consequences to making this change.

From the point of view of the federal government, your business isn't even really undergoing a change. Single-member LLCs are already considered sole proprietorships for tax purposes—you'll still report all of your business income on Schedule C along with the rest of your personal tax return. The switch to LLC is completely invisible to the IRS, and that means no effect on federal income taxes.

Of course, though, the main point of making this change is to add liability protection to your business entity. So the transformation will be clearly apparent to the state government(s) in any state(s) your LLC conducts business. Unlike federal taxation, your state business taxes may (and probably will) change. First, a few states treat LLCs (even those with only one member) like corporations, at least for tax purposes. Second, some states charge unincorporated business taxes. Third, even if the state doesn't explicitly call them taxes, it will charge at least some annual fees in exchange for the privilege of operating as an LLC.

How to Change Your Sole Proprietorship into an LLC

Because of the wide diversity among state statutes, you'll need to check with your home state business development office (usually part of the secretary of state's office) to learn about its exact requirements. But there are a few basic steps you'll need to take no matter where you transform your business structure.

For one thing, you'll have to change the legal name of your company. When you were a sole proprietorship, your name served as the company's legal name. Now the legal name of your company has to include one of the state-approved terms (like "LLC"); this serves as notice to the public that you're using a business entity that limits your personal liability.

You'll also have to fill out all the necessary formation and maintenance paperwork (along with paying all the required fees). Some states make you

Extra Formalities Help Solidify Your Liability Shield

Forming a single-member LLC will do a lot to protect both your personal and business assets from creditor claims. However, single-member LLCs are the most vulnerable to having their liability shields pierced (as you learned in Chapter 22). To keep this undesirable event from occurring, make sure to always treat your company as if it were unconnected to you personally. The more formality you add to the relationship between you and your LLC, the more the courts will uphold the separate entity principle.

Going that extra mile may include performing formalities not required under your LLC's home state law. For example, keeping minutes of meetings (with yourself) can serve as proof that your company is a separate entity.

start from scratch, as if your company hadn't already been in operation at all. In those states, you'll have to file articles of organization, and all the other forms needed to create an LLC. In other states, you'll just have to file some kind of certificate outlining your company's conversion from one entity to another (yes, this simple form probably also comes with a price tag). You'll probably also have to obtain a new state ID number for the LLC.

Make sure to follow the particular guidelines set forth by your company's home state. If you've been conducting business in more than one state, you'll have to register as a foreign LLC in each of the other states in which you do business.

Adding a Second Member Is Pretty Easy

Once you've transformed your business into an LLC, the number of owners is almost irrelevant. Unlike adding a second owner to a sole proprietorship (which dissolves the original entity and creates a new one), adding another member to an LLC usually has no legal implications. Tax implications, yes; but a dissolution and reformation of the entity, no.

This transformation to a multiple-member LLC is made even easier if you've paved the way in your original articles of organization and operating agreement. When the documents are being drafted, tell your attorney that you want to provide for additional membership interests and buy-sell provisions. This will make bringing in a business partner or two much smoother. Plus, you get to decide on your own how things will flow if your future co-member wants out (and that can only help you down the line).

Of course, from a tax perspective everything has changed. Instead of filing the old Schedule C at year-end, now your LLC will have to file a Form 1065, along with Schedules K-1 for each member. You may also have to recognize some gain associated with the sale of an ownership interest, so have your accountant involved in the transaction. He'll also be able to deal with such IRS issues as determining member's basis.

Changing Your Partnership to a Different Form

If you currently have a business that's set up as a general partnership, change it. As you've read (repeatedly) throughout this book, general partners have the highest levels of personal liability for business debts when compared to every other type of business owner. And while partnerships do have some apparent benefits, these are overshadowed by the enormous potential personal liability disaster.

If you're still not convinced, consider this: Every advantage of partnerships is available (at least in some form) in other business entities. Most of the benefits come from the tax laws. The table below illustrates how the current choices of business structures have encompassed some of the great features of partnerships.

PARTNERSHIP BENEFITS SHOW UP IN OTHER ENTITIES, TOO

Entities:	*Pass-Through Taxation*	*Special Allocations Allowed*	*No Double Taxation*
LLP	☑	☑	☑
LLC	☑	☑	☑
S Corporation	☑	☐	☑

Tax Issues When Going from Partnership to LLP

Under most circumstances, converting your general or limited partnership to an LLP can be done without creating any adverse federal income tax implications. Thanks to several IRS private-letter rulings (that really just means IRS permission and confirmation to settle a particular tax issue without involving Congress), the switch is virtually invisible for tax purposes.

Basically, the IRS has said that as long as the business of the partnership did not change, and the type and percentage of ownership interest for each partner stayed the same, they would consider the LLP merely a continuation of the old partnership. So if everything except for the liability stays the same, the entity stays the same for tax purposes.

How to Convert to an LLP

The easiest way to change your existing partnership to an LLP is to simply register as one in your home state and pay the applicable fees. Under most states' laws, the assets and liabilities of the previously existing entity just transfer to the new one.

And here's a very important point to remember: The partners who had personal liability for already existing business debts or obligations of the old entity continue to do so. The liability protection afforded by the LLP applies only to debts incurred after the conversion.

In addition to the registration paperwork, there are a few other administrative tasks to complete. First, the legal name of your business will probably

Don't Forget about Legal Restrictions on LLPs

Remember, not every partnership will be allowed to form an LLP. Some states restrict the use of the LLP form to professional practices; among those, some (such as California) severely limit which forms of professionals can use this entity. Before you get any paperwork underway, make sure that your current firm is eligible to apply for LLP status. If it is, make sure that all general partners are currently and properly licensed in the chosen field.

have to change. You'll have to incorporate one of the official naming conventions (like LLP) into the name of your company. Next, you'll probably have to retitle all of the business assets (including bank accounts) into the new name. You'll have to register your LLP in every state in which your partnership conducts business. And you should probably address the change in your partnership agreement.

Moving from Partnership to LLC

General partnerships can effortlessly shift their business structures to LLCs without experiencing any adverse tax consequences. Making this change will provide all of the partners with the liability protection that was previously lacking in their business entities without causing a taxable event. This is because multimember LLCs are automatically treated as if they were partnerships by the IRS, already reporting their income on Form 1065. So to the federal government, there really is no change taking place.

What does all of that mean in practical terms? You don't need to get a new federal tax ID number for the LLC. You don't have to end the partnership's tax year and start a new one for the LLC—it all just flows over. And, best of all, typically no partners have to recognize gains (meaning pay additional income taxes) due to the conversion. (In some circumstances, however, some partners may need to recognize gains; consult your CPA to find out how your personal tax situation could be affected by the conversion.)

The Mechanics of the Transformation to LLC

How the conversion takes place is a matter of state statute. There are basically three ways the conversion can take place: liquidation and reformation, a technical merger, or merely through paperwork. If your state offers you a choice, go for the paperwork method; if that's not one of the choices, go with merger. (Your professional business advisor should be enlisted to help your company through the transformation if you have to use any method other than simply filing forms.)

Even if your home state allows you to change your partnership to an LLC with just a few strokes of the pen, there still may be some variation in exact method. For example, some states require the filing of articles of organization, just as they would for a start-up business. Others require a simple form, most often called a "certificate of conversion." In some cases, former partnerships must publicly announce their termination before being allowed to officially convert to LLCs.

More Administrative Tasks to Complete

First comes the name change. To keep this as simple as possible, you can simply tack "LLC" on to the end of your former partnership's name. Once that's done, you'll need to retitle all assets in the new name, as they all transfer directly to the LLC. Then comes the numbers game.

All businesses making this change must either transfer their existing ID numbers, licenses, and permits to the new business name, or apply for new ones (clearly, it's easier to roll the old ones over, where permissible). Such items typically include federal and state employer identification numbers, sales tax permits and business licenses. The individual states are more likely to require new numbers (or permits or licenses) than the federal government, since the federal government doesn't really register the change. Check with any offices (state or local) with which your company was previously registered to find out precisely which filings need to be adapted.

Incorporating a Sole Proprietorship, Partnership, or LLC

For existing sole proprietorships and partnerships, converting to a corporation will greatly enhance your personal liability protection—your shield will go from zero to one hundred (percent) in seconds flat. In addition, at certain times and in certain circumstances, operating as a C corporation can perk up your tax situation. But if you want to maintain pass-through tax status, you can always make the S election (as long as all owners are eligible to hold S stock).

> Converting to a corporation will greatly enhance your personal liability protection.

LLCs, by contrast, don't really need added liability protection. And there's really no point to switching an LLC to an S corporation—they both already have pass-through taxation available, and LLCs don't have restrictive ownership guidelines to adhere to. But sometimes, changing the tax status of your LLC to that of a C corporation can be financially advantageous.

From Sole Proprietor to Corporation

If you need some liability protection and for some reason can't form an LLC (for example, you live and work in Massachusetts), a corporate entity will provide the shield you need. Typically, incorporating a sole proprietorship is not considered a taxable transaction. This is mainly because there is no legal distinction between you and your company.

The big ouch here will be in your pocketbook. To ensure your liability protection sticks, have an attorney assist you in the incorporation process. Have him set up your corporation, issue your stock, and transfer the applicable assets.

Now you—along with your accountant—must decide whether to go with C or S status. If your business isn't quite off the ground and pass-through taxation will be beneficial, file your S election. If your business is doing quite well and you'd like to expand it (thereby keeping the lion's share of profits inside the company), you may decide to stick with regular corporation taxation—and take your share out in salary and other ways that can get around the double taxation issue.

From Partnership to Corporation

Incorporating your existing partnership is a fairly straightforward transaction. However, you must make sure to comply with all the points outlined in your partnership agreement as you do it. It's a good idea to involve your

Stay on Top of All the Paperwork

Now that you've gone ahead and incorporated your business, make sure to keep your corporate status intact. The minute your corporation is formed, your obligation to perform all of the legal formalities begins. That means creating a Board of Directors, electing corporate officers, holding shareholder's meetings, and so on. Failing to dot every *i* and cross every *t* will result in a technical termination of your corporation. (For detailed information on corporate formalities, see Chapter 15.)

attorney in the process—and your accountant as well to make sure all the tax bases are covered.

Essentially, you have to dissolve your partnership; theoretically, all assets would be distributed to the partners. You and your partners will temporarily own the assets yourself, then contribute them to the new corporation in exchange for your shares. If you want to get a little more sophisticated, you could retain title to some of the physical assets, then lease them to the corporation—adding a way to get more cash out of the company without involving payroll taxes.

When your new corporation is formed, you'll have to develop bylaws. The easiest way to do this is to "translate" your old partnership agreement into the language of corporations, adapting sections where necessary. (Again, your attorney can easily help you through this.)

From LLC to Corporation

To change your LLC into a corporation, all you have to do is check a box.

You don't need to formally incorporate your business at the state level to add liability protection to your entity—it's already there. So the only reason to make any kind of switch is for tax purposes. There's no point in turning your LLC into an S corporation—you already have pass-through taxation. So such a change must be a time when you and your company (and possibly your co-members) will benefit from regular corporate taxation.

To change your LLC's tax status from the default (partnership taxation), simply obtain IRS Form 8832 (you can download this from the IRS Web site at *www.irs.gov* or ask your accountant for it). Fill out the form. Check the appropriate tax classification box. Sign the form (make sure to include all required signers). Mail the form to the correct IRS office for your home state. You're done.

It Started with One Store in Arkansas

Sam and Bud Walton opened their first Wal-Mart store in 1962. Within five years, they had a total of 24 stores and over $12 million in sales. The next year they expanded their range outside of Arkansas, opening stores in Missouri and Oklahoma. And by 1969, it was time to incorporate.

On October 31, 1969, Wal-Mart Stores, Inc., was officially created. And in 1970, the Waltons went public. By 1972, the stock (originally traded over the counter) hit the big time, and was listed on the New York Stock Exchange. Although Sam and Bud are no longer with us, Wal-Mart Stores, Inc., lives on.

Most S Corporation Terminations Are Involuntary

Unfortunately, many small S corporations are kicked back to regular corporation status even though they didn't want to be. It's pretty easy to lose your S status, so you need to be on the lookout for triggers, such as exceeding the allowed number of shareholders. Luckily, the IRS often waives inadvertent terminations, subject to certain conditions, of course. So if your S status was prematurely ended, contact the IRS and find out what you need to do to set things straight.

Most states follow the federal tax classification of the entity. Check with your state's business office or with your CPA to make sure.

Turn Your S Corporation into a C Corporation

To terminate your company's status as an S corporation, you need to revoke your S election. Once you've made that choice, though, you can't reapply for S tax treatment for at least five years. Plus, the revocation can only go through if shareholders who together own more than 50 percent of the outstanding shares of stock agree to it (if you're the only shareholder, no problem).

When you are ready to change your corporation back to a C, you must send a written statement to the IRS office where your S corporation tax returns were filed. This statement has to include an explicit declaration that the corporation is revoking its S election. It also has to include the total number of shares of outstanding stock on the revocation date. If you want the change to be effective on some future date, you should spell that out in your declaration. Whoever was authorized to sign the Form 1120S must sign the statement.

In addition, you have to attach a consent statement to the revocation. Basically, this should start with something like, "I consent to have this S corporation status revoked." Each consenting shareholder has to list the number of shares he owns as of the revocation date, and sign the statement.

Once the IRS receives and approves your revocation notice, they will send you a letter stating so. The letter will include the effective date of the change.

Change Your C Corporation into an S Corporation

All S corporations started out as C corporations. There's one simple form to fill out when you're ready to make that switch. It's called IRS Form 2553: Election by a Small Business Corporation. As soon as you decide you want your corporation to be an S corporation, file the form. If you do it too late in the year, it won't count until the next tax year.

If you're the sole owner of the corporation, filing the form will be no problem. If you have co-owners, they must unanimously agree to the change and all sign the form. If even one shareholder doesn't want the corporation to alter its tax status, you can't do it. If the form is filled out incompletely or incorrectly, the IRS will kick it back to you (but you can make the corrections and send it back). Once they've accepted your application, they'll send you written notice to that effect.

Remember, S corporations have to adhere to a lot more rules than their C counterparts. If your corporation doesn't fit into the S mold, you won't be able to make the election.

A Reminder Involving Corporate Taxes

S corporations that formerly operated as C corporations may be responsible for paying some corporate level taxes. First is the built-in gains tax that comes into play when assets used by the old C corporation are sold for a profit. Second is the excess passive income tax, which has to do with (you guessed it) passive income combined with previously undistributed earnings (while still a C corporation). The third (called the *LIFO recapture tax*, in case you really wanted to know) has to do with the way inventory was previously valued for tax purposes.

These taxes probably won't affect your company. And they are really more for the accountants to worry about. But don't be shocked if your now S, former C corporation ends up paying a corporate tax now and again.

Recommended Resources

Appendix 1

Appendix 2

Appendix 3

Government Sources

Internal Revenue Service—✐ *www.irs.gov*

This Web site is pretty easy to navigate (believe it or not!). In addition to specific tax information pertinent to your business structure, the IRS site also provides downloadable tax publications and forms. All forms also come with line-by-line instructions on how to fill them out. With special sections for new businesses, and a list of helpful links, this Web site is among the best for small business owners seeking tax information.

Small Business Administration—✐ *www.sba.gov*

This federal agency provides assistance to small business owners through its Web site, in addition to offering live help at its offices (which are all listed on the site—just type in your Zip Code and it will list the offices nearest you). All SBA loan programs are clearly explained here, and application forms can be downloaded to get the process started more quickly. If you're looking for financing for your start-up enterprise, this Web site should be the first stop on your list.

U.S. Business Advisor—✐ *www.business.gov*

Sponsored by the SBA, this Web site for the U.S. Business Advisor was created to help small business owners find the right government agency to assist them—and there are more than sixty existing federal agencies out there established to help small business owners. To save you a lot of phone calls and a lot of time, this Web site will direct you to the proper government agency. Whatever issues you need cleared up (from labor disputes to employee benefits to equal opportunity employer regulations), coming here first will help you avoid being put on hold and transferred around.

BusinessLaw.gov—✐ *www.businesslaw.gov*

Also linked to the SBA, this Web site has a lot of plain English guides to somewhat complex legal issues. These guides cover the legalities relating to all phases of your business. Topics include e-commerce, exports, and even how to hire a qualified attorney. Best of all, this site serves as a gateway to all levels of government that may impact your business, from federal all the way down to local.

Volunteer and Nonprofit Sources

SCORE—✍ *www.score.org*

SCORE is a great organization, dedicated to helping small business owners make their companies successful. Their mentoring group is made up of retired executives and entrepreneurs—these people know what they're talking about. The free services they offer include start-up and planning advice, small business plan preparation, and individual in person or online business consultations. The Web site also includes a contact list of local offices.

FreeAdvice.com—✍ *www.freeadvice.com*

This Web site provides legal counseling for small businesses. The site is very cluttered (mainly because it offers so much information—U.S. federal and state law is vast), but not slow and not difficult to navigate. They have a full section on business law, including a complete state resource center (since state law governs most business legalities, and the laws vary widely among the states). Plus, they have a free question and answer forum and a "find your own lawyer" section. A good place to start when you have legal questions, especially ones concerning basic business start-up issues.

Commercial Sources

Nolo—✍ *www.nolo.com*

The Nolo Web site is chock full of information about the tax and legal questions frequently asked by new small business owners. All of the information is presented in easy to read and understand format, and it is very simple to get from one article to the next. In addition to the vast amount of free information that the Web site provides, Nolo also has an online bookstore. I have found the Nolo books to be particularly well written, in basic everyday language, and full of truly useful information.

CCH Business Owner's Toolkit—✍ *www.toolkit.cch.com*

The CCH Company is well known by accountants, as it provides a very popular tax preparation software system. This trustworthy Web site offers a wealth of legal and tax information, and advice suitable for new business owners. The information is current and reliable (in fact, I often pop over to this Web site to double-check data from other sources). Particularly informative is the "Ask Alice" section of the Web site, as it provides answers to real life questions from real small business owners—the kind of specific answers you would not easily find elsewhere; and if your question isn't covered, send it in.

BusinessTown.com—✍ *www.businesstown.com*

If you are looking for basic information presented in a friendly style, this is the Web site for you. The site is very easy to navigate, and pages load quickly (largely due to the lack of overwhelming advertising in your face). The content is comprehensive, covering essentially all aspects of starting and running a small business. This is a very good place to begin, because the presentation is clear and complete.

The ABC's of Small Business—✍ *www.abcsmallbiz.com*

Similar to BusinessTown with its breezy and light style, this site puts a lot of focus on how to decide whether you want to start your own business. To get started, click on the "Business Basics" section. The topics are clearly listed, and it is very easy to get from one page to the next. This is another good site for beginners to browse.

Bplans.com—✍ *www.bplans.com*

Now that you've decided you want to go into business for yourself, and you have some idea of the type of business you want to start, this Web site will help you pull it all together. It's devoted to helping you research and write a comprehensive business plan. To complete your research, there are several business calculators and a lot of additional links (such as for marketing statistics). Yes, they do want to sell you business plan software—but many people like working from an existing template. Even if you don't want to buy the program, check out the site. They offer free sample plans for about sixty different types of businesses—and one is sure to be similar to yours.

Entrepreneur.com—✍ *www.entrepreneur.com*

Associated with the magazine of the same name, this Web site offers comprehensive advice to small business owners. They have sections focusing on start-up enterprises, franchises, even downloadable market research reports. Although the site is a little slow at times and does have a lot of advertising, the information it provides is worth a little patience.

Small Business Advisor—✍ *www.isquare.com*

This Web site offers advice and assistance to small and home-based businesses. The site provides daily and weekly tips for all facets of small business, like marketing, accounting, and cash management. But their specialty seems to be in offering concrete suggestions to those companies that do business with various U.S. government agencies (such as advice on preparing bids that will get accepted).

Quicken—✍ *www.quicken.com*

The small business section of the Quicken Web site has some good (but limited) information. A lot of their information is derived from Nolo, so it's pretty reliable. This site is pretty cluttered with advertising (a lot of it for Intuit products). But if you click through here to buy Quicken or other related products, you'll pay less for them.

American Express—✍ *www.americanexpress.com*

American Express is well known as a credit card company, with a special section that handles small business credit cards. In addition, American Express has a vast network of highly trained financial advisors who can help you manage and mesh your personal and business finances; they even offer a free initial financial consultation, and they have a lot of discount programs available for new small business owners.

Welcome Business USA—☞ *www.welcomebusiness.com*

This Web site offers a wealth of resources, including a large library of free how-to articles. They have a few business start-up checklists, which can help you make sure you don't overlook any important items when you're setting up your company. They have a large section about e-commerce with a lot of practical advice for how to get your online business up and running. Although there is quite a bit of advertising on the page, their associated vendors (including a lot of big-name business-related companies) offer discounts when you order through the links. This site is closely linked with SCORE.

Good Books (and More) for Further Reading

Profits, Taxes, & LLCs (All Year Tax Guides, 2003) by Holmes F. Crouch. If you're looking for very specific tax advice and information (like the kind you would get from your accountant), this book will help. The book covers some complex tax issues (Crouch books are often used as continuing education texts for CPAs), but it is written in a personal style.

Your Limited Liability Company: An Operating Manual (Nolo, 2002) by Anthony Mancuso. This book is put out by Nolo—and that means the information is reliable. The text focuses on the legal issues specific to LLCs. The book is broken down in a way that makes sense to those of us without legal backgrounds. Its straightforward language makes a tough subject easy to read about.

Small C & S Corporations (All Year Tax Guides, 2000) by Holmes F. Crouch. This book details the ins and outs of small corporations, largely from a tax perspective. Again, the personal style of the author helps make difficult tax issues much easier to follow.

How to Start and Run Your Own Corporation: S-Corporations for Small Business Owners (HCM Publishing, 2003) by Peter I. Hupalo. If you are a do-it-yourselfer, and want to form an S corporation, this book is a good legal and tax guide. The book covers everything from determining the par value for your stock to actually filling out and filing the annual tax return on your own.

The Legal Guide for Starting & Running a Small Business (Nolo, 2003) by Fred S. Steingold and Ilona M. Bray. This book focuses on the common legal aspects that small business owners can expect to face. It includes information about such issues as franchising, resolving legal disputes, and dealing with customers over the Internet.

Keeping the Books: Basic Record Keeping and Accounting for the Successful Small Business (Dearborn Trade, 2004) by Linda Pinson. This is the latest edition of a great guide to accounting for the accounting-impaired. This book will help you take care of the basic bookkeeping for your company—all the way from your check register to financial statements. The author includes worksheets, sample IRS forms, and thorough illustrations for people not as familiar with the inner workings of bookkeeping as they'd like to be.

J. K. Lasser's 1,001 Deductions and Tax Breaks: Your Complete Guide to Everything Deductible (John Wiley & Sons, 2003) by Barbara Weltman. This book is full of practical and comprehensive tax advice for small business owners. The text is part of the J. K. Lasser series—the books that accountants rely on every tax season. On top of explaining each tax deduction in everyday language, the book shows you how to claim the deduction as well as common mistakes to avoid.

Free Money for Small Business and Entrepreneurs (John Wiley & Sons, 1995) by Laurie Blum. Although the latest edition of this book was published a few years back, it's still a great resource for the small business owner who needs external financing. With more than 700 listings from government and private sources, you're sure to find someone to provide you with free or low-cost financing. The guide also provides a primer on how to complete applications and guidelines for writing proposals.

2004 Guide to Federal Grants and Government Assistance to Small Business, put out by the U.S. Government on CD-ROM. (The complete title of this resource would take up half a page.) This catalog of government grants, loans, surplus, and assistance is a great resource for small businesses.

You'll find complete details on how to apply for federal aid, business start-up kits, and government programs.

Working for Yourself: Law and Taxes for Independent Contractors, Freelancers and Consultants (Nolo, 2002) by Stephen Fishman. Now that you have decided to be your own boss, this book will fill in all of the details. It includes such topics as drafting solid contracts, IRS compliance, how to make sure you get paid by your clients, specific tax deductions, and even how to set up your home office. This book gets into the nitty-gritty details of running your business.

Buy-Sell Agreement Handbook: Plan Ahead for Changes in the Ownership of Your Business (Nolo, 2003) by Anthony Mancuso and Bethany K. Laurence. Another entry courtesy of Nolo Publishing, this book is a must have for companies with more than one owner. The book spells out specific legal language to include in your agreements that cover transfers of ownership.

➤ Appendix 2

State Business Development Office Contact Information

APPENDICES

This state-by-state listing includes the appropriate offices for you to contact in order to receive information about the requirements for forming your business entity. Many of the Web sites include fill-in forms for everything from articles of incorporation to applications for state sales tax ID numbers.

When writing to addresses without a specific department name (those listed only as "Secretary of State," for example), add your business type and the word "unit" to reach the correct office (for example, "LLC Unit").

Alabama—✍ *www.sos.state.al.us*

Secretary of State; 11 S. Union Street, State House, Room 207, Montgomery, AL 36103; 334-242-5324

Alaska—✍ *www.dced.state.ak.us*

Corporations Supervisor; P.O. Box 110808, Juneau, AK 99811-0808; 907-465-2530

Arizona—✍ *www.cc.state.az.us*

Secretary of State, Corporation Commission; 1300 W. Washington, Phoenix, AZ 85007; 602-542-3135

Arkansas—✍ *www.sosweb.state.ar.us*

Corporation Commission; Suite 310, Building Services Building, 501 Woodlane, Little Rock, AR 72201; 501-682-3409

California—✍ *www.ss.ca.gov*

Secretary of State; 1500 11th Street, Sacramento, CA 95814; Corp: 916-657-5448, LLP: 916-653-3365, LLC: 916-653-3795

Colorado—✍ *www.sos.state.co.us*

Secretary of State; 1560 Broadway, Suite 200, Denver, CO 80202-5169; 303-894-2200

Connecticut—✐ *www.sots.state.ct.us*

Secretary of State; 30 Trinity Street, Hartford, CT 06106; 860-509-6001

Delaware—✐ *www.state.de.us/sos*

State of Delaware Division of Corporations; 401 Federal Street, Suite 4, Dover, DE 19901; 302-739-3073

District of Columbia—✐ *www.dcra.dc.gov*

Department of Consumer & Regulatory Affairs; 941 N. Capitol Street, NE, Washington, D.C. 20002; 202-442-4432

Florida—✐ *www.dos.state.fl.us*

State Department, Division of Corporations, Corporate Filings; P.O. Box 6327, Tallahassee, FL 32314; 850-245-6052

Georgia—✐ *www.sos.state.ga.us*

Secretary of State, Corporations Division; 315 West Tower, 2 Martin Luther King Jr. Drive, Atlanta, GA 30334-1530; 404-656-2817

Hawaii—✐ *www.businessregistrations.com*

Business Registration Division; P.O. Box 40, Honolulu, HI 96810; 808-586-2744

Idaho—✐ *www.idsos.state.id.us*

Secretary of State;700 W. Jefferson Street, Boise, ID 83720; 208-334-2300

Illinois—✐ *www.cyberdriveillinois.com*

Secretary of State; Suite 328, 501 S. Second Street, Springfield, IL 62756; 217-782-6961

Indiana—*www.in.gov/sos*

Secretary of State, Business Services Division; Room E-018, 302 W. Washington Street, Indianapolis, IN 46204; 317-232-6576

Iowa—*www.sos.state.ia.us*

Secretary of State, Corporations Division; Lucas Building, 1st Floor, Des Moines, IA 50319; 515-281-5204

Kansas—*www.kssos.org*

Secretary of State; Memorial Hall, 1st Floor, 120 SW 10th Avenue, Topeka, KS 66612; 785-296-4564

Kentucky—*www.kysos.com*

Secretary of State; 700 Capitol Avenue, Suite 152, Frankfort, KY 40601; 502-564-3490

Louisiana—*www.sec.state.la.us*

(This Web site is a little tough to navigate, so you may want to try calling the phone number listed below first when requesting information.)

Secretary of State; P.O. Box 94125, Baton Rouge, LA 70804-9125; 225-925-4704

Maine—*www.maine.gov*

State Department, 101 State House Station, Augusta, ME 04333-0101; 207-624-7736

Maryland—*www.choosemaryland.org*

(The state does have an official main Web site at *www.dat.state.md.us*, but this site was much easier to navigate and loaded much faster.)

Maryland Business Assistance, Department of Business & Economic Development; 217 Redwood Street, Baltimore, MD 21202; 1-888-CHOOSEMD

Massachusetts—✍ *http://corp.sec.state.ma.us*

Secretary of the Commonwealth; One Ashburton Place, 17th Floor, Boston, MA 02108; 617-727-9640

Michigan—✍ *www.michigan.gov/cis*

Bureau of Commercial Services; P.O. Box 30018, Lansing, MI 48909; 517-241-9223

Minnesota—✍ *www.sos.state.mn.us*

Secretary of State; 180 State Office Building, St. Paul, MN 55155; 651-296-2803

Mississippi—✍ *www.sos.state.ms.us*

Secretary of State; P.O. Box 136, Jackson, MS 39205-0136; 601-359-1350

Missouri—✍ *www.sos.mo.gov*

Secretary of State; Room 322, 600 W. Main, Jefferson City, MO 65101-0778; 573-751-4153

Montana—✍ *www.sos.state.mt.us*

Secretary of State; P.O. Box 202801, Helena, MT 59620-2801; 406-444-3665

Nebraska—✍ *www.sos.state.ne.us*

Secretary of State; Room 1305, P.O. Box 94608, Lincoln, NE 68509-4608; 402-471-4079

Nevada—✍ *www.sos.state.nv.us*

Secretary of State; 202 N. Carson Street, Carson City, NV 89701; 775-684-5708

New Hampshire—✍ *www.state.nh.us*

Secretary of State, Corporation Division; 107 N. Main Street, Concord, NH 03301; 603-271-3244

New Jersey—✍ *www.state.nj.us*

(This Web site is difficult to navigate, and you may be better off calling for an information packet for your desired business structure.)

Commerce & Economic Growth Commission; 20 West State Street, P.O. Box 820, Trenton, NJ 08625-0820; 609-777-0885

New Mexico—✍ *www.nmprc.state.nm.us*

Public Regulation Commission; P.O. Box 1269, Santa Fe, NM 87504-1269; 505-827-4508

New York—✍ *www.dos.state.ny.us*

State Department, Division of Corporations; 41 State Street, Albany, NY 12231-0001; 518-473-2492

North Carolina—✍ *www.secretary.state.nc.us*

Corporations Division; P.O. Box 29622, Raleigh, NC 27626-0622; 919-807-2225

North Dakota—✍ *www.state.nd.us/sec*

Secretary of State, Department 108; 600 E. Boulevard Avenue, Bismarck, ND 58505-0500; 701-328-2900

Ohio—✍ *www.serfrom.sos.state.oh.us*

Secretary of State; 180 E. Broad Street, 16th Floor, Columbus, OH 43215; 614-466-3910 or 877-SOS-FILE

Oklahoma—✍ *www.sos.state.ok.us*

Secretary of State; Room 101, 2300 N. Lincoln Boulevard, Oklahoma City, OK 73105-4897; 405-521-3912

Oregon—*www.filinginoregon.com*

Corporation Division; 255 Capitol Street NE, Suite 151, Salem, OR 97310-1327; 503-986-2200

Pennsylvania—*www.dos.state.pa.us/corps*

State Department; 206 North Office Building, Harrisburg, PA 17120; 717-787-1057

Rhode Island—*www.state.ri.us*

Corporations Division; 100 N. Main Street, 1st Floor, Providence, RI 02903-1335; 401-222-3040

South Carolina—*www.scsos.com*

Secretary of State; P.O. Box 11350, Columbia, SC 29211; 803-734-2158

South Dakota—*www.state.sd.us/sos*

Secretary of State; 500 E. Capital Avenue, Suite 204, Pierre, SD 57501-5070; 605-773-4845

Tennessee—*www.state.tn.us/sos*

Division of Business Services; 312 8th Avenue N, 6th Floor, William Snodgrass Tower, Nashville, TN 37243; 615-741-2286

Texas—*www.sos.state.tx.us*

Secretary of State, Corporations Section; P.O. Box 13697, Austin, TX 78711; 512-463-5583

Utah—*www.commerce.state.ut.us*

Division of Corporation and Commercial Code; 160 E. 300 S., Salt Lake City, UT 84111; 801-530-4849

Vermont—✍ *www.sec.state.vt.us*

Secretary of State, Corporations Division; 81 River Street, Drawer 09, Montpelier, VT 05609; 802-828-2386

Virginia—✍ *www.state.va.us/scc*

State Corporation Commission; P.O. Box 1197, Richmond, VA 23218; 804-371-9967

Washington—✍ *www.secstate.wa.gov*

Secretary of State; P.O. Box 40234, Olympia, WA 98504-0234; 360-753-7115

West Virginia—✍ *www.wvsos.com*

Secretary of State, Corporations Division; Building 1, Suite 157-K, 1900 Kanawha Boulevard E, Charleston, WV 25305-0770; 304-558-8000

Wisconsin—✍ *www.wdfi.org*

Corporations Section; Third Floor, P.O. Box 7846, Madison, WI 53707-7846; 608-261-9555

Wyoming—✍ *http://soswy.state.wy.us*

Secretary of State, Corporations Division; State Capital, Room 110, 200 W. 24th Street, Cheyenne, WY 82002-0020; 307-777-7311

Accounting and Business Terms Every Business Owner Should Know

This book does not focus on accounting, as that's best left to the accountants. However, in order to understand what your accountant is talking about, you need to have a working knowledge of accounting and business lingo.

account:
A grouping of related transactions; typical accounts include Cash, Property, Long-Term Debt, and Sales.

accounting period:
A specified length of time, such as a month or a year, covered by a financial statement.

accounts payable:
Money your company owes to vendors for goods or services received.

accounts receivable:
Money due to your company from customers for credit sales (not credit card sales).

accrual accounting:
A method of bookkeeping that posts revenues when earned and expenses when incurred regardless of payment date.

accumulated depreciation:
The cumulative decline in value for a physical asset, from its first date in use through the present.

active member:
One who materially participates in the business of an LLC.

active partner:
One who materially participates in the business of a partnership.

actual authority:
Any rights expressly granted to business owners or managers in an operating agreement.

adjusted basis:
Regarding business assets, the original cost of an asset plus any expenditure made to permanently improve the asset, less total accumulated depreciation.

alternative minimum tax (AMT):
A 20 percent flat tax on refigured taxable income; tax preference items subject to inclusion in the income recalculation include accelerated depreciation, passive activities, and certain loss limitations, among other things.

amortization:
The allocation of the total cost of an intangible asset over the periods it benefits.

annual meeting of shareholders:
The meeting at which all (or effectively all) of the shareholders of a corporation vote on the board of directors and other corporate issues; most states require that shareholders meet at least annually.

apparent authority:
The appearance to unknowing third parties that a business owner or manager has the right to conduct business on behalf of the business, regardless of whether he has actual authority.

articles of incorporation:
The main document that begins a corporation's existence, filed according to state law.

articles of organization:
The state form required to create an LLC.

assets:
Economic resources owned by a company for the purpose of creating or enabling operations, including such things as cash, furniture, inventories, and patents.

at-risk rules:
Tax provisions that limit the amount of deductible loss for a partner or LLC member to the amount that he can personally lose; the amounts considered at risk for a partner or member include both the combined value of cash and the adjusted basis of property contributed to the business plus any amounts borrowed by the business for which he is personally liable for repayment.

authorized shares:
The total number of shares of stock that may be issued by a corporation, as specified in the articles of incorporation (not all authorized shares need be issued; a corporation can have authorized but unissued shares that will be distributed in the future).

balance sheet:
A financial statement that shows your company's assets, liabilities, and equity on a specific date; also called a Statement of Financial Position.

basis:
The value of an ownership interest in a business, calculated for tax purposes, based on the amount of capital contributed and the owner's change in personal liability responsibility; also, the historical cost of a business asset, including any expenditures necessary to prepare the asset for use (such as shipping and installation charges).

board of directors:
A group, elected by the shareholders, who preside over the affairs of the corporation; in small corporations, there may be only one director.

buy-sell provisions:
Terms within a business agreement that control the transfer of ownership interests.

C corporation:
A standard business corporation taxed under subsection C of the IRS tax code.

capital:
See equity

capital account:
The measure of each partner's or member's ownership interest.

capital asset:
Property purchased for long-term use.

capital gain:
The excess of sale price over adjusted basis of an income-producing asset.

cash basis accounting:
A method that records revenues only when cash is received and expenses only when cash is paid out.

cash flows statement:
A financial statement showing the movement of cash into and out of your business; also called a Statement of Changes in Financial Position.

certificate of authority:
A state document issued to a foreign corporation allowing it to transact business within that state.

chart of accounts:
A numbering system for all accounts maintained by a business.

close corporation:
A form of corporation, allowed by law in some states, which has the following attributes: a small number of shareholders, substantial active participation in the business by the majority shareholders, and no readily available market for the corporation's stock.

common stock:
The primary class of stock for a corporation, which allows shareholders the right to vote on corporate issues and receive a proportional share of dividends.

corporate bylaws:
An internal document that contains the rules, regulations, and detailed operations of the corporation, generally including such items as the rights and duties of both shareholders and board members; bylaws are private documents, not subject to state filing.

corporate officers:
A group of individuals, appointed by the board of directors, responsible for the day-to-day operations of the corporation (in most states, one person can assume all officer roles); the four standard corporate officers are president, vice president, treasurer, and secretary.

corporate record book:
A book or file that contains the articles of incorporation, the corporate bylaws, and all minutes of each meeting of the directors and of the shareholders.

corporate seal:
A metal or rubber stamp of the corporate name and/or logo used to authenticate corporate documents.

corporation:
A separate legal entity formed under state law; this entity can conduct business, enter into contracts, sue and be sued, and be held accountable under the law.

cost of goods sold:
The price paid by a retailer for the merchandise he has sold.

DBA (Doing Business As):
A name, other than the legal name of the entity, under which a company transacts business (for example, Smith and Jones, LLC DBA Green Gardeners).

depreciation:
A physical asset's decline in value over time; considered a deductible expense for tax purposes.

dissolution:
The termination of a company's legal existence.

distributions:
Transfers of cash and/or property from a business to one of its owners; for partners or LLC members, distributions are taxable only when they are either guaranteed payments, they are in excess of the partner's or member's basis, or they are considered a liquidation or sale of his ownership interest in the company; for C corporation shareholders, distributions are taxed as dividends.

distributive share:
The portion of any items of income, deduction, gain, loss, or credit allocated to a partner or LLC member.

Employer Identification Number (EIN):
A tax registration number required for any business that has employees, maintains certain retirement plans, or files certain tax returns (such as excise or fiduciary).

entity:
A business structure, such as a corporation or an LLC.

equity:
Ownership of a business, calculated by subtracting the company's total liabilities from its total assets; also called capital.

ERISA:

The Employee Retirement Income Security Act, a federal law governing the administrative side of employee benefit and retirement plans.

estate tax:

An assessment, by both the federal and state governments, based on the current value of a decedent's assets.

estimated tax payments:

Quarterly tax remittances made by taxpayers on any income not covered by withholding taxes; required of sole proprietors, general partners, active LLC members, and C corporations.

expenses:

Costs incurred in association with running a business.

federal unemployment tax (FUT):

An assessment on companies by the federal government to cover unemployment compensation for terminated employees.

FICA:

The nickname for the combination of Social Security and Medicare taxes.

financial statements:

A group of reports that display accounting information grouped in a useful manner.

fiscal year:

Any twelve-month accounting period; it does not need to coincide with a calendar year.

fixed asset:

A physical asset purchased by a company for long-term use; examples include equipment and vehicles.

foreign corporation:
A corporation transacting business in a state other than the state in which the corporation was formed.

foreign LLC:
An LLC conducting business in a state other than the one in which the LLC was formed.

Form 1065:
The annual informational return filed with the IRS by a partnership or an LLC taxed like a partnership for federal tax purposes to report its income and other financial information.

Form 1099-MISC:
The form on which miscellaneous payments are reported to both the IRS and the payee, completed by the payer. Miscellaneous income includes such things as payments of $600 or more to a nonemployee for services rendered to a business, royalty payments of $10 or more, or rent payments of $600 or more.

Form 1120:
The annual tax return that must be filed by LLCs treated as corporations for federal tax purposes.

Form 1120S:
The annual informational return filed with the IRS by an S corporation to report its income and other financial information.

Form 5500:
The IRS form that has to be filed annually for all profit-sharing, money purchase, and defined benefit retirement plans that cover multiple persons or otherwise do not meet the requirements to file Form 5500-EZ.

Form 5500-EZ:
The IRS form that must be filed annually for a profit-sharing, money purchase, or defined benefit retirement plan that qualifies as a single-participant

plan and holds total plan assets of more than $100,000 (plans owning less than $100,000 of assets do not have to file any forms).

Form 8829:
The tax form on which expenses incurred for the business use of a personal residence are reported; the information on this form carries to Schedule C for sole proprietors and single-member LLCs.

Form 8832:
The IRS form on which a business entity can make a tax treatment election.

Form W-2:
The form on which an employer reports annual wages and withholding taxes to each employee; it is used to prepare the employee's tax return.

franchise tax:
A state tax levied on a corporation for the privilege of transacting business in that state; different states charge the tax on different bases, but it is generally based on earnings, the value of outstanding stock, total assets, or total revenues.

fringe benefits:
Items, such as health and life insurance, provided to business owners and employees by the business on top of regular salaries or other earned income.

general partner:
An owner of a partnership interest who is personally fully liable for all partnership debts.

going concern:
The accounting notion that assumes a business entity will stay in operation indefinitely (provided there is not evidence proving otherwise).

goodwill:
The portion of the purchase price of a company over and above the fair market value of its listed assets; the value of a company's reputation.

gross margin:
The difference between net sales and cost of goods sold; it may also be referred to as gross profit.

guaranteed payments:
Distributions to a partner in exchange for services or use of capital which are determined without regard to partnership income; these do not include a partner's regular distributive share of partnership profits.

historical cost:
The original purchase price of an asset.

holding company:
A corporation whose sole function is owning stock in and supervising the management of other companies.

income statement:
A financial statement that summarizes income earned and expenses incurred by your company for a specific period of time; also called a Profit & Loss Statement (or P&L).

incorporator:
The person (or other entity) who prepares, files, and signs the articles of incorporation.

indemnity:
The right to be reimbursed for amounts paid out; for example, if one partner paid more than his fair share of a debt, the other partners would be required to pay him back for the excess.

installment sale:
An asset transfer wherein a series of payments are made over time rather than in one lump sum.

intangible asset:
A property without physical form that can be owned by a business; examples include patents, trademarks, franchises, copyrights, and goodwill.

inventory:
Goods held for resale.

invoice:
A written bill that includes a description of goods or services delivered and the terms of payment.

journal:
A complete sequential record of all of a company's transactions.

ledger:
The book that contains all of a company's accounts.

liabilities:
Debts and obligations your company owes, whether in the form of money, goods to be delivered, or services to be performed.

limited liability:
A legal theory that caps the amount a business owner can lose to his investment in the company; no business creditors can therefore collect from the owner's personal assets.

limited partner:
An owner of a partnership interest whose personal liability for partnership debts is limited to his investment in the partnership.

liquidating distribution:
The assets given to a member upon dissolution of an LLC.

liquidation:
The selling off of business assets, usually for the purpose of paying debts.

liquidity:
The state of having enough cash on hand to pay debts and obligations as they come due.

LLC (Limited Liability Company):
A business engaged in for profit by one or more individuals (except in Massachusetts, where at least two owners are required by state law) that provides its owners with the desirable pass-through taxation feature of partnerships plus the advantageous limited liability protection offered by corporations.

LLLP (Limited Liability Limited Partnership):
A limited partnership that has specially registered with its home state to provide the general partner with limited liability protection.

LLP (Limited Liability Partnership):
A business engaged in for profit by two or more individuals that provides its owners with the desirable pass-through taxation feature of partnerships plus at least some level of the limited liability protection offered by corporations; all LLPs offer their partners protection from obligations arising from the tortious acts of other partners at the very least, and some states give the partners the same level of protection as LLC members.

long-term debt:
Regular business liabilities that have due dates longer than one year.

management:
The person or people who have the overall responsibility to operate a business on a day-to-day basis.

material participation:
Taking part in the business on a regular, continuous, and substantial basis.

member:
An individual owning an interest in an LLC; no person or entity is barred from becoming a member under U.S. law.

membership interest:
The relative ownership percentage of an LLC by an individual.

minutes:
A written record of all notable corporate events such as shareholder meetings; these records are typically filed in the corporate record book.

net loss:
The excess of a company's expenses over its revenues.

net profit:
The excess of a company's revenues over its expenses; also called net income.

net sales:
The total proceeds from the sale of merchandise minus any returns or discounts.

nondiscrimination rules:
Regulations covering retirement plans specifically stating that contributions made or benefits provided cannot favor highly compensated employees (plans not in compliance cannot be considered "qualified plans").

nonqualified plan:
Deferred compensation arrangements (including retirement plans) that do not meet all requirements of qualified plans under ERISA and therefore don't enjoy full and immediate tax benefits and legal protections; *See also* ERISA.

no-par-value stock:
Stock with no stated minimum value.

operating agreement:
A written contract entered into by all members that will govern the conduct of the members and the LLC.

operating expenses:
The costs of running a business other than inventory costs; typical operating expenses include utilities, telephone, and office salaries.

overhead:
Expenses that don't directly relate to the production or sale of goods or services (such as the bookkeeper for a plumbing contractor).

par value:
The stated minimum amount for which a share of stock may be sold.

partner:
An individual owning an interest in a partnership; no person or entity is barred from becoming a partner under U.S. law.

partnership:
A trade or business engaged in for profit by two or more individuals that is not incorporated or formed as an LLC.

partnership agreement:
A written contract entered into by all partners, which will govern the conduct of the partners and the partnership.

passive activity loss limitations:
Rules under the IRS that disallow losses from passive activities to be offset against other types of income when determining tax liability.

passive member:
One who does not actively participate in the business of the LLC.

passive partner:
One who does not actively participate in the business of the partnership.

pass-through taxation:
The phenomenon by which the business entity pays no taxes on its income, instead passing all items of income, deduction, gain, loss, and credit directly through to its owners for reporting on their individual tax returns.

payment terms:
The part of a sales agreement that outlines payment responsibilities; for example, terms of *net 30* would mean the balance of an invoice must be paid in full in thirty days.

phantom income:
The phenomenon unique to pass-through tax entities that require an individual with ownership interest to have a tax liability for business income when he has not received any distribution.

posting:
Transferring information from the journal (which stores transactions in chronological order) to the ledger (which groups transactions by account).

preferred stock:
A class of stock that generally grants its shareholders preferential payment of dividends but no voting rights; preferred stock must be authorized in the articles of incorporation.

prepaid expenses:
Expenses that have been paid in advance and not yet used up (like magazine subscriptions and insurance).

professional corporation:
A business incorporated for the purpose of engaging in a licensed or learned profession, such as accounting or law.

proxy:
An authorization to vote on behalf of a shareholder.

Qualified Family-Owned Business (QFOB):
An IRS classification for small family-owned businesses, which allows extra estate tax exemptions and an installment option for paying any estate taxes due.

qualified plan:
A retirement plan that complies with all federal guidelines and requirements (under ERISA), and therefore is entitled to special tax benefits; requirements include such things as nondiscrimination and specific vesting standards based on the type your company has; *See also* ERISA, vesting.

quorum:
The minimum number of individuals required to attend a meeting so that business may be conducted; quorums may be measured as simple majorities or stated percentages.

registered agent:
A person designated by a company to receive service of process and other official documents.

registered office:
The business location, stated in the articles of incorporation or organization, where the registered agent can be reached; this office need not be the principal place of business of the corporation or LLC.

resolution:
A formal decision made for the corporation by either the shareholders or the board of directors; resolutions should be filed in the corporate record book.

revenues:
Earnings that result from the operation of a business; also called sales.

RULPA (Revised Uniform Limited Partnership Act):
A body of statutes developed to offer guidelines to the states when they drafted their limited partnership laws.

S corporation:

A corporation that has made an election to be taxed under Subchapter S of the Internal Revenue code, which allows the business and its owners to use beneficial pass-through taxation.

Schedule A:

The tax form on which personal deductible expenses are reported as part of a personal tax return.

Schedule C:

The tax form on which the business revenue and expenses of a sole proprietor or single-member LLC owner are reported as part of his personal tax return.

Schedule C-EZ:

A short, simplified tax form for reporting business revenue and expenses.

Schedule E:

The form on which a partner's or member's share of the ordinary income of the partnership or LLC (when the LLC has chosen to be treated as a partnership for federal tax purposes) is reported; this schedule is included as part of each partner's or member's annual individual tax return.

Schedule K-1:

The form prepared by an S corporation, a partnership, or an LLC taxed as a partnership for each shareholder, partner, or member to report his share of income, deductions, gains, losses, and credits. The business must also file a copy of the schedule with the IRS.

SCORE:

The Service Corps of Retired Executives; associated with the SBA, this association, run by volunteers, offers a management assistance program for small business owners.

Securities and Exchange Commission (SEC):
The U.S. federal government office that regulates the issuing, buying, and selling of securities (primarily stocks); all publicly held corporations must adhere to the agency's strict reporting requirements.

self-employment taxes:
The combination of Social Security and Medicare taxes due on an active member's share of the LLC's net ordinary income, 15.3 percent of the first $87,900 of income plus 2.9 percent of any income greater than that threshold for 2004.

separate entity:
A business that is distinct from its owners—financially, legally, or both.

share:
A unit of ownership of a corporation.

shareholders:
Individuals or entities that own shares of stock in a corporation.

sole proprietorship:
A business owned by one person that is formed neither as a corporation nor an LLC.

source document:
The underlying paperwork that serves as proof of a transaction (like a receipt).

special allocations:
A method by which items of income, deduction, gain, loss, and credit will be shared by the partners or a partnership of the members of an LLC and taxed like a partnership other than in direct proportion to their respective ownership interests; such distributions must be detailed in the partnership or LLC operating agreement and meet specific IRS requirements to be held valid.

statement:
A written summary of outstanding invoices, often used as a reminder to a customer that a payment is due.

stock:
The capital of a corporation, measured in shares, with each share representing a unit of ownership of the company.

stock certificate:
A written instrument that establishes ownership of shares of a corporation.

stock transfer book:
A listing of all owners of shares of stock of a corporation.

stockholder:
See shareholders.

substantial economic effect:
The IRS requirement that the actual economic burdens and benefits to a partner correspond to a special allocation.

Tax Matters Partner (TMP):
A general partner designated by the partnership to deal directly with the IRS.

tax-deferred:
Typically associated with retirement plans, this refers to the fact that paying taxes on earnings is put off until the assets are withdrawn for use.

trade discount:
A reduction in list price, often in excess of twenty percent.

transaction:
An exchange of value between independent parties.

treasury stock:

Shares of previously outstanding stock in a corporation that have been bought back by that corporation.

trial balance:

A summary of all ledger accounts; it serves as a check on their accuracy.

Uniform Limited Liability Company Act (ULLCA):

A model body of law for LLCs; many states do not conform to these guidelines, which were modeled on the Uniform Partnership Act.

Uniform Partnership Act (UPA):

The model law governing partnerships on which all states' statutes regarding partnerships are based.

unlimited liability:

Complete personal responsibility of a business owner for all of the debts and obligations of his business; sole proprietors and general partners are subject to unlimited liability.

vesting:

Usually associated with retirement plans, this is the means of acquiring a nonforfeitable right to money that has been set aside for an employee by an employer.

voting rights:

The decision-making powers granted to an LLC member by the operating agreement.

Index

Accountant. *See* Certified public accountant

Accounting system, 29. *See also* Bookkeeping; Recordkeeping
cash basis
changing to accrual basis, 53
compared to accrual basis, 51, 110–111
in general, 50–51
timing of income/expenses, 52–53
who can use?, 51–52
corporations, 176–177
LLCs, 241
partnership, 110–111

Alter ego theory, 268–269. *See also* Liability issues

Asset protection. *See also* Liability issues
corporation
in general, 199–200
minimum cash strategy, 200–201
with multiple entities, 202–203
transferring cash out of corporation, 201–202
LLC
in general, 263–264
minimize liquid assets, 264–265
multiple entities, 265–266
trust, 79–80

Attorney, 5. *See also* Professional help
choosing, 27
in general, 26
services to client, 27–28

Bankruptcy, LLC, 270

Bookkeeper. *See also* Bookkeeping; Certified public accountant
functions of, 29, 30

Bookkeeping. *See also* Accounting system; Recordkeeping
accounts payable, 54–55
accounts receivable, 55
in general, 53
inventory tracking, 53–54

Bottom Line/Personal, 284

Business license, 18

Business name
business structure affects name, 17
DBA name, 15, 18
determining name availability, 16–17
in general, 15
registration, 18
domain name registration, 19

Business plan
in general, 12–13, 15
break-even analysis, 13
cash flow forecast, 13
profit and loss forecast, 13, 14–15
number crunching for, 13–15

Business structure. *See also specific structures*
changing, in general, 9–10
choosing
factors affecting, 6–7, 285–288
in general, 5–6, 282
legal factors, 289
personal factors, 8
taxes affecting, 286–287
dissolution/transfer, 7
in general, 2–3
types
corporation, 4–5
limited liability company, 5
partnership, 4
sole proprietorship, 3–4

California, LLCs, 228

Cash flow forecast, 13

Cash flow statement, 102

Certified public accountant (CPA), 5, 180. *See also* Accounting system; Professional help
choosing, 30–31
in general, 28–29
services to client, 29–30

Charging orders. *See also* Liability issues
corporation, 207
defined, 137
LLC, 269–270
partnership, 137–139

Contracts, 28

Corporation
accounting system, 176–177
asset protection
in general, 199–200
minimum cash strategy, 200–201
multiple entities, 202–203
transferring cash out of corporation, 201–202, 206–207
board meetings, 157–158
corporate resolutions, 178
minutes, 177–178
quorum, 157–158
board of directors, 157–158
business name, 17
businesses appropriate for, 164
bylaws, 155–156
discussed, 172–173
C corporation, 4, 174, 176
compared to S corporation, 300–301
converting S corporation to, 314
converting to S corporation, 315
discussed, 160–161, 298–299, 302–303
taxes, 180, 181–187
compared to LLC, 301–303
compared to partnership, 298–300
compared to sole proprietorship, 293–294
corporate officers
in general, 158–159
president, 159
secretary, 160
treasurer, 159
vice president, 159
dissolving
final taxes, 219–220
in general, 216–219
insurance needs, 219
S corporation, 220
in general, 4–5, 154
incorporation
articles of incorporation, 170–171
bylaws, 155–156, 172–173
costs, 171

Partnership—*continued*
incorporating, 311, 312–313
liability issues
charging orders, 137–139
examples, 133–134
in general, 132
liability for acts, 132–133
limited liability partnership, 135–136
limited partnership, 132, 134–135
limited liability limited partnership, 95
discussed, 97, 295, 296
limited liability partnership, 4, 94–95, 130
changing to, 309–310
charging orders, 139
discussed, 97–98, 108–109
interstate business, 110
naming requirements, 109–110
registered agents, 110
limited partnership, 4, 130
charging orders, 138–139
discussed, 96, 108, 294–295
liability issues, 132, 134–135, 138–139
naming conventions, 144
partnership agreement
contents of, 104–105
in general, 104
indemnity clause, 133
selling
changing partners creates new partnership, 142–145
limited partnership interest, 145–146
taxes, 111
advantages, 126–128
audit risk, 129
benefits, 121
buying into partnership, 128
disadvantages, 129–130
estimated taxes, 119–120
expenses/deductions, 120–121
in general, 118–119
IRS classification, 123–124
limited partnership/limited liability partnership, 130
limits on losses, 121–122
"material participation", 123–124
"nonrecognition rule", 126

pass-through taxes, 118
passive activities/tax losses, 122–123
separate tax treatment, 125–126
tax forms, 124–125
transfer of appreciated property, 126–128
transactions with partner, 113–114
types
family limited partnership, 94–95, 96, 97
in general, 94–95, 284, 294
general partnership, 4
limited liability limited partnership, 95, 97
limited liability partnership, 4, 94–95, 97–98, 130
limited partnership, 4, 130
Payroll service. *See also* Taxes
in general, 31–32
Personal service corporation (PSC). *See also* Corporation
discussed, 4–5
Professional help. *See also* Attorney; Certified public accountant
in general, 26

Recordkeeping. *See also* Accounting system; Bookkeeping
business/personal finances
business checking account, 42, 48
business credit card, 43, 48
in general, 42
moving cash between, 43–44
corporation, 205
mileage logs, 49–50
receipts
for cash purchases, 49
constructive receipt rule, 52
in general, 47–49
Retirement plans, 32
choosing, 24
defined benefit plans, 23
defined contribution plans, 22–23
in general, 21–22, 278
Social Security, 45, 119, 190
Revised Uniform Limited Partnership Act (RULPA), 104, 108, 138
RULPA. *See* Revised Uniform Limited Partnership Act

SBA. *See* Small Business Administration
Securities law, 176
Shareholder, corporation, 155–156
Small Business Administration (SBA), 20, 36
Social Security, 45, 119, 190. *See also* Retirement plans
Social Security number, 39–40
Sole proprietorship, 9. *See also* Liability issues
business name, 17
changing to LLC, 306–308
changing to other structure, 35
compared to corporation, 293–294
compared to LLC, 292–293
defined, 3, 34
dissolving business
cleanup tasks, 84–85
exit strategies, 85
in general, 84
family issues
children as employees, 45–46
in general, 44, 85–86
spousal co-ownership, 44–45
tax issues, 46–47
transfer of power, 86
transferring assets, 87
in general, 3–4, 34–37, 282–283
businesses appropriate for, 37–38
businesses not appropriate for, 38–39, 76
getting started
in general, 39
permits, fees, taxes, 39–40
home-office deduction, 66–69
incorporating, 311, 312
reclassification as hobby, 70
recordkeeping suggestions, 42–44
selling business
confidentiality issues, 90–91
in general, 89
tax consequences, 91–92
who will buy it?, 89–90
tax issues, 39–40, 69–70
estate taxes, 87–89
family employees, 46–47, 86–87
sale of business, 91–92

Taxes. *See also* Payroll service
accumulated earnings tax, 186
alternative minimum tax, 185–186

STREETWISE® BOOKS

Newest Arrivals!

Crash Course MBA
$19.95 (CAN $29.95)
ISBN 1-59337-210-8

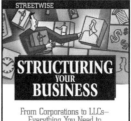

Structuring Your Business
$19.95 (CAN $29.95)
ISBN 1-59337-177-2

Also Available in the *Streetwise*® Series:

24 Hour MBA
$19.95 (CAN $29.95)
ISBN 1-58062-256-9

Achieving Wealth Through Franchising
$19.95 (CAN $29.95)
ISBN 1-58062-503-7

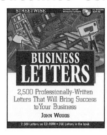

Business Letters with CD-ROM
$29.95 (CAN $47.95)
ISBN 1-58062-133-3

Business Valuation
$19.95 (CAN $31.95)
ISBN 1-58062-952-0

Complete Business Plan
$19.95 (CAN $29.95)
ISBN 1-55850-845-7

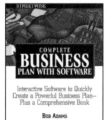

Complete Business Plan with Software
$29.95 (CAN $47.95)
ISBN 1-58062-798-6

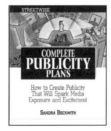

Complete Publicity Plans
$19.95 (CAN $29.95)
ISBN 1-58062-771-4

Customer-Focused Selling
$19.95 (CAN $29.95)
ISBN 1-55850-725-6

Direct Marketing
$19.95 (CAN $29.95)
ISBN 1-58062-439-1

Do-It-Yourself Advertising
$19.95 (CAN $29.95)
ISBN 1-55850-727-2

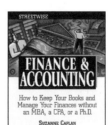

Finance & Accounting
$19.95 (CAN $29.95)
ISBN 1-58062-196-1

Financing the Small Business
$19.95 (CAN $29.95)
ISBN 1-58062-765-X

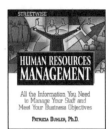

**Human Resources
Management**
$19.95 (CAN $29.95)
ISBN 1-58062-699-8

Independent Consulting
$19.95 (CAN $29.95)
ISBN 1-55850-728-0

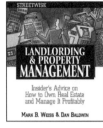

**Landlording & Property
Management**
$19.95 (CAN $29.95)
ISBN 1-58062-766-8

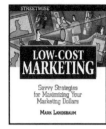

Low-Cost Marketing
$19.95 (CAN $31.95)
ISBN 1-58062-858-3

**Low-Cost Web Site
Promotion**
$19.95 (CAN $29.95)
ISBN 1-58062-501-0

Managing a Nonprofit
$19.95 (CAN $29.95)
ISBN 1-58062-698-X

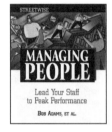

Managing People
$19.95 (CAN $29.95)
ISBN 1-55850-726-4

Marketing Plan
$19.95 (CAN $29.95)
ISBN 1-58062-268-2

**Maximize Web
Site Traffic**
$19.95 (CAN $29.95)
ISBN 1-58062-369-7

**Motivating & Rewarding
Employees**
$19.95 (CAN $29.95)
ISBN 1-58062-130-9

Project Management
$19.95 (CAN $29.95)
ISBN 1-58062-770-6

**Relationship Marketing
on the Internet**
$17.95 (CAN $27.95)
ISBN 1-58062-255-0

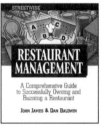

**Restaurant
Management**
$19.95 (CAN $29.95)
ISBN 1-58062-781-1

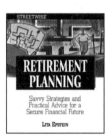

Retirement Planning
$19.95 (CAN $29.95)
ISBN 1-58062-772-2

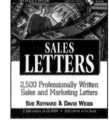

**Sales Letters
with CD-ROM**
$29.95 (CAN $44.95)
ISBN 1-58062-440-5

Selling Your Business
$19.95 (CAN $29.95)
ISBN 1-58062-602-5

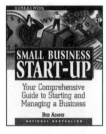

Small Business Start-Up
$19.95 (CAN $29.95)
ISBN 1-55850-581-4

Time Management
$19.95 (CAN $29.95)
ISBN 1-58062-131-7

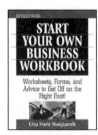

**Start Your Own
Business Workbook**
$9.95 (CAN $15.95)
ISBN 1-58062-506-1

Available wherever books are sold.
For more information, or to order, call 800-872-5627 or visit www.*adamsmedia.com*
Adams Media, an F+W Publications Company, 57 Littlefield Street, Avon, MA 02322